W9-AGX-311

Harare

World Cities Series

Edited by
Professor R. J. Johnston and Professor P. Knox

Published titles in the series:

Forthcoming titles in the series:

Other titles are in preparation

Harare

Inheriting a settler-colonial city: change or continuity?

Carole Rakodi
University of Wales, Cardiff, UK

INDIANA-
PURDUE
WITHDRAWN
MAR 2 6 1999
'ORT WAYNE

HT
384
.Z552
H377
1995

JOHN WILEY & SONS
Chichester • New York • Brisbane • Toronto • Singapore

ACE 4/06

Copyright © 1995 Carole Rakodi

Published 1995 by John Wiley & Sons Ltd,
        Baffins Lane, Chichester,
        West Sussex PO19 1UD, England

        National   01243 779777
        International (+44) 1243 779777

All rights reserved.

No part of this book may be reproduced by any means,
or transmitted, or translated into a machine language
without the written permission of the publisher.

Other Wiley Editorial Offices

John Wiley & Sons, Inc., 605 Third Avenue,
New York, NY 10158-0012, USA

Jacaranda Wiley Ltd, 33 Park Road, Milton,
Queensland 4064, Australia

John Wiley & Sons (Canada) Ltd, 22 Worcester Road,
Rexdale, Ontario M9W 1L1, Canada

John Wiley & Sons (SEA) Pte Ltd, 37 Jalan Pemimpin #05-04,
Block B, Union Industrial Building, Singapore 2057

Library of Congress Cataloging-in-Publication Data
Rakodi, Carole.
    Harare : inheriting a settler-colonial city : change or continuity? / by
Carole Rakodi.
        p.   cm. – (Belhaven world cities series)
    Includes bibliographical references and index.
    ISBN 0-471-94951-5
    1. Urbanization – Zimbabwe – Harare.   2. Colonial cities.
    I. Series.
    HT384.Z552H377   1995
    307.76'096891–dc20   95-3850
                                                                          CIP

British Library Cataloguing in Publication Data

A catalogue record for this book is available from the British Library

ISBN 0-471-94951-5

Typeset in 10/12pt Palatino from author's disks by
Mayhew Typesetting, Rhayader, Powys
Printed and bound in Great Britain by
Biddles Ltd, Guildford and King's Lynn

*This book is printed on acid-free paper responsibly manufactured from
sustainable forestation, for which at least two trees are planted for each one used
for paper production.*

Contents

List of figures

List of tables

Preface

For those of us who lived in Zambia following the Unilateral Declaration of Independence in Southern Rhodesia and the boundary closure which followed, that country was an unknown quantity. I left Zambia in 1978 but took the opportunity afforded by a return visit in 1981 to satisfy my curiosity by visiting what was by then independent Zimbabwe. That visit marked my first contact with the Department of Rural and Urban Planning at the University of Zimbabwe. The possibility of a link with the department was not followed up until 1985, but then was pursued with considerable interest on the part of that department and my own. Between 1987 and 1993, the British Council funded a series of staff exchanges in both directions under its Academic Links programme. In 1990, funding was obtained from the Economic and Social Research Committee of the Overseas Development Administration for a research project on land, housing and urban development in Harare and Gweru. Over that period, on a succession of visits to teach and carry out research, I spent a total of nearly a year in Zimbabwe. My own interests and the particular focus of that research help to explain the emphases embodied in this book about the city of Harare.

Thanks are due to many people for their support and assistance during those visits. Firstly, I would like to thank Professor Naison Mutizwa-Mangiza, who initiated the link from the Zimbabwe end, collaborated with me on a review of research on housing in Harare in 1987/8, and was kind enough to read the manuscript of this book in 1994. His successors as chairmen of the Department of Rural and Urban Planning, Professor K. Wekwete, Dr C. Rambanapasi and Dr L. Ndhlovu, continued to support the link and provided the larger research project with a home. These and other members of staff in the department, not least the technical staff, were generous with ideas, contacts, time and practical assistance.

Approval for the research and access to relevant information was given by the Ministry of Local Government and Rural and Urban

Development, the Ministry of Public Construction and National Housing, and Harare City Council. The major task of administering and analysing household surveys and other data collection was carried out by the Research Associate, Ms Penny Withers, who was based in Harare for a year. She was assisted by a team of interviewers drawn from among the students in the Department of Rural and Urban Planning at the University of Zimbabwe. Other aspects of the research were undertaken by colleagues from that department, namely Oscar Musandu-Nyamayaro and Vincent Hungwe. Some of the more technical aspects of the research have been reported elsewhere.

I am indebted to my friends Ian and Alison Love, also staff members at the University of Zimbabwe, for their support and hospitality on many visits. Completion of this book would not have been possible without a period of study leave from my own department. In particular, the support of Somas Kandiah, who took on my administrative duties and some of my teaching in my absence, and Janice Cole and Geraldine Davies for the graphics, is acknowledged. Finally, thanks to my sons for cheerfully putting up with my absences and for spending two summer holidays in Harare, where periods of boredom alternated with the excitement of game parks and other tourist attractions.

The account of Harare given here reflects my own interests, disciplinary background and approach to understanding the urban development process. It would have been impossible to write a book on Harare by relying solely on published sources. The account draws on unpublished reports and statistics provided by central and local government, and above all on the results of the research undertaken between 1990 and 1992, especially the household sample surveys. The focus of this research on land and housing markets and policy, together with my own interests as a city planner, explain the considerable emphasis given in the account to the urban development process and its management without, I hope, neglecting the people who live in the city. To them, housing is second only to work in assuring a decent quality of urban living. This does, I think, justify the considerable attention given in this book to housing and its occupants. My own view that cities, and the activities of the agencies that administer them, cannot be understood without reference to wider political, economic, social and cultural forces is reflected in my attempt to show how the changing national political economy has provided a context which must be understood in order to explain the process of urban development and the outcomes of urban policy.

Carole Rakodi,
Department of City and Regional Planning,
University of Wales, Cardiff UK
July 1994

Exchange rates

June 1981	Z$1	=	US$1.4327	or	£0.7381
Dec. 1982	Z$1	=	US$1.0876	or	£0.6710
Dec. 1983	Z$1	=	US$0.9047	or	£0.6225
Dec. 1984	Z$1	=	US$0.6656	or	£0.5711
Dec. 1985	Z$1	=	US$0.6093	or	£0.4227
Dec. 1986	Z$1	=	US$0.5959	or	£0.4055
Dec. 1987	Z$1	=	US$0.6013	or	£0.3234
Dec. 1988	Z$1	=	US$0.5147	or	£0.2874
Dec. 1989	Z$1	=	US$0.4388	or	£0.2783
Dec. 1990	Z$1	=	US$0.3793	or	£0.1968
Dec. 1991	Z$1	=	US$0.1996	or	£0.1092
Dec. 1992	Z$1	=	US$0.1869	or	£0.1200
Dec. 1993	Z$1	=	US$0.1460	or	£0.0980
Dec. 1994	Z$1	=	US$0.1177	or	£0.0786

1

The political and economic context of Harare

Urban development in Zimbabwe, as elsewhere in the world, is shaped by the way in which the country is integrated into the world economy, but also, and uniquely, by the particular socio-economic circumstances of that society. The interplay between geographical setting, colonial legacy, post-independence trends and pressures, and a country's attempts to achieve developmental and other objectives shapes the urbanisation process. In this book the relationships between these forces and the urban characteristics to which they have given rise in Harare, the capital of Zimbabwe, will be analysed.

Colonialism and urbanisation

At the time of settler occupation of the area that is now Zimbabwe, the population was entirely rural. The same was true in much of sub-Saharan Africa, although there were, in some parts of the subcontinent, pre-colonial urban settlements which had been the administrative headquarters of kingdoms and empires, as well as trading centres not just on domestic trade routes but also in international trade. Trade across North Africa, trans-Saharan trade, and trading routes southwards along the Nile Valley and East African coast were associated with the spread of Islam. Portuguese mercantilism expanded into Africa from the mid-fifteenth century and was followed by British and French trade in the sixteenth century. Initially in gold, trade expanded into other products, especially slaves, with devastating effects on the West African kingdoms (Winters 1983). Ports were founded in western, southern and southeastern Africa, but the early European presence was generally confined to defence and trade in coastal settlements. Although there was little penetration inland, European trade shifted the focus of existing economies, especially in West Africa, towards the coast.

The earliest settlers in Zimbabwe, from about 200 BC on, were Bantu iron-working agriculturalists. By AD 1000 an empire had been established by Shona speakers which extended to the coast to the east. New groups established rival states, but by the nineteenth century, pressure from the Portuguese who had established the ports of Lourenço Marques and Beira in Mozambique, slave trading, and Nguni raids from the Zulu state to the south had led to their decline. The best known of the small Shona urban settlements, Great Zimbabwe, had been abandoned. An offshoot of the Nguni, the pastoralist Ndebele, became established in the south and west of the country in the second half of the nineteenth century (Stoneman and Cliffe 1989).

Deep in the interior of the subcontinent, Zimbabwe had thus been relatively little affected by the early incorporation of Africa into Arab and European mercantile trade. However, the development of capitalism in Europe gave rise to a search for cheap raw materials and agricultural produce and for markets for manufactured exports. In West Africa, the destructive effects of the slave trade on pre-existing social formations made it possible to shape a system of large scale production of goods such as cocoa, palm oil, timber and rubber by organising trade monopolies, taxing peasants, providing support to local rulers and forced labour. Large parts of central Africa were opened up to plunder by concessionary companies. In southern and parts of central and eastern Africa, colonial capital wished to exploit minerals and also to engage in agriculture. To obtain a cheap labour force, land was expropriated, taxes imposed and African agriculture discriminated against. It was as part of this Africa of the labour reserves that Southern Rhodesia, now Zimbabwe, was settled. The driving force behind the economic penetration of southern and central Africa was the search for gold and minerals for European manufacturing industry. Exploitation of the goldfields of the Rand in South Africa, and rumours of the supposed wealth of the gold-, copper- and iron-working Shona people, fuelled expectations of more discoveries. In 1890, a 'Pioneer Column' of Rhodes' British South Africa Company moved northwards across the Limpopo River. Despite violent opposition from the Ndebele, which spread to Shona-speaking parts of the country and was only put down in 1897, British South Africa Company administration was established.

There are indeed significant mineral deposits. However, these are scattered and, except for coal and chrome, small. Exploitable deposits include gold, asbestos, copper, chrome, nickel and tin. However, it soon became obvious that no 'second Rand' was going to be discovered and many of the settlers opted for farming. While in parts of Africa, as noted above, the most profitable means of exploiting agricultural potential was to induce peasant farmers to produce tradable crops, elsewhere the colonists themselves sought land to cultivate. Those excluded from access to land by European land ownership and inheritance systems, or fleeing poverty and lack of economic opportunity, perceived opportunities in the production both of exports, such as the coffee of Kenya, the tea of Nyasaland or the sisal of Tanganyika, and of food for the growing local urban population. Land in Southern Rhodesia was appropriated from the local inhabitants by the Company and apportioned to individuals and companies in large blocks at ridiculously cheap prices, especially in the areas of the country most favourable to agriculture.

Much of the country is plateau, declining in height from over 1200 metres in the centre towards the River Zambezi to the north and the Sabi–Limpopo river basin to the south. The undulating plateau is in places broken by hills and rock formations, especially the Great Dyke, but only in the Eastern Highlands, which rise to over 1800 metres, are these significant. Although the country is situated in the tropics, the climate is modified by altitude (Weiner 1988; Stoneman and Cliffe 1989). Soils and climate, especially rainfall, vary considerably, affecting agricultural potential. Good soils occur throughout the country, but high proportions of the better soils are on the plateau or highveld in the centre of the country. There is a single rainy season (November to March), with more prolonged rain only in the Eastern Highlands. The latter area is suitable for intensive farming (Natural Region I, see Figure 1.1) but accounts for only 2% of the total land area. The rainfall is also relatively reliable and soils generally good in the highveld (Natural Region II), which is also suitable for intensive agriculture based on maize, tobacco, cotton, livestock and other grains. Rainfall is less in terms of quantity and reliability both in the western and southern highveld (Natural Regions III and IV) and in the lower regions to the north and south (Natural Region V), where temperatures are also higher. Agriculture is thus riskier in the middleveld, which is suited to semi-intensive livestock and sometimes crop production, and is marginal in the lowveld, where rainfall is sufficient only for extensive livestock production. The country is liable to drought every few years, and the areas of lower rainfall are particularly vulnerable.

The areas with greatest agricultural potential (the highveld and Eastern Highlands) were those most attractive to the settlers. Black farmers, already supplying miners with food, were displaced from these areas to the middleveld and lowveld. Thus, while in 1903 African agriculture accounted for over 90% of the marketed output, by 1922 64% of the African population were confined to the reserves (Astrow 1983: 7).

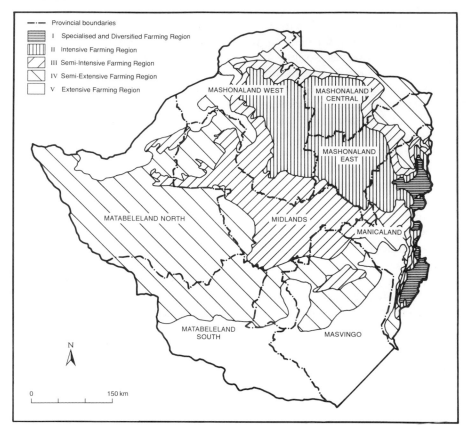

Figure 1.1 Agro-ecological zones in Zimbabwe. Source: Surveyor General, Harare, Zimbabwe, 1984

Measures to ensure a supply of black labour to mines and white farms were instituted, including, in the early days, forced labour, and also the imposition of hut taxes, in addition to the disruption and destruction of peasant agriculture (Riddell 1978). Dispossession, confinement to reserves, and measures to ensure a supply of migrant male labour typified the pattern of colonialism throughout southern, central and eastern Africa. As local populations were squeezed onto more and more limited land areas, over the years the capacity of families to support themselves diminished, reinforcing the migrant labour system (Cokorinos 1984; Stoneman and Cliffe 1989).

Colonial urban settlements developed not as industrial centres, but to facilitate the extraction of commodities and the politico-administrative system on which this depended. Many coastal settlements that were already engaged in international trade, for example Dar es Salaam and Lagos, expanded (Mehretu 1983). With the establishment of European mining and then agriculture, small urban centres began to evolve around the mines and to serve the agricultural population. Urban centres developed as transhipment points for the export of raw materials and distribution centres for imported consumer goods. In 1890 the Pioneer Column reached what is today Harare (formerly Salisbury) in search of gold. Although the initial intention was to settle at Mount Hampden, 12 kilometres to the northwest, where there was a good defensible site, doubts about water supply led to the choice of the present site. Initially a defensive and trading centre, this 'frontier' town was located on what was to become the main axis of development, along which agricultural land was allocated to settlers and other towns were established. Transport infrastructure, especially railways, was everywhere in Africa developed to connect ports to their hinterlands (Gugler and Flanagan 1978; Coquery-Vidrovitch 1991). Thus in Kenya, Nairobi was established on the rail line from Mombasa, to serve the main area of European farming, the White Highlands. In Northern Rhodesia and the Congo, exploitation of copper in Katanga and the Copperbelt was made possible by the railways, and towns such as Ndola and Chingola were established. Between 1897 and 1902 the railways from South Africa and Mozambique reached Rhodesia. The routes chosen favoured the main watersheds, which coincided both with the location of many mineral deposits and with the best land. The earliest routes, from the southwest to Bulawayo and from Beira to Harare, consolidated the position of these two settlements (Figure 1.2). The railway was extended from Bulawayo to Harare and later to Hwange (Wankie) and Zambia (Northern Rhodesia), and branch lines were extended to the larger mines.

Zimbabwe's urban system, including Harare, is, typically of eastern, central and southern Africa, a colonial creation. As such, these systems were carefully planned and precisely administered from the outset, initially in many cases by colonial capital with political sanction from the mother country. While economic competition was responsible for the penetration of African economies, it was paralleled by political competition. In the scramble for partition and political control, which coincided with or followed and was related to economic transformation, colonial rule was established by a combination of persuasion and coercion; often arbitrary boundaries were drawn; and interaction between the colonial administration and indigenous rulers had an important influence on the type of administrative system established. The doctrine of assimilation underlay direct centralised control in French, Portuguese and Belgian territories, while British paternalist

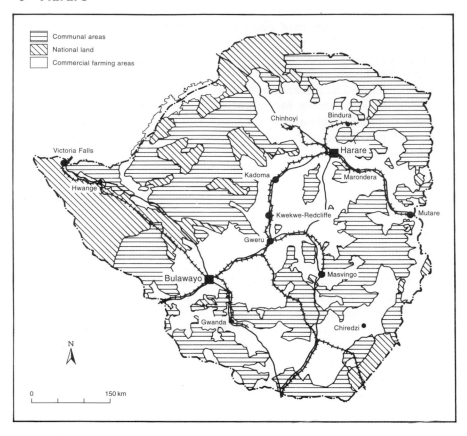

Figure 1.2 Land distribution and the urban system

philosophy found expression in decentralised administrative practice in, for example, the Gold Coast, Nigeria and Northern Rhodesia.

Where the new European population saw themselves as settlers, however, they demanded not only opportunities for accumulation, but also political and other rights. In these areas, influence and control over indigenous economies, cultures and socio-political systems was more extensive and tighter (Bell 1986). In the settler colonies, including those of Portugal (Angola and Mozambique), France (Algeria), Britain (Kenya, Southern Rhodesia) and Britain and the Netherlands (South Africa), the European population had more to lose from independence and resisted majority rule more strongly and for longer, forcing the indigenous population into bloodier struggles for independence. The political and economic legacies of early settler colonialism and the settler state are reflected in countries' economies, politics and social and urban systems.

Independence or continued dependence: the end of colonialism?

African countries had a similar legacy at independence, which influenced the pattern of urban settlements, the nature of the urban built form and the processes by which urban development is administered. However, for some, independence was gained in the 1960s or before. By the 1990s there had been three decades for their economies, polities and urban settlements to escape from colonial patterns of economic integration, political dominance and urban management. In the 1960s and early 1970s, some progress was made: economies grew, based on healthy world prices for primary commodities; a process of import substitution industrialisation commenced; political independence was granted; democracy was established and the franchise extended; and administrative systems were brought under indigenous control.

However, a series of external economic shocks halted and even reversed progress in the 1970s, especially oil price increases and declining terms of trade for primary commodities; domestic shocks, especially drought; political instability; and expectations of the public sector which exceeded its financial and administrative capacity to deliver. Political autonomy was threatened by superpower interest in some parts of the continent and regional interference in others; countries continued to depend on primary commodity exports and became increasingly marginal to the world trade system; flows of foreign direct investment were limited; aid dependence increased; and state capacity to manage the economy proved elusive. Borrowing to deal with what were seen as temporary balance of payments problems (or, for the few oil exporters, to develop their oil reserves), however, precipitated a crisis in the early 1980s when interest rates were increased and the world plunged into recession. Stepping in to help stabilise, adjust and diversify countries' economies, the IMF and World Bank imposed a set of policies which have not succeeded in solving economic problems and in many cases have exacerbated them (Jesperson 1992; Woodward 1992). Worsening economic problems have not encouraged political stability, nor have they produced conditions conducive to effective planning and management of rapidly growing urban areas. While neither all these problems nor all the characteristics and mistakes of post-independence regimes can be attributed to the colonial legacy, they are rooted in the colonial economic, political and administrative system, the influence of which persists.

In Zimbabwe, which did not achieve majority rule until 1980, the influence of the settler-colonial legacy is exceptionally strong. It left the new government with a particular economic structure, based on a particular pattern of land and business ownership, and a permanent European population; these have combined, along with external economic and political factors, to limit its room for manoeuvre. The urban planning concepts adopted, and the administrative system devised to ensure their implementation, were not only central to the settler economic and political enterprise, but remain basic to urban development today, unlike in many other countries, where towns and cities existed for centuries prior to colonialism and where planned and controlled urban development is but a small proportion of all urban development. To understand Harare, we need to understand the political, economic and administrative structure and evolution of what was not only a British colony in Africa, but also a long-lived settler state. The attainment of majority rule seems to be a critical turning point in the history of any country and might be expected to have a dramatic impact upon government policies and the pattern of urban development. In some respects, it has been significant and momentous changes have followed independence. In other respects, however, the post-independence period in African countries has been characterised by continuity rather than change, both at national and city levels. Explanations for the balance between continuity and change in a particular place must be sought both in the terms on which it is integrated into a changing world economy and polity, and in the constraints on and potential for policy change posed by configurations of domestic interests. These are predicated upon and acted out within a particular geographical context and natural resource system.

The city of Harare is the product of a settler-colonial political economy, which aimed to reorganise existing African societies so that exports could be produced with only minimal returns to local labour (Amin 1971), by means of restructuring peasant agriculture, introducing a new administrative system and establishing urban settlements. The city has been influenced by its geographical context, the historical evolution of a specific settler society, and the nature of the post-independence state. Before exploring the evolving political and economic systems of Southern Rhodesia / Zimbabwe and the histories of urban local government and planning, with which the remainder of this chapter will be concerned, I will sketch a portrait of the city.

Harare: a brief sketch

Harare is located on the highveld or watershed plateau between the Limpopo and Zambezi Rivers, the topography of which is formed by the flat African erosion surface, above which a few remnants of the higher post-Gondwana erosion surface are visible. The site is generally flat or undulating, with tiny remnants of the post-Gondwana erosion surface at Mount Hampden to the northwest and as large granite boulders near

Epworth. The African erosion surface extends over much of the site, forming watersheds between the Umwindsi (now Mabvindzi), Mazowe and Gwebi rivers and between the southward draining tributaries of the Hunyani (now Manyame) river, the Ruwa, Marimba and Makabusi (now Mukuvisi) rivers (Figure 1.3). The original site, 2 kilometres northeast of an isolated hill (the Kopje) and just to the north of the Mukuvisi river, promised a defensible site, good water supply and a pleasant climate.

The two erosion surfaces are juxtaposed on scarps or more gradual transition zones. To the northeast the Mabvindzi River drops 120 metres to the lower post-African erosion surface in less than 5 kilometres, giving rise to pronounced scarps and ridges. Only low density development is possible in this more broken country. Elsewhere, the basic topography is modified by rock type, giving rise to undulating topography in the northern part of the area, flatter land south of the railway, and hills where harder rocks are more resistant to erosion, for example Kopje and Emerald Hill (Lister 1975). Mineral deposits in the vicinity of the city are generally too small to be worked, but there is a variety of building materials, including limestone, clay, gravel and granite. Poorly drained areas occur in some of the river valleys and in quite widespread vleis (poorly drained depressions with soils which are waterlogged in the rainy season and crack when dry, causing cracking in structures). The high water table also gives rise to problems with sewage disposal (Tomlinson and Wurzel 1977). Development in these areas has been inhibited by the physical difficulties. Other than the vleis, much of the area was originally forested, but only a few pockets of woodland remain, most notably in the Mukuvisi Woodland Reserve not far to the southeast of the city centre. The city is situated at an average altitude of 1550 metres. This has a beneficial influence on its climate, which has mild to hot days and cool nights, and an average of 2900 hours of sunshine each year. Rain falls between November and March, varying from 470 to 1350 millimetres per annum, with an average of 820 millimetres. Prior to the rainy season, temperatures and humidity are high, while some frost occurs in winter (June/July). Prevailing winds are from the northeast (Tomlinson and Wurzel 1977).

On this site, which in the early days appeared to be constrained by neither physical difficulties nor shortage of land, a spacious, orderly settlement was developed. Five not always compatible concerns were paramount: the desire for a sanitary and pleasant environment for the white settler population; the need for land and efficient infrastructure to enable the city to fulfil its administrative, industrial and service functions; the desire for profit, preferably speculative; the need to ensure a cheap and easily controlled black labour force; and a preference for the

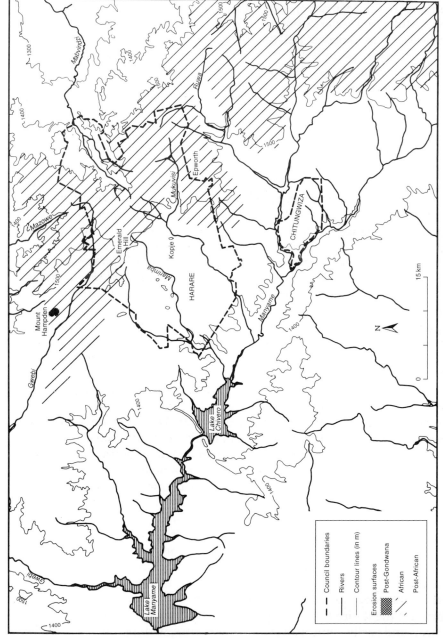

Figure 1.3 The site of Harare. Based on Surveyor General 1985; Lister 1975, p. 36

city to be financially self-supporting. These are reflected in both visible and invisible features of Harare today. In a central business district (CBD) laid out on a grid street pattern, low rise commercial buildings are gradually being superseded by medium and even some high rise offices and commercial development. Around the CBD to the north, east and west sprawl residential suburbs. Densities are low, individual houses on large plots the norm, open spaces for parks and recreation extensive and greenery abundant. Mixed land uses, street selling and other features typical of African cities are closely regulated. Few buildings are more than seventy years old and utility services operate to high standards.

Out of sight of the clean, pleasant, orderly high income suburbs are the industrial areas, themselves very formal, located along the railway line west and east of the city centre and operating as a buffer zone between the former European and former African housing areas*. The latter, although built to much lower standards than the areas just described, are orderly and well serviced, compared to typical low income areas in many other African cities. Extensive areas of almost identical one-storey detached houses seem to stretch as far as the eye can see. Generous plot sizes and road reserves give an impression of low densities, though most of the houses contain more than one family. Compared to the roads of the high income suburbs, the streets and shopping centres of these housing areas are busy and lively, especially at weekends. The most distant and most extensive, Chitungwiza, to the south, is a legacy of late settler ideology of separate development and paranoia about controlling the urban African population. Only near the city centre, in and around Mbare, however, do higher densities, backyard shacks, bustling streets, markets, buses and taxis combine to give a sense of the pulsating life and chaotic environment of bigger, older African cities. Lacking distinctive features or a metropolitan feel, Harare is, rather, a pleasant garden city of one and a half million people, in which there is an almost complete absence of squatter areas, strict control over small businesses, little air pollution, and functioning services. However, it is also characterised by inefficient land use patterns, as well as standards and opportunities which differ widely between income groups.

---

* Before independence, the indigenous occupants of Southern Rhodesia were referred to by the colonists as Africans, blacks or whites. Since 1980 the terms black and white have been used of Zimbabweans, although European still persists, strictly to describe the racial origins of whites, both Zimbabweans and expatriates. There are few Asians or Coloureds (people of mixed race) in Zimbabwe.

The political economy of Southern Rhodesia and Zimbabwe

The settler state

In the nineteenth century and the early years of the twentieth, as noted above, exploitation of Africa's resources was instigated by external economic organisations, including the trading, mining and railway companies. Competitive relations between European states around the time of the First World War, however, and the desire to ensure control over the resources important to their economies, led to the establishment of colonial administrations. In parts of Africa where existing state structures could be coopted, this took the form of indirect rule. Elsewhere, the absence of existing political and administrative systems capable of delivering what the colonial powers required, led to the institution of direct rule by political appointees and members of the civil service of the home country. Those who regarded themselves as settlers demanded a more direct say in territorial government. Although the influence of the home country remained strong, a degree of self-government gave more say to the settlers, more scope for influencing the country's development path and more responsibility for financing government and development.

In 1923 the settlers in Southern Rhodesia were given the choice of becoming part of the (then) Union of South Africa or internal self-government. To avoid Afrikaner dominance they opted for the latter. A state developed whose primary purpose was to foster European settlement and advancement. Mining and agriculture required infrastructural development and support, and a state apparatus evolved to provide these. There was investment in railways and later in roads and electricity, as well as in industries such as iron and steel and agro-processing. Unlike in most other African countries, the interests of domestic capital and the settler population were served by adding value to primary products, for both domestic use and export. Agriculture and, to a lesser extent, other sectors were supported by credit programmes, research, marketing and other services, plus protection against competition, especially from African farmers. Measures were taken to ensure a continued supply of cheap black labour, and the privileged position of white settlers was reinforced by policy, legislation and administrative practice related to migration and place of residence, labour conditions, etc. Although, as elsewhere in eastern, central and southern Africa, blacks were largely excluded from opportunities in trade and commerce, there were plenty of settlers anxious to exploit them and it was not necessary to import Asian traders, as was done in Kenya, Uganda and Zambia, to prevent the emergence of an African commercial class. The white working class, drawn to Southern Rhodesia mainly from Britain and South Africa to take up jobs in mining, transport and services, depended for their high wages and privileges on ensuring the confinement of blacks to unskilled and low paid work, and thus had interests in common with the farmers and mine owners. As we will repeatedly see in subsequent sections, the policies and practices designed to support European settlers and colonial enterprises had dramatic impacts on the pattern of urban development.

A strongly interventionist state represented the interests of settler farmers, local mining, industrial and commercial capitalist interests, subsidiaries of multinational capital, white middle classes and white workers (Stoneman and Cliffe 1989). It played an important role in the development of the capitalist economy and the maintenance of racial domination and privilege, attempting to transform African social formations to accomplish these aims (Cokorinos 1984). Close management of the economy was achieved by extensive state ownership and regulation of many activities by State Boards.

All sections of the white-controlled economy shared an interest in ensuring a cheap and compliant black labour force, and this was the primary influence on labour and urbanisation policy until the 1940s (see below). After that, however, interests to some extent diverged. While agricultural settler capital and individual white households seeking domestic labour continued to give high priority to cheapness, multinational and industrial capital were interested both in the beneficial productivity effects of a stable urban labour force and in its potential as a market to enable continued capitalist expansion (Cokorinos 1984; Stoneman and Cliffe 1989). Despite opposition from semi-skilled whites, limited training for the black industrial workforce was instigated and creation of a higher income black market for industrial and consumer goods initiated by fostering black small scale commercial farmers in the 'African Purchase Areas' and other middle class elements.

In 1954 Southern Rhodesia was joined with Northern Rhodesia (now Zambia) and Nyasaland (now Malawi) in a Federation designed to increase the economic viability of the small component states; to make the initiation of major development projects, such as the Kariba hydro-electric power scheme, easier to realise; to block the rise of African nationalism; and to enlarge the market for Southern Rhodesian manufactures (Gann 1986). This enabled Southern Rhodesia to increase investment in infrastructure and industry, ostensibly on behalf of the whole Federation but in practice to the disadvantage of Northern Rhodesia and the advantage of its own manufacturing sector (Riddell 1992). Harare benefited from the enlarged administrative, financial and industrial functions that resulted. Overcapitalisation in manufacturing ended the boom at the end of the 1950s (Bond 1993b).

By the 1960s those white elements which were threatened by the desire of some capitalist interests to foster limited black enterprise and improved wages backed the right wing Rhodesian Front party, which was elected to power in 1962 and reversed some of the earlier trends, slowing down black advancement in business and industry (Stoneman and Cliffe 1989). Opposition to the Federation from Northern Rhodesia and Nyasaland, which saw it as a means of prolonging white rule, led to its breakup in 1963, followed a year later by independence for Zambia and Malawi. A year after that, in 1965, Southern Rhodesia's Rhodesian Front party, unwilling to accept a political system based on black majority rule, announced its Unilateral Declaration of Independence.

Left only with South Africa as an ally and (open) trading partner, Southern Rhodesia was forced into increasing its economic self-reliance, though its economic dependence on South Africa also increased. Its existing agricultural and industrial base, abundant raw materials and relatively well organised and coherent state enabled considerable progress to be made. Although some local industrial and agricultural capital benefited from the availability of this protected market, the very limited possibilities for trade served the interests of multinational capital less well and ultimately imposed a brake on economic expansion due to the impossibility of developing an extensive capital goods industry for such a small domestic market. In the mid-1970s, crisis again followed the development of excess capacity in manufacturing (Bond 1993b) and the impact of oil price increases (Riddell 1992). A period of under-investment followed, and by 1980 much industrial plant and transport and communications equipment was outdated, limiting productivity, though the economy of both the country as a whole and its urban areas was much less import dependent and more diversified than was typical for Africa. However, few economic opportunities were made available to blacks. Black businessmen were fewer in number than professionals (teachers and medical staff) and were almost entirely confined to rural areas and small settlements.

Although there had been African opposition to settler rule earlier, modern political parties emerged, just as in other British colonies, in the 1950s; the Zimbabwe African People's Union (ZAPU) was formed in 1962 and the breakaway Zimbabwe African National Union (ZANU) in 1963. On UDI the parties were banned and went into exile, with many of their leaders in detention. Small scale armed incursions from Zambia in the second half of the 1960s were relatively easily contained by the Rhodesian armed forces. However, from 1972 onwards ZANU, from bases in Mozambique, adopted a new approach based on the estab-lishment of a politicised popular base for armed struggle in the northeastern areas of the country, some distance from Harare, let alone other urban centres. Although the liberation and establishment of an alternative government structure in whole regions of the country was prohibited by the fragmented pattern of African reserves, more or less clandestine administrative structures were established in many of these areas, and increasing military success was achieved.

Complex conflicts within and between the parties, despite a formal alliance between 1975 and 1979 (the Patriotic Front), led to the eventual association of ZAPU with Ndebele speakers and ZANU with Shona speakers, despite their original multi-ethnic composition. Although both parties had their radical wings, and ZANU in particular a radical rhetoric, in broad ideological terms there was little difference between them. Nevertheless, fear of a liberation struggle that could mobilise support for a radical transformation of society led to various unsuccessful British and international efforts to facilitate agreements between the Smith regime and the nationalist parties during the 1970s (Stoneman and Cliffe 1989). In the later 1970s Rhodesian and South African economic and military pressure was brought to bear on Zambia and Mozambique, to such an extent that these countries had to insist that the Patriotic Front reach some agreement, even though its bargaining position was thereby weakened.

In the Lancaster House Conference, convened and strongly influenced by Britain, and the Agreement which emerged, covering provisions for a ceasefire, elections, the transition to independence and a new constitution, the Patriotic Front was forced to make a number of concessions. In particular, the new government was only permitted to acquire property on a willing seller basis, with the partial exception of 'underutilised' agricultural land for resettlement or other public purposes. Such land had to be acquired at market value and the compensation was remittable in foreign exchange. Although changes could be made after ten years, the lack of provision for payment of compensation as government bonds or in instalments, exacerbated by the failure of overseas donors to provide any volume of foreign exchange, limited the ability of the government to tackle perhaps the most pressing issue—that of unequal access to agricultural land. The elections were relatively open and fair. Contested separately by ZAPU and ZANU (and other political parties), a surprisingly decisive win by ZANU enabled it to form a government (Stoneman and Cliffe 1989). The ZANU government and Zimbabwe's political economy since independence will be discussed in the next section.

Independent Zimbabwe

In the 1980 elections, ZANU obtained more than 80% of the votes in the provinces where they had had a strong guerilla presence, a large majority in Midlands and Mashonaland West (Figure 1.1), but only one seat out of sixteen in the two Matabeleland provinces (Stoneman and Cliffe 1989). A rapprochement with ZAPU was therefore necessary, and the party was brought into the government. Politically vulnerable despite its electoral majority, the government was faced with immediate threats and organisational demands, as well as the need to consolidate its political support and tackle outstanding developmental problems. Faced with threats from the Rhodesian army and South Africa, it had to construct a national army out of three formerly hostile forces. It was keen, following the experience of Mozambique, to avoid a white exodus, especially as it had to cope with the feeding of a million people displaced by the war, many of them to Harare, for which it was dependent on surpluses produced by white commercial farmers. Although there was large scale out-migration of whites around 1980, reducing the population to less than half the pre-independence peak of 275 000 by the mid-1980s (Lloyds Bank 1985: 3), a policy of 'reconciliation' reassured those remaining that neither their economic interests nor their (largely urban) way of life were seriously threatened.

The approach taken by the new government to urban areas can only be understood in the context of the severity of the problems of the rural black population, which needed both immediate and longer term solutions, and the dependence of not only the national but also the urban economy on agricultural production. Much infrastructure in the reserves (Tribal Trust Lands (TTLs), renamed Communal Areas (CAs)) had been destroyed in the war, and administrative structures had broken down. Reconstruction was the immediate priority, followed by the creation of a rural administrative structure. Resentment by blacks of the disproportionate access of whites to land was one of the main grievances which fuelled the independence struggle. At independence 40% of the land was European agricultural land (about 400 ha per head), 42% TTLs (about 12 ha per head) and a small proportion (4%) had been distributed to small scale African commercial farmers in the African Purchase Areas (Figure 1.2) (Moyo 1986: 168; Auret 1990).

Not only was the quantitative distribution of land very unequal, but white farmers had commandeered a disproportionate amount of the land in the areas of greatest agro-ecological potential (Table 1.1). The European or large scale commercial farming (LSCF) areas comprised about 6000 farms with an average size of 2200 ha. However, they occupied nearly three-quarters of the best land, while the Communal Areas, roughly equal in area, occupied only a fifth of the best land and yet had to accommodate nearly half the total population, nearly 60% of whom were living in marginal zones (Natural Regions IV and V) (Table 1.2). Zimbabwe's food self-sufficiency had to be protected, agricultural

Table 1.1   Access to land

	% of all land	% of best land: Natural Regions	
		I & II	I–III
Communal areas	41.8	21.5	30.5
Small scale commercial farming areas	3.6	4.0	5.8
Large scale commercial farming areas	40.1	72.5	57.8
Forest	2.4	1.1	1.5
National land	12.0	0.9	4.4
Total	100.0	100.0	100.0

Source: Zimbabwe 1989: 171.

Table 1.2   Share of land by natural region

Natural Region	Communal Areas	LSCF	Resettlement[a]		SSCF	State
			Model A	Model B		
I	0.7	3.0	0.4	21.7	0.5	8.2
II	8.7	28.6	18.5	48.9	17.8	1.3
III	17.1	17.5	46.9	29.4	37.9	18.6
IV	47.6	25.2	30.9	–	36.9	28.7
V	25.9	25.7	3.8	–	6.9	43.2
Total	100.0	100.0	100.0	100.0	100.0	100.0

Source: Weiner et al 1984.

LSCF Large scale commercial farmers; SSCF Small scale commercial farmers.
[a] Model A resettlement provides for individual land holdings (1.669 million hectares by 1984), Model B for producer cooperatives (0.067 million hectares by 1984) (Auret 1990: 74).

inputs to domestic manufacturing assured and export earnings maintained (Herbst 1990: 38). Agricultural production by the LSCF sector thus had to be maintained, at the same time as agricultural policy was reorientated towards meeting the diverse needs of Communal Area farmers, in order to improve their livelihoods and deter rural–urban migration; and the grossly unequal access to land had to be addressed. The first and last of these aims were in opposition. Progress in transforming the agricultural sector has been limited. The LSCF sector has continued to dominate production, though there is general agreement among analysts that at least half the land owned by these farmers is underutilised (Riddell 1978; Zimbabwe 1982; Libby 1984; Moyo 1986; Auret 1990). The Communal Areas suffer from increasing population pressure and land degradation. Because of the long history of male migration, many of the households are headed by women (Moyo 1986). Policies since independence have resulted in increased production for sale, but the farmers who benefited were those with access to land and labour and were spatially concentrated in the areas of greater potential (Drakakis-Smith 1987a; Auret 1990). Although agriculture's share of GDP has been decreasing (Table 1.3), as has its share of formal sector employment, these remain substantial, and would be much greater if those working in agriculture in the CAs were taken into account. Despite the sector's important and increasing share of export earnings, a significant proportion of CA households are landless and many very poor, fuelling continued migration to urban areas. A more determined effort has been made to redress inequalities of social service provision. The increased priority given to public expenditure on health and education and to the rural areas resulted in improved access to social services by large numbers of rural residents (Auret 1990), but also added to a burgeoning budget deficit.

Quite an extensive urban manufacturing sector had developed by the 1970s, assisted by Southern Rhodesia's isolation during the Second World War and the markets provided by Northern Rhodesia and Nyasaland during Federation. The desire of industrial capital to expand the size of the domestic market by increasing black incomes had been hindered by the retrogressive policies of the Rhodesian Front, but UDI had also provided, as noted above, a stimulus and an opportunity for further and more diversified import substitution industrialisation to compensate for sanctions, as well as some new export development (sanctions busting via South Africa). In addition, foreign owned firms which could not remit funds reinvested them. While production grew until 1973, the country was adversely affected first by the 1973 oil price increase and then by escalating civil unrest, as well as by overcapacity (Bond 1993b). The results were falling rates of return, capacity utilisation and employment in the sector (Green and Kadhani, 1986). At independence, therefore, Zimbabwe inherited low foreign debt and a diverse urban industrial base, but one operating with outdated plant and well below capacity. Mining's significance in export terms has declined during the 1980s because of recession and declining terms of trade (Ncube 1991). It is geographically very dispersed, but underpins urbanisation by supplying cheap power, raw materials and a market for engineering products (Table 1.3). Although the role of manufacturing in the national economy and its relative importance in employment terms has increased only slightly in the twenty-year period shown in Table 1.3, it is more significant than in any other sub-Saharan African country, with the exception of South Africa and Zambia.

Table 1.3 Sectoral shares in the economy

	Share of GDP[a]			Share of wage employment			Proportion of export earnings		
	1974	1980	1990	1970	1930	1990	1970	1980	1990
Agriculture, forestry and fishing	17.6	14.2	12.9	34.9	32.4	24.3	n.a.	39[c]	51
Mining and quarrying	7.6	8.8	8.2	6.7	6.6	4.3	n.a.	15[d]	8
Manufacturing	23.5	24.9	26.4	13.4	15.8	16.5	n.a.	46[e]	41
Electricity and water	2.3	2.2	3.3	0.7	0.7	0.7	–	–	–
Construction	4.6	2.7	2.2	5.0	4.2	6.4	–	–	–
Services[b]	44.4	47.2	47.0	39.3	40.3	47.8	–	–	–
Total	100.0	100.0	100.0	100.0	100.0	100.0	100.0	100.0	100.0

Sources: CSO 1987a, 1990: 10, 1991: 8; Zimbabwe 1989.

n.a. Not available
[a] Source: Zimbabwe 1989: 101. Gross domestic product at factor cost at current prices; Services treated as residual category.
[b] Including financial services, insurance and real estate; distribution, restaurants and hotels; transport and communications; public administration; education; health; private domestic service; and other.
[c] SITC categories 0 Food, 1 Beverages and tobacco, 2 Crude materials derived from agriculture and forestry; Source: calculated from CSO 1987b: 22–4; 1991: 20.
[d] Standard International Trade Classification (SITC) categories 2 Crude materials (minerals), 3 Mineral fuels, related products and electricity.
[e] SITC categories 4 Animal and vegetable oils and fats, 5 Chemicals and related products, 6 Manufactured goods classified by materials, 7 Machinery and equipment, 8 and 9 Miscellaneous manufactured goods.

At independence the European population (3% of the total) received nearly two-thirds of national income, both from wages and salaries and from profits, and, together with foreign interests, owned nearly all the capital in industry and mining. The benefits of earlier economic growth were, therefore, extremely unevenly distributed (Bratton 1981; Stoneman and Cliffe 1989). As a result, continued economic health depended on domestic and foreign white capital, which was divided about 70:30 between foreign and settler interests, and the production structure was biased towards production of goods for a minority market. Not only were blacks estimated to control only 12% of the productive capacity of the economy, but also all the sectors of production were dominated by large scale producers (Bratton 1981; Ushewokunze 1982).

Although the need for structural transformation of the economy and radical redistribution of wealth and income was recognised in the government's political platform, expressed as a strategy of 'growth with equity and transformation' (Zimbabwe 1982: 24), expedience, real constraints and a predisposition towards relatively conservative fiscal management on the part of Chidzero, the Minister of Finance, Economic Planning and Development, and others, limited the changes which were made. Initially, rapid economic growth, fuelled by reopened trade and an inflow of loan funds, helped to reinforce both the adoption of an essentially capitalist economic development strategy, and reliance on anticipated continued inflows of foreign loans, while masking the relatively limited nature of the redistributive measures adopted. However, by 1982 the post-independence boom had turned into crisis (Green and Kadhani 1986).

Emergence of a budget deficit led to recourse to the IMF, so 'policy choices came to reflect a compromise between a conventional economic stabilization program and a political commitment to redistribution in the form of subsidies, transfer payments and expenditures on social services' (Bratton and Burgess 1987: 204). Despite the latter commitment, subsidies were gradually reduced from 1983 on and, especially since 1988, post-independence minimum wage increases have been eroded by inflation, expenditure on social services has been reduced and fees have gradually been extended and increased. Meanwhile, the failure of anticipated foreign investment to materialise and the difficulties of penetrating export markets have limited the availability of foreign exchange and hindered the replacement of existing capital equipment, much of it long obsolete. Continued deterioration in the economic situation by the end of the 1980s, combined with pressure from the international agencies, led to the adoption of a fully fledged structural adjustment programme in 1991 (Zimbabwe 1991a). Similar in content to those adopted earlier by other African countries (Seralgeldin 1989;

Jesperson 1992), short term pain (in the form of public and private sector redundancies, higher interest rates and other fiscal reforms, elimination of remaining subsidies, reform of parastatals, and so on) would, it was hoped, result in healthier economic structures and renewed economic and employment growth by the mid-1990s.

To understand why Zimbabwe's policies have been far from radical, a number of factors must be considered. The struggle for independence was essentially a nationalist struggle, though ZANU's rhetoric promised a socialist transformation, embodying a redistribution of wealth and assets and equalisation of access to opportunities and services. Progress has been made with the latter, but 'the Mugabe government has been . . . distinctly wary of dispossessing capitalist classes of their property' (Bratton and Burgess 1987: 200). Faced with very real constraints, even where there was scope for choice, the government has plumped for caution. Explanations for this rest in the nature of the struggle for independence, the inherited economic structure, the political and administrative systems, the regional situation and the global economy.

Destruction of an existing political economy is a prerequisite for radical transformation. The independence struggle in Zimbabwe, however, was geographically remote from the main European agricultural areas and urban industrial areas, including Harare, and the settler economy survived almost intact. Its economic and political vulnerability meant that the government had to reach an accommodation with the powerful economic interests on which it depended to feed much of the black population, to provide employment and revenue and to earn foreign exchange (Bratton 1981; Shaw 1989). As blacks were drawn into better paid niches in the economy, both in public and private sector enterprises, often in token roles rather than as skilled managers and professionals, they also developed a vested interest in maintaining the basic nature of the economic system. Even if the involvement of blacks in the formal large scale sector is marginal and often symbolic, and the black small business sector remains relatively small, the emergence of this group inevitably makes it more difficult for the majority of blacks to challenge the structure of the system.

Even amongst the radical wings of ZANU and ZAPU, which merged in 1987, what a socialist transformation might look like was never fully worked out (Lemon 1988; Shaw 1989). Although some radical policies have been espoused, neither the capacity and technical expertise to formulate a coherent development strategy nor grass roots organisation sufficient for authoritative claims to represent the voice of the people have been developed by the parties. Party organisational capacity to influence policy and get things done is, therefore, limited (Bratton and Burgess 1987; Herbst 1990). Although the merger of the two parties implied a virtual one-party system in much of the country, Mugabe was dissuaded from formally declaring a one-party state by pressure from international and national sources, including newly formed opposition parties (Stoneman and Cliffe 1989). One of the latter, the Zimbabwe Unity Movement (ZUM), contested the 1990 elections. By capitalising on popular discontent, it won 17% of the vote (though only two seats), but proposed policies to the right of the government's as a solution to the economic problems it identified (Sachikonye 1990).

Strong, extensive and centralised state structures have meant that the civil service has been influential in policymaking, including urban and housing policy. Although in the early years after independence the conservatism of this influence could be attributed to the dominance of whites in senior civil service ranks, rapid promotion of many blacks has not changed the basic nature of the state apparatus. The strongly developed state apparatus also meant that at independence, the government inherited the capacity to regulate the economy, run certain economic enterprises and service the formal private sector. The conservative positions that civil servants tend to adopt also reflect the embourgeoisement of an element of the black population (Mandaza 1986a) and, given the earlier lack of opportunities for developing business interests, a situation in which the state apparatus is potentially a major avenue of access to other opportunities and assets. As elsewhere in Africa, these range from access to credit to the allocation of scarce commodities such as serviced plots, and there is scope for mutual favours and rewards for support. The interests of an emerging black petite bourgeoisie which has ties with the domestic and international bourgeoisie and the domestic white petite bourgeoisie are, Mandaza asserts (1986a, 1986b), in opposition to the interests of workers and peasants.

The Zimbabwe government's autonomy in policymaking has been limited not just by local interests, but also by the nature of its relations with surrounding countries and the global economy. Civil war in Mozambique has threatened its link with the port of Beira. Maintaining protection for the road and railway and for the oil pipeline, and accommodating Mozambican refugees, have imposed a considerable drain on government resources. Relationships with South Africa, with which Zimbabwe's white population has close family, social and business ties, have been complicated. The government's support for political change was counterbalanced in the 1980s by its continued economic dependence on South Africa and the latter's capacity for destabilisation in the region and even within Zimbabwe.

In common with other African countries, external economic dependency reduces the state's capacity for autonomous action and is self-reinforcing. Zimbabwe's debt position is far worse than it was in

1980—debt service as a proportion of export earnings increased from 3.8% in 1980 to 32% in 1992, well above the sub-Saharan average of 20% (World Bank 1994: 206–7). However, even with Zimbabwe's advantages over other African countries, attracting foreign investment and increasing export earnings have both proved difficult, and so the government is forced to borrow in order to achieve its economic aims (Sibanda 1988). Borrowing implies conditionality, thus imposing a further constraint on autonomous policy choices.

Neither economic transformation nor redistribution of wealth and income were possible without challenging, in particular, white ownership of assets, something for which aid funds were certainly not going to be made available. The perceived needs not to upset the mainstays of the economy, especially large scale commercial farmers, but also the mining, manufacturing and private services sectors, to adhere to the Lancaster House Agreement, to maintain its creditworthiness, and to satisfy its most important political constituency (black smallholders in the Shona-speaking parts of the country), have led the government to adopt policies that have favoured the perpetuation of the existing economic system. Although gains in terms of access to education and health services were safeguarded during the economic policy shifts of the 1980s (Davies and Sanders 1988), these have been more seriously threatened by the structural adjustment programme of the 1990s, the impact of which was exacerbated by the severe drought of 1992. Real GDP fell dramatically in the short term (−7.7% in 1992, compared to 4.9% growth the previous year) (CSO 1993). Employment in both the private and public sectors fell, as a result of both the adverse effects on industries of economic liberalisation and the loss of agricultural raw materials, and the lifting of restrictions on making workers redundant.

Overall, there has been relatively little change in the structure of Zimbabwe's economy since independence. This discussion of the main sectors of economic activity is relevant in different ways to urban development. The situation of farmers, particularly those in the CAs, and with particular respect to access to land, is crucial to understanding patterns of rural–urban migration and the continuing rural ties of the urban population. Mining is scattered and workings have rarely given rise to urban settlements, but it supplies inputs to manufacturing, which, together with services activity, is predominantly located in urban areas. Manufacturing is well developed but the structural weaknesses of the sector have resulted in periodic underutilisation of capacity. At these times, capital has flowed instead into the built environment, especially into commercial investment. Thus the capital, locational and labour requirements of the manufacturing and services sectors have been a primary influence on the evolution of the pattern of urban development, both between and within urban settlements. This will be explored in the next section.

The history of urban development

The services for miners and farmers located in the towns provided support for a white population which was always predominantly urban (56% by 1921) and became more so as the urban economies developed, reaching 86% at the time of the 1969 census. The interests of the urban white population were paramount both in the labour policies and practices adopted and in approaches to planning and housing. The first of these aspects of urban development will be discussed in the next section, and then more information presented on the demographic aspects of urban development and the pattern of urban settlement which has resulted. Approaches to planning and housing will be analysed in Chapters 2, 5 and 6.

Historical development of the urban labour force

The white urban population that was engaged in mining, the provision of services to miners and farmers and later manufacturing industry, was gradually supplemented by black labour, initially for domestic servants and later as unskilled workers in other sectors. Similar mechanisms to those used to ensure a supply of black labour to agriculture were used for urban labour: that is, taxes, and then, when tax demands were met by increased sales of maize and cattle by African farmers, by unfavourable maize pricing policies for black producers. As in the mining and European farming areas of other colonies, especially Zambia and South Africa, black male workers were recruited on short term contracts, not only from the rural areas of Rhodesia, but also from Malawi, Zambia and Mozambique, and were expected to return home at the end of their contracts, on losing their jobs or on retirement. Wives and families had to be left in the rural areas, thus enabling urban wages to be kept low. At the same time, the exodus of labour from the rural areas and the development of import substitution manufacturing destroyed craft production and increased rural demand for manufactured goods, reinforcing the reliance on cash income.

> The colonial form of production organisation was based on very tight control over black unskilled and semi-skilled labour by white managements. White workers, on the other hand, formed a labour 'aristocracy',

which possessed the skills and jealously guarded their 'skilled' jobs. The state not only propelled the industrialisation process but also shaped the conditions for cheap black labour while acting as a bulwark for the white skilled workers. (Moyo 1988: 206)

As in other labour reserve colonies, especially South Africa, this tight control over black workers and protection of white workers was achieved by a succession of laws. The white working class was badly hit by the depression of the 1930s and this led in 1934 to the Industrial Conciliation Act, which formalised racial discrimination in urban jobs, and in 1936 to the Native Registration Act, which required all black residents to possess valid registration documents only obtainable if they were legitimately employed (Mazur 1986/7). The 1941 consolidated Land Apportionment Act provided, *inter alia*, for the creation of black townships by municipal councils, and this became compulsory under the 1946 Natives (Urban Areas) Accommodation and Registration Act (Simon 1986). Employers were obliged to provide housing, mostly in hostels, and the control was backed up by a Vagrancy Act which gave the authorities power to return black residents to their rural areas of origin if they were unemployed.

Increasing demand for black labour from the growing manufacturing sector after 1945 led to changed policy emphases. A continued supply of migrant labour was ensured by the Land Husbandry Act of 1951 which limited the size of African agricultural landholdings (Drakakis-Smith 1987b). Manufacturing capital also began to require more skilled labour. How to provide this was an arena for struggle between the owners of capital and the white working class. Manufacturing capital favoured the training and stabilisation of black labour—as did mining capital in Katanga and the Copperbelt (Coquery-Vidrovitch 1991)—but in Zimbabwe this was strongly resisted by white skilled workers concerned to protect their disproportionately high wages and other privileges. Job fragmentation was used to create semi-skilled jobs for blacks out of skilled trades (Moyo 1988). The Industrial Conciliation Act was amended in 1959, not to facilitate the growth of African trade unions, which rapidly increased in numbers and membership, but as a means of controlling unregistered trade unions. It also barred unions from engaging in political activity. Minimum wages were introduced in 1947 (Mazur 1986/7). However, these provisions only involved industrial workers—domestic servants' labour conditions were still regulated under the Masters and Servants Act, while still in 1975 only 10% of the blacks employed outside agriculture received a wage sufficient to support a family of six above the poverty line (Riddell 1978: 15).

As in countries to the north, and despite the continued control over residence (unlike in South Africa where influx control was more draconian), the black urban population continued to grow. The ratio of black to white urban residents in Zimbabwe increased from 1 : 1 in 1904 to 3 : 1 in 1960 and to 5 : 1 in 1980, when there were about 234 000 whites in the fourteen main urban centres (Whitsun Foundation 1980: 3), compared with a total African urban population of 0.1 million in 1936, 0.2 million in 1946 and 1.2 million in 1977. Despite this growth, only 17% of the black population lived in urban areas by 1979.

UDI, as we have noted, was the political expression of the interests of agrarian capital and the white urban working class. The government acted after 1965 to further protect white skilled jobs and workers and to restrict black trade unions (Moyo 1988). Thus between 1959 and 1980 there was not one legal strike by black workers (Herbst 1990). Trade union leaders were cultivated by white employers and did not overtly oppose the Anglo-Rhodesian settlement proposals in 1972. However, the Pearce Commission, sent to find out if the proposals were acceptable, was met by strikes and demonstrations called contrary to the instructions of union leaders. Unrest was also associated with later attempts at political settlement between 1976 and 1979. While some union leaders were imprisoned, others prevented generalisation of strikes and other actions, resulting in a weakening of the potential power of black urban workers.

> It is scarcely surprising that in the 1960s and 1970s a dark cloud hovered over trade unionism in Zimbabwe. A decimation of the leadership of unions through its incarceration in detention or exile, the onerous labour laws, in addition to the dubious role of international labour institutions . . . had a general weakening impact on the unions. (Sachikonye 1986: 251).

While white unions were well organised and recognised as bodies with whom employers could negotiate, black unions were unable to improve either the working or the living conditions of black workers and so many blacks did not become members. White unions obtained higher wages for white employees, by the creation of a shortage of skilled workers rather than by negotiating minimum wages, by representing jobs filled by blacks as less skilled than they really were, and by job reservation (Raftopoulos 1986). However, the relatively high wages so won meant that increasingly by the 1970s white workers were pricing themselves out of jobs, while the supply of skilled labour was reduced by conscription and emigration. Although in 1972 only 5% of the workforce were classified as black semi-skilled workers, many were doing similar jobs to whites on much less pay, as illustrated by the outcome of regrading exercises in the early 1980s which resulted in 27% of the workforce being designated semi-skilled (Wood 1988). Meanwhile, the reliance on continued white in-migration for the supply of skilled workers hindered the development of in-country technical training capacity.

By the time of the independence struggle in the 1970s, therefore, repression of the urban black labour force had reduced its potential to undermine the government. Poverty and job insecurity discouraged militancy, while many union leaders were imprisoned (Wood 1988). Expectations that organised labour could be the channel for destabilisation of the government were not to be realised, while the centrality of land to the nationalist struggle and the base of exiled political parties to the north and northeast of the country, far from white commercial agriculture, industry and mining, ensured that the guerrilla struggle was predominantly a rural affair. This history, and the ambivalent feelings towards organised labour that have resulted, help to explain post-independence attitudes to the urban labour force.

In the late 1970s emigration of whites increased, the economy was increasingly badly affected by the war, investment slackened, and the end of racial discrimination was anticipated. While the white population of Harare, for instance, decreased from an estimated 118 300 (20% of the total) in 1977 to 91 100 (13%) in 1981 (Davies 1986), in-migration from rural areas, already substantial because of the stagnation of rural wage employment and continued population pressure in the CAs, was swelled by people fleeing from the fighting. The rescinding of legislation restricting black movement, residence and property ownership helped to further increase in-migration, while the movement of wives and families to join their menfolk already working in the towns gradually changed the gender composition of the urban population.

There is a variety of potential sources of power for urban populations. In a democratic system, they have electoral power, both at the central government level and at the local government level in the election of councillors. The presence of formal sector jobs in urban areas also makes organised labour potentially powerful, though the extent to which this potential is realised will depend on the structure of capitalist interests, the importance of the formal sector *vis-à-vis* the informal sector, links between employment and other services such as health and housing, and government attitudes to worker organisations. It is this last aspect which has been considered in this section. The relations of labour with employers and government help to determine policies and practices related to working conditions and wages and so, in an urban economy in which the majority are wage employees, critically influence the living conditions of the urban majority. Trends in wages and incomes in

Harare will be discussed in Chapter 3 in the context of the changing relationship between capital, labour and the state in post-independence Zimbabwe.

Patterns of urban settlement

Despite the extractive nature of colonial economies, the limited development of manufacturing, and the attempts at influx control, urban areas in Africa had been growing at between 4% and 6% per annum in the 1950s, except in southern Africa. Nevertheless, at the beginning of the 1960s less than a fifth of Africa's population lived in urban areas. While in a few countries the proportion of people living in urban areas was well above this (for example in South Africa, Zambia and Senegal), the remainder of African countries had very low levels of urbanisation (UN 1991). At independence, influx control became unacceptable and the rate of urban growth, which had been accelerating prior to the main wave of countries attaining independence, continued to do so. At the same time, newly independent governments set out to improve the health of their populations and to increase their access to education. Investments in health care and basic services such as water and sanitation led to reduced infant and child mortality and increased life expectancy. At the same time, fertility remained high for a variety of reasons, including household labour needs, female disadvantage in terms of access to educational and economic opportunities, and uneven access to family planning services. Thus in sub-Saharan Africa as a whole the fertility rate was 6.5 in 1970 and 6.1 in 1992; infant mortality fell to 142 per 1000 live births in 1970 and 99 per 1000 in 1992; the population per physician decreased from nearly 32 000 in 1970 to 20 000 in 1990; and life expectancy increased by seven years, from 45 in 1970 to 52 in 1992 (World Bank 1994). Rates of natural increase therefore steadily increased, reaching 2.5% per annum for Africa as a whole in the early 1960s, 2.6% per annum later in the decade and 2.7% per annum in the early 1970s.

Rates of urban growth have, on average, been roughly double the rates of natural increase. The most marked increases in urban growth rates occurred, on the whole, in the least urbanised countries, including those which attained independence without significant urban centres (including, for example, Mauritania, which was previously governed from Senegal). In contrast, slower rates of urban growth were experienced in some countries which inherited oversized capitals—for example Congo and Senegal, where Brazzaville and Dakar had been the administrative centres for the whole of French Equatorial and West

Africa respectively (O'Connor 1983). A number of changes associated with independence increased the attraction of cities. The growth of civil services and attempts to industrialise gave a boost to rural–urban migration. The centralisation of politics and bureaucracy formed a further attraction to investors who needed access to the state machinery. What urban centres there were became the locus of power and investment, and new states invested heavily in their capitals because of their international and national visibility (Gugler and Flanagan 1978; Mehretu 1983; Skinner 1986). The creation of additional subnational units gave rise to a further impetus to develop new administrative centres, for example the new states in Nigeria; while some states, where the colonial settlement pattern was considered to be particularly inappropriate, embarked upon the construction of new capitals. The exploitation of new resources led to growth in cities such as Port Harcourt, centre of Nigeria's oil industry, while other mining centres declined in relative terms, for example in Zaire and Zambia. In the later 1960s urban growth rates reached 8% per annum or more in nine countries and by the early 1970s these countries had been joined by at least four more. In the eight, mostly Francophone, countries of West Africa examined by Zachariah and Condé (1981), almost half the urban growth between the mid-1960s and the mid-1970s came from migration, mostly from the rural areas. The anticipated inhibiting effects of urban residence on fertility were outweighed by the relatively young age profile of migrants, the lower mortality rates in urban areas, and the increase in family migration (Standing 1984; Salau 1990). By 1970 there were eight cities with populations of one million plus in Africa: four in North Africa, two in South Africa, and only two elsewhere in the continent (Lagos and Kinshasa). Other large cities with particularly rapid growth rates (10% per annum or more) in the 1960s and early 1970s included Abidjan, Conakry, Tripoli and Dar es Salaam, along with many of the smaller capital cities. A pattern of increased concentration of rural–urban migration in the largest city within a country was widely evident (Zachariah and Condé 1981).

Despite Africa's marginal position in the world economy and the economic difficulties experienced more or less consistently since the mid-1970s, urbanisation has continued. By 1990 it was estimated that a third of the population was urban, compared to a quarter in 1975. United Nations figures suggested that the rate of urban growth in the 1980s was even higher than in the 1960s, running at around 5% per annum, and that the number of cities with more than a million people had grown from 8 in 1970 to 24 in 1991, in 18 countries (UN 1991). As in the earlier period, rates of growth in the least urbanised regions (East and West Africa) were above the average for the continent as a whole. However, there were major difficulties with these figures: of the 56 countries, less than half had conducted a census since 1980 and only three of the largest countries had reasonably recent semi-reliable censuses, while two (Nigeria and Zaire, estimated to contain over a fifth of the continent's total and urban populations) had never conducted a reliable census. The inability of so many African countries to carry out regular and reliable censuses is a symptom of their poverty and underdevelopment, as well as of civil war and political instability. As a result, much of the analysis of recent urbanisation trends is based on unreliable data or estimates. Nevertheless, it is clear that the proportion of the population which lives in the largest city is high and increasing, while secondary cities and small urban centres continue to be underdeveloped (Rondinelli 1988). Despite Africa's economic difficulties, cities have continued to grow: rates of natural increase are high, despite the spread of AIDS and evidence of recent fertility declines in some countries; they are transport and communications hubs; and they are often the seats of government. Their location as the place of residence for politicians, senior civil servants and diplomats has helped to bias public expenditure on specialist health and other services and infrastructure towards them; this and the need for access to government offices has in turn made them the most likely choice for both transnational and domestic investment in manufacturing and for the offices of multinational corporations (MNCs) with mining or agricultural enterprises elsewhere in the country.

Zimbabwe had a total population of about five million in 1969, rising to seven and a half million in 1982, spread over an area of about 391 000 square kilometres. A fifth of the total population was urban in 1961/2, a similar proportion to the overall average for Africa; by the early 1980s this had reached a quarter, below the average for Africa as a whole (28% in 1980) (UN 1991; and see Table 1.4). It is quite likely, however, that all the censuses undercounted the urban population. At the time of writing, urban totals from the 1992 census were not yet available. However, estimates in 1989 suggested that 2.5 million people were living in urban and semi-urban areas (Zimbabwe 1991a: Annex III).

Zimbabwe's largest city is Harare, followed by Bulawayo (Figure 1.2). Of the total urban population in 1982, 58% was in these two centres, which had both grown at about 4.5% per annum since 1969, reaching a population of 656 111 in Harare and 413 814 in Bulawayo. However, Chitungwiza, a satellite town established to the south of Harare and part of the latter's economy, should really be added to the population figure for Harare, giving a total of 829 000 at least. Chitungwiza, from a population of only 15 000 in 1969, grew 20.7% per annum to reach 172 600 by 1982. By 1992 the total population of the conurbation had reached 1.45 million (1.18 million in Harare, 0.27 million in

Table 1.4   Urbanisation in Zimbabwe

	Total population		Urban population[a]				
	(000s)	% p.a.	White (000s)	Black (000s)	Total (000s)	% p.a.	% of total
1961/2	3857.5		188	533	764.7		19.8
		4.1				2.5	
1969	5099.3		203	676	945.4		18.5
		3.1				5.5	
1982	7546.1		n.a.	n.a.	1941.6		25.7

Sources: Censuses as reported in Mutizwa-Mangiza 1986: 148. Source for white and black population is Whitsun Foundation 1980: 32. Figures do not add up to the total due to later adjustment of census totals. By 1982 census results for urban areas no longer reported by racial group.

[a] Defined as localities with at least 150 people in which the majority of adult males were in non-agricultural occupations in 1961/2 and 1969. If this definition is used, figures for total urban population in 1969 would be 900.0 and in 1982 1730.0. Figures given are using the 1982 definition of urban which is all places with a population of 2500 or more.

Chitungwiza), representing a growth rate of 5.8% per annum. Harare grew considerably faster than Bulawayo (4.7% per annum), which reached 621 000; only Mutare (6.6% per annum) and one or two smaller centres grew faster than Harare (Zimbabwe 1992). Despite the remnants of influx control and economic recession, relaxation on black urban residence and migration from areas affected by the liberation war resulted in a rate of urban growth in Harare which was similar to that of Africa as a whole, though well below that in countries with the most explosive rates of urban population growth.

Although Harare and Bulawayo remain the largest settlements, they are not as overwhelmingly dominant in the settlement size distribution as are the largest city or cities in many other countries. However, the dominance of Harare is increasing, as illustrated by its relative size in comparison with Bulawayo: the population of Bulawayo was 68% of Harare's in 1962, 63% in 1969, just under 50% in 1982 if Chitungwiza's population is added to that of Harare itself and 43% in 1992 (Davies 1987; Zimbabwe 1992). Harare and Bulawayo were also considered to be dominant in terms of their central place functions, with service areas estimated to cover two-thirds and one-third of the country respectively (Heath 1990).

Separate estimates of the rate of natural increase of the urban population are not available, but Table 1.4 shows that in the 1960s it was growing less rapidly than the national population, reflecting the effectiveness of migration controls at that time, while between 1969 and

1982 the urban population was growing at 5.5% per annum compared to the national population at 3.1%, implying that roughly 56% of urban growth could be attributed to natural increase and the remainder to migration, not unlike the rest of Africa. Further discussion of Harare's economic role will be postponed to Chapter 3 and of the demographic and migration characteristics of its population to Chapter 4. First, the arrangements by which the city is administered and, in the next chapter, the physical dimensions of the city's growth will be elaborated.

Urban administration

The evolution of the urban local government system under the settler government

Health concerns and the need to provide colonial administrators and early settlers with an acceptable living environment gave rise to environmental sanitation measures and the establishment of rudimentary local government throughout colonial Africa (King 1990). Urban local authorities were established early in the history of Southern Rhodesia, as the European settlements began to grow. Initial administration was by the British South Africa Company, which reserved and administered land around the towns, initially in its own ownership. A Sanitary Board was set up in Harare in 1891, and in the following year another was established in Masvingo. Even though there was not at that stage a legislative basis for these administrative arrangements, the Boards held elections and started collecting property taxes (rates) in order to provide infrastructure and environmental sanitation services. Harare and Bulawayo became municipalities in 1897.

The urban areas were managed by and for the benefit of their European populations. Whereas local councils in French colonies were run by appointed administrator-mayors (Skinner 1986), in British colonies white property owners were enfranchised. Local authority functions were designed to provide a healthy environment for the white population.

> God, Greed, Gold and the Flag motivated all settler activity. Amongst this strongly class conscious imperialist group the indigenous African was generally considered a backward, illiterate heathen unworthy of social intercourse as an equal, fit only for menial labour and the object of charitable works ... The distinct racial differences of colour and appearance served to emphasise ethnic-cultural differences and to facilitate the creation of unsympathetic stereotypes ... The apparent and obvious 'differentness' [sic] between the two groups progressively exacerbated intergroup relations, reinforced attitudes and justified planning policies of separate development. (Dewar 1987: 42).

The settlers' conviction of their cultural superiority and African inferiority led them to believe that blacks had neither the intellectual skills nor the educational attainment to understand democracy (Mungazi 1992). However, black labour, as described in the previous section, was required. Land segregation on the basis of race, similar to that instituted in other colonial countries (Simon 1992), was introduced in 1894. Under a series of subsequent enactments, provision was made to set aside land for townships, to which those blacks permitted to live in urban areas (with the exception of domestic servants) were confined. As the numbers of urban blacks grew, various provisions were introduced to administer the areas in which they lived and in 1935 Harare became a city.

During the 1960s, administration of the larger urban centres became increasingly disjointed, creating problems for planning and service provision. By 1967, 26 Town Management Boards had been set up to manage private subdivisions, some with their own African townships (Whitsun Foundation 1980). At the beginning of the 1970s, the boundaries of the two cities of Harare and Bulawayo were extended and rationalised. The redrawing of boundaries was followed in 1973 by the Urban Councils Act, intended to rationalise and replace earlier legislation. This Act, in its amended form, is the basis for urban local government today. The Act, modelled closely on the British local government system, gives urban local authorities, including city, municipal and town councils, a wide range of mandatory and permissive powers. The city is divided into wards, each of which elects a councillor. A mayor is elected annually from among the councillors, chairs the council, represents it to the public and leads negotiation with other bodies (Jordan 1984). Only white, Asian and coloured ratepayers were given the vote, in addition to the spouses of ratepaying owners and occupiers, and representatives of businesses and bodies which owned or occupied property. Most councillors were independent and, despite its efforts to do so, the Rhodesian Front did not gain a majority (Jordan 1984): 'there existed a great degree of perceived homogeneity within the European society, of value consensus and unanimity derived from shared experience and permeation of similar ideas and information' (Dewar 1987: 43). Thus informal contacts substituted for formal political lobbying, and Dewar notes that in Harare in 1970 only one ratepayers' association was registered.

While the approval of the full council is required for financial matters, making by-laws, the alienation of land and the appointments of the principal officer and heads of department, other matters may be delegated to standing committees. The council has wide discretionary powers to provide utilities and services and may make by-laws. It is also the local planning authority. The government aimed to make urban councils financially self-sufficient, with the exception of government grants for preventive health care and the maintenance of main roads. Revenue is derived from rates on property (see Chapter 5); receipts from trading accounts, such as the sale of water; fees for services; and registration fees, especially vehicle licences. Capital expenditure is financed from the council's own funds or central government loans, while the larger local authorities were given the right to borrow from building societies or the private sector and to issue bonds. Proposed by-laws and capital borrowing are subject to central government approval. While similar in structure to urban local government in other British colonies, the needs and wealth of the relatively large white settler population ensured and enabled greater institutional and financial capacity in urban areas in Zimbabwe than elsewhere (Stren 1989).

As in other colonial cities, such as Nairobi, Lusaka or Johannesburg, African housing areas were spatially separated from but administered by the city council. Although black labour was needed, black Africans were regarded as only temporary urban dwellers, and did not have the vote; influx was to be controlled; cultural differences were thought to be unbridgeable; and social control was vital to the settler government. Despite the requirement for housing to be provided, and a levy on urban employers between 1961 and 1976 which was used to subsidise housing and transport services, living conditions in black townships were poor. In 1967, parallel with similar but more extreme moves in South Africa, an attempt was made to provide more autonomy to the townships, to develop skills in self-management and to eliminate subsidies to them by establishing a lower tier of local government with certain assigned responsibilities. The first Township Board was established in 1971. The Boards had

> a measure of executive authority to operate minor services (e.g. markets), to provide and maintain welfare, recreational and entertainment services and facilities, to assist voluntary groups and institutions and to coordinate voluntary effort to meet community needs. They were empowered to prepare budget estimates, to raise finance from beer sales, service fees and accommodation levies, and they could also borrow money and accept . . . grants. However, the budget estimate still had to be approved by the City council. Boards could also appoint or dismiss staff subject to council ratification. The municipality retained control of the landlord-estate function and of major services. The all-Black membership was partly elected and partly nominated by the Minister of Local Government and Housing. (Dewar 1987: 44)

Attitudes towards the Boards varied from strong opposition to apathetic acceptance. Criticisms were voiced both by Europeans, who considered that Africans preferred paternalistic forms of government, and by Africans, who viewed the Boards as an attempt to entrench a policy of separate and unequal development. In 1979, African townships were renamed Local Government Areas, and the Township Boards became Area Boards with observer status on the urban councils (Whitsun Foundation 1980).

Although the Boards were elected, they were mainly consultative, with very limited powers and limited popular backing (Patel and Adams, 1981). While in theory, Boards could progress to becoming municipalities in their own right, only that for Chitungwiza, to the south of Harare, did so after independence (see Chapter 2). Although the other townships were an integral part of the urban economy, they had separate financial arrangements, were administered by a separate department of the local authority, and were subject to decisions made by the local authority in which they had no right to a say. Revenue to cover the cost of services was raised from supplementary charges paid monthly per plot, user charges for water and (until 1987) electricity, and the brewing and sale of opaque beer. Found in other cities in British colonies, for example Lusaka, the local authority beer monopoly, the revenue from which was used for the provision of services and housing, was initiated as a way of controlling illegal beer production and sales. It provided substantial revenue for welfare and services, thus avoiding the need for subsidies from the European to the African population, but also acted as a means of social control. The services provided were limited by the revenue available, though additional funds for house construction were available from central government loans (Whitsun Foundation 1980).

Changes since independence: revolution or evolution?

The inherited philosophical, legal and financial basis and institutional system for planning and managing urban development changed only incrementally in most countries in the early years after independence. The balance between continuity and change, Simon (1992) suggests, was influenced by the nature of the anti-colonial struggle; the fate of the ex-colonial elite; the policies pursued by the new elite with respect to national integration and relations with the world economy; national modes of production and means of social reproduction; and the extent to which urban legislative change was instituted. Governments were preoccupied with national political and economic issues and generally paid relatively little attention to urban administration. Where centralised structures existed, these persisted, especially in Francophone Africa

(Stren 1989). Where urban local government on the British model had been established, apart from a rapidly enlarged franchise at independence, it was retained more or less intact. However, in some cases the scope of urban local government functions was reduced before independence by the establishment of separate statutory bodies. In other cases, previously local functions were taken on by central government after independence for ideological and practical reasons, particularly education and the police. The potential contradictions inherent in central–local government relations led to the erosion of local government autonomy in most post-colonial societies (though the extent to which this occurred and the form which it took varied between and even within countries). This erosion was exacerbated by the lack of administrative capacity at the local level. The inherited British ideology of impartial officials guided by notions of technical rationality, advising elected councillors who viewed the exercise of power as a moral non-political activity—a poor description of the authoritarian and self-interested reality even in colonial times—was particularly inappropriate in a post-independence situation in which political office was used to fulfil traditional social obligations, to further personal interests and to increase popular support and power bases (Rakodi 1986).

In addition, the speed of urban growth far exceeded the capacity of the institutional system to adjust, not only in political but also in administrative, technical and financial terms. The result has been environmental damage, deteriorating living conditions, especially for the urban poor, and lack of the political legitimacy needed to improve revenue collection and regulatory processes. Recognition of urban bias in spatial investment and non-spatial policies by the 1970s led to an over-reaction, as flows of government expenditure and aid switched to rural development. Central and local governments, despite the political power of urban populations, had declining volumes of resources and often misdirected them into ineffective or prestige investment. The result was that local administration and services deteriorated.

Zimbabwe, in contrast, inherited a fragmented, racially divided but relatively well developed urban local government structure at independence, especially for urban areas. The capacity of African Councils (the local government units in TTLs) to provide services for the local population was limited by their small size, limited financial capacity and lack of autonomy, and had been further damaged by the destruction and disruption of the war. In comparison, although urban councils had had to deal with an increased influx of refugees and migrants, because of their significance to capital and European residents they had retained their powers, economic base and infrastructure more or less intact.

At independence, the Local Government Areas (LGAs) around Harare were incorporated into the city council under an amended Urban Councils Act. The immediate aim, of enfranchising those previously disenfranchised, was relatively easy to achieve and urban local government elections have now occurred four times (in 1980/1, 1984, 1987 and 1991). Prior to 1980, as I have described above, only ratepayers could vote, but many of them owned or occupied more than one property (residential and business, or in different wards) and so had more than one vote. Non-ratepaying residents in low and medium density (former European) areas (that is, adult children, servants and lodgers) still do not have the vote. In the LGAs (high density residential areas), despite the principle that any person paying taxes to a local authority is entitled to vote, the political need for haste in 1980 led to the voters' rolls being based on the housing register—that is, including owners, tenants and registered lodgers, but not unregistered lodgers (Jordan 1984). The logic of this franchise is that all those paying taxes to the local authority should have the right to vote, but considerable sections of the population, who pay for and consume services, are still disenfranchised, leading to the interests of property owners being overweighted in the electoral system (Jordan 1984; Zimbabwe 1986a).

In the 1980/1 elections, candidates were put forward by ZANU (PF) and PF (ZAPU), and the city council returned a majority from the former and a minority (mainly white) of independents (Jordan, 1984). The ratio of black to white councillors in all urban areas following the elections was 5:3 and the city council included some members who had previously been councillors, so there was some degree of continuity (World Bank 1985). A cooperative relationship was established with experienced and knowledgeable white officials prepared to accept change and to work with black councillors (Pasteur 1992). Elections were held again in 1984 and, following an amendment to the Urban Councils Act to require four-yearly elections, in 1987. In both elections, the majority of candidates were unopposed and where opposition did occur, it tended to be from independents in low density areas. The 1991 elections were marked by a mixture of inertia and controversy. More seats were contested, but voter turnout was very low in uncontested seats. To some extent, this may have been due to controversy surrounding the approval of candidates, which was forthcoming only at the last minute. Candidates had to be approved by the Returning Officer (the Town Clerk), giving rise to some concern about bias against non-ZANU candidates, especially where the Town Clerks were themselves party officials. ZANU (PF) uses primary elections in each ward to select its candidate, though some primary candidates, disgruntled at not being selected, stood against the official candidate and some won. Many previous councillors were not re-elected (Pasteur 1992). Whites continued to stand in a minority of low density areas, mainly as independents in the earlier tradition. The main new feature of the 1991 elections, however, was the number of ZUM candidates who stood in both low and high density areas, though only two in Harare were successful (out of 42 wards) (newspaper reports; Pasteur 1992).

The new government aimed to integrate the administration, finances and physical development of urban areas. Implementation of the 'One City' concept implied the merging of previously separate administrative departments responsible for LGAs and former European areas, merging budgets and accounts, and moving towards a uniform system of revenue generation by replacing supplementary charges with rates following the valuation of property in the former townships (see Chapter 5). At the same time, central government has emphasised the need to achieve financial self-sufficiency in urban local government; the need to control major revenue sources and borrowing, in order to ensure that central government requirements are met and that resources are devoted to priority sectors (World Bank 1985); and the need for greater decentralisation and participation in urban as in rural areas. The financial basis for local government is vital, and will be discussed first. This inevitably raises issues about the relationship between councils and central government. It also relates to the internal organisation of local government and to its relationships with urban residents and their organisations.

Urban local authorities are responsible for making a wide range of capital investments, for providing services and for various regulatory functions. Fire and ambulance services are the responsibility of the Town Clerk's department, as also is the administration of the municipal police, a force originally concerned with the protection of municipal property and providing support to the police, which was enlarged at independence, on government instructions, by taking on ex-combatants. The health services provided by the council concentrate on preventive health, based mainly on local clinics, and also include environmental health, including inspection of premises, monitoring of air pollution, and rodent and malaria control. In the past, control of street vending was seen as a hygiene issue and was the responsibility of the environmental health department, but this is now one of the duties of the Department of Housing and Community Services, which also administers markets. However, this department's main task was originally the administration of African townships. Today it still combines policy and programmes for new low cost housing and the management of high density housing areas (though infrastructure maintenance is actually carried out by Works departments), and welfare, including the provision and running of libraries, halls, sports facilities and vocational training. The liquor undertaking has now been taken over by a separate marketing department.

The largest council department is Works, which is responsible for all new construction, road maintenance, building control, town planning, solid waste disposal, open spaces and water supply and sewerage. In 1975 water resources were taken under central government control (now the Ministry of Energy, Water Resources and Development), but the council continues to be responsible for piping water from dams, treatment, and distribution, to Chitungwiza as well as Harare. Urban councils also have primary responsibility for public transport. Until 1987 the council was also responsible for electricity distribution, and had a separate City Electrical Engineer, but now its only function in this respect is to collect electricity charges on an agency basis on behalf of the Zimbabwe Electricity Supply Authority. In the same year, an educational function was added. As yet the council's responsibility for building and equipping new schools, operating and maintaining them, and providing consumables is partial, while central government supplies teachers, controls the curriculum and runs schools established before 1987. Although the intention is eventually to pass full responsibility over to the local authorities, they are concerned at the financial burden and are resisting this (Mutizwa-Mangiza 1991a; Pasteur 1992).

Finally, in order to manage the financial aspects of these extensive operations, the City Treasurer is responsible for budgeting and accounting. Local government share of total recurrent expenditure was 25% in 1979, increasing to 28% in 1981—twice as much as in Britain and more than in the average developing country (Zimbabwe 1986a: 327). A sample of city and municipal councils taken in 1981/2 showed that 20.3% of income was derived from local taxes (rates and a share of supplementary charges), 73% from non-tax revenue (nearly 28% from beer profits, and also fees, licences, rents and interest from the councils' large reserves) and only 6.7% of revenue was made up of transfers from central government (grants, mostly for the provision of health services, and vehicle taxes) (Zimbabwe 1986a: 327).

Councils prepare revenue and capital estimates on an annual basis and a rolling three-year capital development plan. While central government has always exercised a degree of control over the latter, control over the former has been increased since independence. The Ministry of Local Government and Town Planning (now Local Government and Rural and Urban Development) retained control over the setting of supplementary and other charges in high density areas after independence, ostensibly to protect the interests of low income residents. In addition, the retail price of and excise duty on beer have been controlled by central government, which has periodically frozen the former and increased the latter since 1980, reducing the profits from beer sales and adversely affecting local government revenue. Central government has provided grants to local authorities to enable them to provide additional services (health care, especially free health care to those earning less than Z$150, from 1980, and primary education since 1987). Initially, the grant towards health care covered 100% of the cost, but government financial difficulties in 1982/3 led to a reduction in the level of support, and councils were instructed to find an increased share. Their ability to do so has been limited by the decreased revenue from beer sales, and government restrictions on permitted increases in other charges and taxes.

The main source of funds for new development has been central government, which operates separate funds for housing and infrastructure investment (see also Chapter 6). As the demands on general revenue have increased and the government has increasingly faced financial problems, the funds available for borrowing have been markedly less than local authority demand. Although Harare can issue bonds, and borrow from the private sector, government concern to control borrowing has limited this in recent years. The reduction in capital loan funds available in absolute and relative terms has given rise to a backlog in desirable investment (World Bank 1989; Pasteur 1992).

Recognition of the increasing problems in urban local authorities but also of their potential for financial self-sufficiency is reflected in the 1991 economic reforms, which call upon urban councils to become more efficient and self-sufficient, to make better use of existing investment to postpone new investments, and to balance maintenance with the need for new infrastructure (Zimbabwe 1991a). In return they were promised greater financial independence. Reviews of operations occurred towards the end of 1991 and gave rise to proposals to retrench staff and rationalise administrative operations. Parallel to the discussions of economic reforms, discussions were taking place on a second World Bank urban project. This reflects a shift in World Bank thinking that has occurred since the early 1980s, from funding housing and infrastructure projects to developing local institutional capacity. It takes on board the two main issues: improving local authority financial management to regain solvency on a sustainable basis, and providing access to additional capital development funds. In order to qualify for access to the loan funds, local authorities were required to prepare financial plans and to adhere to these over an agreed period (World Bank 1989). Invariably, these required substantial increases in rents, fees and charges, which, despite grumbling and undoubted hardship for the poor, councillors have been willing to back and residents, at least initially, to pay. Unlike in other African cities, the continued ability of the local authority to provide services has maintained its political legitimacy. Implementation was intended over the five-year period from 1989/90 to 1993/4, but delays occurred on both sides. As the effects of the structural adjustment programme deepen and declines in real wages and increases in unemployment continue, the contradiction is likely to intensify. Widespread default among low income urban residents is possible as a direct result of World Bank approved structural adjustment policies and will, if it occurs, threaten both the aims of its own urban project and the legitimacy of local councils.

The current reforms and the Urban II project are concerned with financial viability rather than equity. It was pointed out by the Tax Commission that the inherited financial system was regressive, as beer trading was mostly in the high density areas, while the 20% of population in the low density areas contributed, together with commercial uses, only 8% of the revenue by means of rates (Zimbabwe 1986a: 327). Progress towards a more progressive structure has been hindered by the maintenance of separate accounts, which have made it difficult to equalise standards and tax burdens (Zimbabwe 1986a); the need to maintain roads and services in extravagantly laid out low density areas now inhabited by blacks as well as whites; and the political quiescence of poor urban residents.

Aspects of the changing relationship between central and local government have been touched on above. After 1980, as in other newly independent ex-colonies, central government was concerned to consolidate its position politically and demonstrate its grip on the economy and the civil service (Tordoff 1984). The Ministry of Local Government and Rural and Urban Development is responsible for the supervision of local government budgets and administration, providing financial assistance, especially for city-wide infrastructure projects, and physical planning. Meanwhile, housing, which had been under the same ministry as urban local government prior to independence, was separated into a Ministry of Public Construction and National Housing, a separation which gave rise to some confusion in the early 1980s as the two ministries tried to carve out areas of influence and competence. Since 1986, central government has also exercised control over senior local authority appointments. The policy shift towards greater central government control, in which Zimbabwe is typical of other newly independent African countries, has had some beneficial outcomes, in that government has been able to suspend individuals and councils that have misbehaved (Mutizwa-Mangiza 1991a). However, centralisation has been accompanied by increased bureaucracy and delay, giving rise to legitimate complaints from local authorities about the problems caused for them by central government and the lack of scope for them to experiment with innovative solutions to local problems.

A counter-trend was the recognition in the mid-1980s, embodied in the Prime Minister's 1984 directive on decentralisation, that people needed to be involved in decision making and development at the local level. In the African townships, some Area Boards remained after independence, but by 1984 only one was operational in Harare (Jordan 1984; Dewar 1987). In European housing areas ratepayers' and residents' associations were common and formed links between residents and councillors. Many continued to do so (Pasteur, 1992). ZANU (PF) has developed an urban organisation based on cells, branches and districts (approximately 100, 500 and 5000 families respectively), but this is not necessarily based on ward boundaries. Dewar (1987) suggested that district chairmen ran as candidates in local government elections in the 1980s, and that the cell executives were active in social welfare, ensuring adherence to party principles, and resolving conflicts between residents and sometimes between employers and employees, for example in domestic service. Pasteur, on the contrary, considers that the party has developed only a small role in urban affairs, compared, for example, to the United National Independence Party during Zambia's one-party state in the 1970s and 1980s.

Instead, following the 1984 directive, Area, Ward and Neighbourhood Development Committees were supposed to be established, to provide a basis for community organisation and a link between residents and the council via the elected councillors. NEDCOs (representing about 1000 people) are comprised of four directly elected members, and nominees of the Women's and Youth Leagues of the party. They in turn send representatives (chairs and secretaries) to the WADCO, which is chaired by the councillor, also includes Women's and Youth League representatives, and thus represents about 5000 residents (Pasteur 1992). In 1987 Harare City Council decided to implement this system, as a means of improving communications and organising developmental activities at the community level. An early evaluation of the system in one of the few areas in which it had been implemented (Glen Norah) found that the Committees mostly responded to consultations, had limited financial bases, were used for political education and had provoked relatively little resident participation (Dizanadzo 1987). By 1989, in only 5 of 38 wards was a full set of NEDCOs operating. There has been no subsequent evaluation, but few seem to operate effectively.

Today, local councils are expected to conduct business on party lines, but the ZANU (PF) majority is so clear that in practice, decisions are mostly reached on a non-party basis. The role of the mayor has sometimes been controversial. His role as chairman of the council is both political and ceremonial, but on the whole, a 'strong mayor' role has not been favoured, and not only mayors but also councillors remain heavily dependent on officers for policy initiatives (Pasteur 1992). Although during the 1980s white officers in both managerial and professional positions have retired and been largely replaced by blacks, the operating mode of local authorities has concentrated on service delivery and has remained very traditional. The committee structure, sectoral departments and general administrative culture have a very British flavour, dating from the 1950s and 1960s. There is no formal structure for corporate or strategic management, though there are some elements of this—for example the preparation of Capital Investment Programmes and, more recently, Financial Performance Plans; the preparation and review of land use plans (see Chapter 5); and the coordinating role of general purposes committees (Pasteur 1992). Although council meetings are open to the public and minutes of committee and council meetings are available, Jordan by 1984 detected 'a growing tendency towards less openness in local government'. By the early 1990s, newspaper coverage of local government affairs appeared to be divided roughly equally between factual reporting of operations and critical reporting on council misdeeds and mistakes, while the lack of resident involvement was reflected in the decreasing voter turnouts in elections and the ineffectiveness of WADCOs and NEDCOs.

Despite these problems, the local urban administrative system in Harare retains considerably more capacity to ensure the provision of an environment conducive to business, the maintenance of the lifestyles of the better off, and basic urban services to low income residents than many other African local authorities. These functions and their outcomes will be examined in more detail in subsequent sections and it will emerge that, despite the positive picture that is painted, pressures and strains on the system which are typical of African countries that won their independence a couple of decades before Zimbabwe are starting to emerge.

2

Urban structure

In this chapter, the focus will be on the physical creation and development of the city of Harare. The production of an urban built environment and a particular arrangement of land uses, and the movement needs and patterns to which these give rise, have a physical manifestation, but are related at least as much to political and economic influences as to physical conditions. In the first section of the chapter, the historical development of Harare up to 1980 will be described. The subsequent section will explain the establishment of the dormitory suburb of Chitungwiza, to the south. Before examining current land use patterns, a more detailed examination of infrastructure issues will be carried out. However, a city is not simply a static arrangement of land uses—it provides the environment within which residents live and enterprises operate. A livable and efficient environment for its users depends on the availability of adequate means of movement and thus on the relationship between land uses and transportation. The transport system in Harare is discussed in the penultimate section. Finally, the administrative process of planning, which has been a particularly important instrument for the production of the built environment in Harare, is described.

Salisbury, 1890–1979

Beginnings

On the arrival of the British South Africa Company police in 1890, a military settlement was built on the site which is now the main square (Africa Unity Square) in the central business district (CBD) and was named Fort Salisbury after the then Prime Minister of Great Britain. The fort and surrounding area were laid out, as were many settlements founded by colonists, as a grid aligned to the magnetic north. It was subdivided into large plots (stands) with very wide roads, and some administrative buildings were erected (Figure 2.1). The area was named Causeway, after the causeway which connected it to the Kopje area to the southwest, where a second survey at about the same time laid out another grid of wide roads, this time aligned parallel to the hill, where members of the disbanded Pioneer Column began to establish commercial enterprises (Christopher 1977). As a result, not only did the two grids meet at an odd angle, but also wagon drivers heading for Masvingo or Bulawayo tended to drive straight across the area, which although laid out was still largely undeveloped. People erected buildings along the routes, which thus became fixed (Manica and Charter Roads and Julius Nyerere Way) though they cut across the two formal grids. The two parts of the new settlement therefore developed according to differentially aligned street grids separated by a marshy stream draining southwards to the Mukuvisi River. The sites of the original settlements form today's CBD, bounded by the railway to the south (see below) and the Kopje to the west (Zinyama 1993).

The British South Africa Company reserved 8150 hectares of land surrounding the settlements as town reserve or commonage. Rights were granted, on the payment of fees, for pasture, firewood, quarries and brickworks (in the south) (Figures 2.1 and 2.2). Market gardening was also permitted on short leases. These 'townlands' permitted controlled land use and the reservation of extensive sites for public uses, including industrial areas, an airfield, police, prison and army headquarters, agricultural and veterinary research stations, schools and sports facilities. In the 1970s a quarter of the area was still undeveloped and considerable areas are still unused. Beyond the commonage, members of the Pioneer Column staked out farms of 1500 morgen (1250 hectares), together with the 15 mining claims to which each was entitled. Most were more interested in the latter, so many of the farms were sold to speculators, often for as little as £100. In addition, land, which was mostly bought by companies, was sold cheaply by the British South Africa Company.

Within the commonage, 2548 stands were demarcated in Salisbury Township between 1891 and 1894. Those in the south and centre were between 600 and 800 square metres in area, while further north, in the area which became known as the Avenues, larger stands of between 2000 and 3000 square metres were demarcated. In addition, an area on the northern edge of the Kopje area was alienated as a special grant and subdivided into small plots. In 1897 a municipal council took over administration of the settlement from a Sanitary Board and was given title to the remaining British South Africa Company land within the

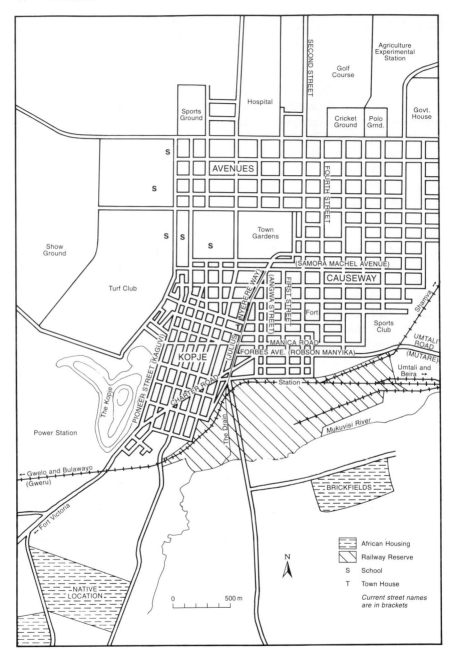

Figure 2.1 Early Salisbury. Sources: base map from Surveyor General 1986; Christopher 1977, p. 15

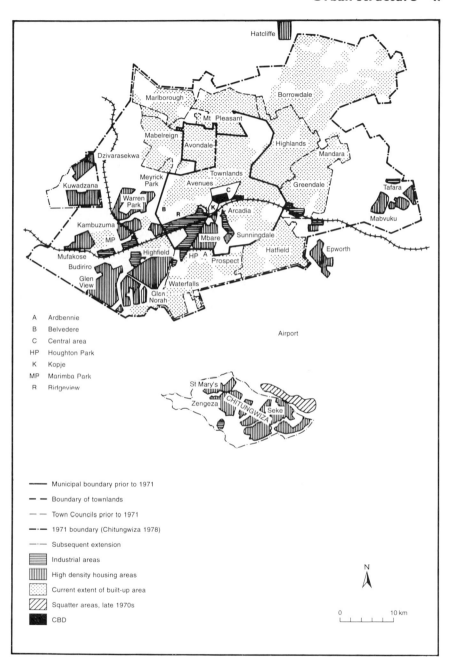

Figure 2.2 Historical development of the city of Salisbury

commonage. By the end of the century, the railway had reached the new settlements and the initial mud and thatch buildings had begun to be replaced by brick and iron, though many stands were undeveloped—partly because of the sheer youth of the settlement, partly because of speculation (38% of the alienated stands in the central grids were owned by five companies) (Christopher 1977), and partly because of African unrest and economic depression (Jackson 1986). Although the vlei (marshy area) between the two settlements had been drained, development had not yet occurred.

Land prices for residential stands varied, with those near Government House fetching one and a half times as much per unit area as the smaller plots near the city centre. Already by 1900, land prices in the CBD had risen to nearly five times those in the surrounding residential area and throughout the township land values often exceeded the value of buildings on the plots. Beyond the Townlands, maximum prices on average tended to be about 1.5% of those in the residential areas surrounding the CBD. For example, in 1904 land in Mount Pleasant was selling at between 0.2% and 2.5% of values near the city centre (Christopher 1977). Further general information on land values is not available for many years, though we know that alarm at the proportion of stands in the township kept vacant for speculative reasons prompted the Township council to introduce higher rates for land than improvements early in the twentieth century (Christopher 1973). The arrival of the railway led to the development of light industry and wholesaling in the southeastern part of the Kopje grid, though the commercial pre-eminence of the area was lessening, as larger shops shifted nearer to government and better residential areas (Christopher 1977).

Initially, black African workers were allocated an area or compound on the fringe of the subdivided areas where they could erect huts. The 1894 Town Management Ordinance empowered the local authority to establish and manage housing areas for employed blacks, but it was not until 1906, in accordance with the Native Locations Ordinance, that the first African township was established, to the south of Kopje (Figure 2.1). Nicknamed 'Ma Tank', this started off as 50 huts and a brick barracks, was later named Harari and is today Mbare (Davies 1986; Jackson 1986; Zinyama 1993). In 1930 the Land Apportionment Act withdrew the right of all blacks to acquire land outside the reserves and provision was made to set aside land for townships, managed by the adjacent council. The first African Advisory Board was established in Mbare in 1937, comprising six African members (four elected by occupiers and two appointed by the Salisbury council), and two nominated European members. Its role was consultative and not decision making (Dewar 1987). Prior to 1930, some African workers had lived on farms outside the commonage, but following the Land Apportionment Act this became more difficult. In 1935, in response to increased squatting, 453 houses were built at Highfield, a farm 9 kilometres from the centre (Figure 2.2).

Between the wars

Realisation of the vulnerability of the economy following the First World War led to the establishment of more import substitution manufacturing as well as agro-processing industries. Most of these early larger industries, together with a power station, were developed on sites set out alongside the railway to the southwest of the town centre, where flat land was available, the area was both downstream and downwind of European residential areas, and raw materials such as clay and limestone were available (Trinder 1977). The locations of the early African housing areas were chosen to be near the developing industrial areas and because the prevailing wind, as noted in Chapter 1, was from the northeast.

Because of the strict control over publicly owned land, private sector development occurred outside the commonage, from the 1920s onwards, by the subdivision of commercial farms. The first subdivision was at Avondale, in 1920 (Figure 2.2). In an attempt to control development, it was incorporated into the Townlands and administered as a suburb. Otherwise, during the depression years development was slow, with only 700 stands beyond the original grids by 1940, 131 to the east and the rest to the north and west.

Renewed growth

A new wave of migration after the Second World War led to growing pressure on land and more development had to be allowed in the Townlands, especially on plots of 2000 square metres south of the railway in Hatfield and Waterfalls. At a greater distance (20–40 kilometres away), areas of land were reserved for African use, as Tribal Trust Lands (TTLs) and African Purchase Areas. In between, further subdivision of farms started to occur, increasingly concentrating to the north, where areas were physically more attractive and further away from African housing areas.

Cheap land (£15 per hectare in Mount Pleasant in 1903 compared with £1000 for a similar *area* of residential land within the township), large plots, freedom from rates on developments, and a semi-rural environment seem to have been the principal early attractions of the area beyond the Townlands. These seem to have more than compensated for the greater distance from town and the lack of municipal services . . . (Christopher 1977: 21).

Township Management Boards were established to administer each of the suburbs, subject only to central government guidance which specified a minimum plot size of 1 acre (4000 square metres) if septic tank sanitation was used, gave approval to subdivisions into holdings of less than 40 hectares and, if a township was proposed, specified minimum access and open space requirements. Between 1945 and 1966, 223 private subdivisions, averaging only 52 stands each, were made (Christopher 1977). To administer this piecemeal development, Town Management Boards and, later, councils were established. By the 1960s eight such boards were in existence (in Greendale, Hatfield, Highlands, Mabelreign, Marlborough, Mount Pleasant, Meyrick Park and Waterfalls), while Borrowdale was administered by a rural council (Figure 2.2). With the exception of Mabelreign, where cheap houses were provided on plots of between 1000 and 2000 square metres by the central government for postwar immigrants, the townships were developed with stands of at least 4000 square metres and often more, freehold land ownership and septic tank sanitation. European ownership was universal, though every stand had servants' quarters and the European suburbs accommodated nearly a third of the African population at the end of the 1960s (Smout 1977a). The boards each had between six and twelve councillors, elected by ratepayers (the European population), and a small administrative staff, but relied on the government and Salisbury Municipality for services that they could not provide themselves (Dewar 1987).

The earlier African housing areas proved inadequate to accommodate the African population (see also Musekiwa 1993). From 1946 employers were obliged to provide accommodation for blacks in townships, or to pay rent for the accommodation occupied by their employees, and local authorities were obliged to build further accommodation to rent, mainly to single male migrants. Salisbury council set up a Department of African Administration and embarked upon a construction programme of hostels, as well as some small family houses, in the Mbare area. By 1969, this area accommodated over half the African population within the municipal boundary (approximately 60 000 people), though other townships of small family houses to rent had been built outside the then municipal boundary at Mabvuku, some distance to the east, and Mufakose, an equal distance to the west (Figure 2.2). The government also established African housing areas, outside the municipal boundary: for example St Mary's was built in 1956 to house employees at the airport, while Dzivarasekwa, 13 kilometres to the west, was developed in 1961 to house domestic servants (Patel and Adams 1981).

The 1946 African (Urban Areas) Accommodation and Registration Act continued the provision for the establishment of Advisory Boards in the townships, though most blacks disdained to serve on them. These boards, as in Mbare, comprised four elected and two appointed African members, two nominated European members, and, ex officio, the chairman of the council's Native Affairs and Finance Committees. However, Africans, because of their subservient status, lacked the skills and confidence to negotiate strongly, while Europeans believed that they knew and understood the African mind and could therefore prescribe for blacks (Dewar 1987).

Federation and beyond

During the 1950s and early 1960s, the government's efforts to ensure that the benefits of Federation flowed to Southern Rhodesia encouraged the diversification of mining capital into manufacturing, foreign investment, and large scale borrowing for infrastructure investment. The growing industrial and finance sectors concentrated in Salisbury, the new buildings constructed for their use changing the character of the CBD. The restricted size of markets for manufactured goods soon limited expansion of productive activities again, and financial resources were directed into property development for commercial and financial institutions, as well as speculation, fuelling property price rises in the CBD which outstripped and outlasted those for residential and industrial land and buildings (Bond 1992). However, the end of the speculative boom, followed by the breakup of the Federation, UDI and sanctions in the 1960s, resulted in a crisis of confidence, which led to the first collapse in land prices and a virtual halt to new private construction (Christopher 1973).

> The consequences, during the long downturn of the early 1960s, included the collapse of finance-driven property speculation, [and] a shake-out of the financial sector in which hire purchase contracted by 25% while the number of building societies shrunk from eight to three. (Bond 1992: 14–15).

Pressure from industrialists facing increased costs of accommodation for their black workforces led to relaxation of the prohibition on home ownership and government encouragement to the building societies to lend to black families. Despite abundant funds at the end of the 1950s, the building societies were unenthusiastic and low wages held back effective demand. The attempt by manufacturing capital to engineer a shift from direct supply of employee housing to an indirect supply, even with state backing, made little progress and eventually failed, following the early 1960s recession and capital flight (Bond 1993a).

As described in Chapter 1, the interests of agrarian capital and working class whites came to the fore with UDI, and in 1969 the Land Apportionment Act was replaced by the Land Tenure Act. A number of changes occurred. Black housing areas were designated in what were considered to be European urban areas and attempts made to con-centrate blacks in these districts. Thus after the 1969 census showed that the number of black residents exceeded that of whites in Highlands, a low density suburb to the northeast of the town centre, many blacks were rehoused in Tafara and Mabvuku, while municipal regulations were passed which forbade employers to house non-employees, forcing many domestic servants to send their families to live in the townships or back to the rural areas (Patel and Adams 1981). Native Advisory Boards were replaced by Township Boards with more resources, powers and responsibilities, which by 1973 had all-black memberships (Dewar 1987). Although there were no restrictions on their residence, Asian and Coloured populations (about 10 000 people by 1981) had tended to concentrate in small suburbs south of the railway line or in the Kopje area (Davies 1986). In the 1970s, separate areas were allocated to these groups for the first time: Belvedere and Ridgeview, to the west, for Asians, and Arcadia and Ardbennie, to the south of the railway, for the Coloured population (Patel and Adams 1981; Zinyama 1993) (Figure 2.2). In a concession to African discontent and in an attempt to foster the emergence of a middle class, the first home ownership area for blacks was laid out in Marimba Park, with stands of between 2000 and 4000 square metres and a minimum building clause in the regulations governing development in the area sufficient to ensure reasonably good quality building (Teedon 1990; Zinyama 1993). The municipal boundary was extended in 1971 to incorporate a wide range of both government administered African housing areas, including Marimba Park, and independent European suburbs (Figure 2.2).

The development of land and housing since the late 1970s will be examined in more detail in Chapters 5 and 6. In this chapter, as stated at the outset, the analysis will concentrate on physical aspects of the city's development. By the mid-1970s, escalation of the struggle for inde-pendence led to an influx of refugees into the capital. A municipal transit camp was set up at Musika, the long distance bus station near Mbare, with temporary plastic and later concrete pole and panel dwellings for rent. To provide somewhere for the people to go, the International Red Cross provided temporary relief housing of wood and sun-dried brick, with asbestos roofs, but, in line with the policy of decentralisation of black residential areas, the government forced this to be located some distance to the south. Small squatter areas had occasionally developed in earlier years. For example residents from Hunyani, where about 2000 people had settled on the banks of the Manyame (Hunyani) River in 1962, were resettled by government on serviced plots in St Mary's nearby. An increased volume of squatting resulted from the refugee influx. It was observed, for example, in Chirambahuyo-Derbyshire, a small squatter settlement of about 200 people which had existed on land owned by a granite quarry since 1958, that the population increased within a few months in 1976 to 12 000. These residents were resettled in Zengeza, adjacent to St Mary's, to the south, on plots of 95 square metres laid out for self-help construction, but were then moved again, into new two-room semi-detached houses in Seke, not far away (Figure 2.2). However, as soon as the Zengeza houses were vacated, other residents moved in (Patel and Adams 1981). At independence, these squatter areas south of the city were still in existence, in addition to 19 very small settlements within the municipal boundary. Another growing squatter settlement, with a population of between 20 000 and 40 000, was Epworth, on mission land just outside the boundary to the east (Davies 1986; Zinyama 1993) (Figure 2.2). St Mary's and the new housing areas of Zengeza and Seke formed the core of a new town which was also established in the 1970s, and which will be described in the next section.

Chitungwiza

The initial proposal to establish a township in the Seki TTL to the south of Salisbury was made in 1951, to allow local people to acquire stands for residential and business purposes. In 1954 2600 hectares were set aside and a village laid out, with the intention of it becoming a growth point. Growth points were part of general government attempts to address the problem of uneven regional development, but were fated to almost universal failure (Bond 1993b). Some industries were set up in an industrial area in Seki and the village was later declared a township. In the 1970s, as I have described above, there was also a major Salisbury City Council house building programme in St Mary's and Zengeza (Zinyama 1993).

Following the 1969 Land Tenure Act, a feasibility study was commissioned to ascertain the best pattern of development for the city of

Salisbury, given the desire to segregate African residential areas from the European city for ideological reasons similar to those advocated in South Africa and which were increasingly underlain by security concerns. Without waiting for the results of the study, in 1974 the central government decided to establish a new town adjacent to the existing Seki township. A central government team was given the responsibility of preparing the development plan and implementing a large low cost housing programme, even though the choice of site was opposed by the government's own Chief Planning Officer because it was unnecessary, given that existing townships could have accommodated the forecast additional numbers of African households, at least until the late 1980s; it was unviable; it was not integrated with Salisbury; and it would give rise to long journeys to work as well as problems of sewage disposal (Sparrow 1979; Teedon 1990).

The reservations of the project team are evident in its report, though it proceeded to make the best of a bad job.

> No firm terms of reference were given, nor was clear policy guidance made available save that a new town should be established in the northwest part of the Seki TTL . . . to provide initially for the housing demand arising from employment in Salisbury . . . However, it was clear from the start that if the new town was to have any meaning in social and economic terms, it should be designed so as to enable it to become, over a period of time, a self-contained entity generating from within itself substantial employment opportunities as a result of the establishment of increased industrial, commercial, service and agricultural activities . . . The proximity of Salisbury . . . raises difficulties in respect of the practical realization of any economically and socially acceptable new town structure. The new town will have great difficulty in building up an independent identity. In particular it will have difficulty in creating a suitable industrial and commercial base . . . (Seki Project Team 1976: 3, 10)

Nevertheless, the team aimed to create ' a varied vital and liveable environment for the inhabitants' (ibid: 1), economic self-containment, and 'a "rural city", in which the close relationship between the urban workforce and the rural tribal trust land has been fostered' (ibid: 18). Before examining the urban form which was supposed to enable the achievement of these goals, the physical characteristics of the site will be briefly described.

The gazetted site was a low ridge between two rivers, with intersecting streams cutting the ridge into narrower sections separated by extensive, poorly drained, shallow valleys, extensive granite rock outcrops and poorly drained vleis. Overall, only 60% of the area was considered to be suitable for building. Most of it drains north to the Manyame river, while St Mary's-Zengeza and the northwestern part of

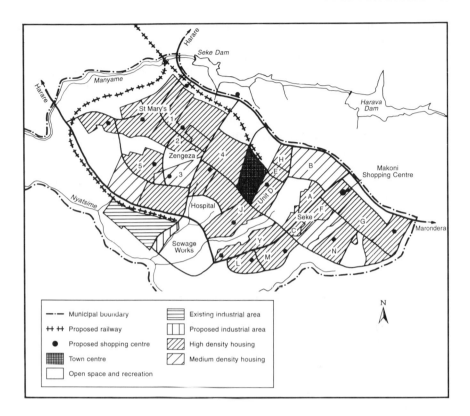

Figure 2.3   Chitungwiza in 1991. Source: HCMPPA, draft written statement 1991

the site drain to the Nyatsime River. In 1976 the government confirmed that planning should proceed for an area sufficient for 65 000 houses. Of these, 32 000, accommodating a population of perhaps 190 000, would form the first stage, for completion by 1980. It was expected that most of the development would be by the public sector, including major infra-structure and social facilities, though it was also expected that private sector investment could be encouraged in housing, commerce and industry.

The topography led to the adoption of a linear form for the new town, with the transport network forming a skeleton for a grid of residential communities along a spine road (Figure 2.3). The watercourses, it was considered, were suitable only for open space, and would thus (some wishful thinking) require planting and management. Aligned with the valleys, a hierarchy of roads was planned, with a largely separate cycle/pedestrian system. Along the spine road, residential communities were planned, each made up of on average 10 000 housing units and self-contained in terms of everyday services. Each was divided into smaller community or village units and each had a local centre, while of six planned district centres, the existing Seki and St Mary's-Zengeza centres were the first. Land for industry was set aside near the existing industrial area, and the route for a rail link with Salisbury was reserved. Outside the Phase I area, to the southeast, land was allocated on the spine road for the main civic, commercial and cultural centre of the town.

Initial progress with basic infrastructure and house construction was rapid, despite the war, with over 20 000 units being completed by 1979 (Sparrow 1979). In 1978, after much discussion, an urban council was appointed to administer Chitungwiza, taking over responsibility for Seke, as well as St Mary's and Zengeza, from Salisbury City Council, though the latter retained responsibility for water supply and sewage treatment, and the central government was still responsible for house construction and major infrastructure installation. The council was initially comprised of representatives of the existing Township Boards, but elections took place the following year and again in 1981. Despite a very low poll in 1979 (13%), 18 councillors were elected and three senior white civil servants were seconded to handle the administration. Almost all those in work commuted to Salisbury, a journey which absorbed between 12% and 25% of their incomes and took between 10 and 12 hours a week (Patel and Adams 1981). By 1981, 26 schools and two colleges had been built to serve the population, which reached 172 000 (at least) in 1982. However, only 13 concerns were operating in the industrial estate (Davies 1986); other social and commercial facilities were undeveloped and there have been no resources to develop the open space.

Before discussing infrastructure for both Harare and Chitungwiza and present day land use patterns in Harare, Chitungwiza's story will be brought up to date. During the 1980s social facilities were gradually improved. However, provision did not keep pace with population growth. Phase I of the town centre was not started until 1989, when the first group of shops was built for letting by the Old Mutual insurance group and the Urban Development Corporation, a parastatal. Little progress has been made in achieving the goal of economic self-containment (Zinyama 1993). Of the 55 hectares of industrial land available, only 21 hectares have been developed, and some sites allocated to industrialists have had to be repossessed when investment did not materialise. Although the population had reached at least 274 000 in 1992 (Zimbabwe 1992), only 5000 local industrial jobs were available. The intention has always been to attract investment from national and international firms, but despite the granting of growth point status in 1986, with its accompanying incentives, little success has been recorded, and increasingly emphasis is shifting to local businesses and the fostering of emergent businesses (small scale enterprises with black owners). Despite the rapid rate of house construction, the council is unable to keep pace with demand, as illustrated by the waiting list, which had reached 30 000 households in mid-1991 (*Herald*, 23 August 1991), and the growth of backyard shacks for renting. It was estimated that 18% of the population lived in outbuildings in 1987 (HCMPPA 1989), while the waiting list was certainly an underestimate of housing need. Growth in population had not been matched by revenue growth. The absence of industrial and commercial activity and high income residents meant that the local authority was the only large urban local authority to be dependent on central government for its basic revenue, and funds were insufficient to maintain services at an adequate level, let alone to extend the area of land serviced and the provision of social services. Already, by 1983, the physical infrastructure was under strain. Sewage disposal is a particular problem.

By the beginning of the 1990s, Chitungwiza was no closer to solving its problems. However, a new and more dynamic mood seemed to be emerging. Councillors from the 24 wards were increasingly inclined to speak out about the raw deal they considered the town to be getting from both central government and Harare City Council. An emerging local business interest group (which was often in conflict with political interests) was expressing its resistance to the monopoly of opportunities by outside firms, particularly in the main town centre, though their claims of discrimination have also been dismissed as sour grapes at being undercut (*Herald*, 28 February 1991). In 1991, this group, headed by a local industrialist and hotel owner, set up a development company to erect factories for local emergent entrepreneurs intending to enter manufacturing, and appealed for investors (*Herald*, 19 April 1991). Since the mid-1980s the council has adopted a more proactive role in attempting to attract industrial and commercial development, as well as emphasising the need for local initiative. Resentment at the allocation of the contract for, and retail units in, Phase I of the town centre to large and outside businesses has resulted in provision for local investment in Phase II and promises that local businessmen will be given priority when new units are let. It is hoped that the valuation exercise completed in May 1991, and the phased replacement of supplementary charges by rates, will result in increased revenue. Meanwhile, the council is trying to progress infill development to make the most of its existing land, and actively seeking to acquire land for further extension, though the search has been hindered by the reluctance of the Harava District Council, which adminsters the area to the east and south of Chitungwiza, to sell any of its land (see Fig. 2.3). Funds have not been available to construct the planned rail link with Harare, though widening of the main road link started in 1991.

Water and waste in Harare

Both the constraints on and patterns of urban development are related to the provision of infrastructure and utilities. These are, in turn, influenced by topography, institutional arrangements and policy priorities. The crucial utilities needed to serve urban areas, notable by their inadequacy in most cities in developing countries (Stren and White 1989), are water supply, sanitation and solid waste management. The relative success of Harare in providing its growing population with high quality services can be attributed to the city's political history, the financial and engineering capacity resulting from its sizeable and privileged European population and diversified economic base, and restrictions on urban growth (especially unauthorised development).

Water supply

Water supply in Harare is influenced both by its climate, with a long dry season and high rate of evapotranspiration, and by its location on a watershed, with only small and seasonally erratic streams and limited aquifers. The earliest settlement relied on springs, supplemented by collection of water from roofs, while from 1891 onwards, wells and boreholes were sunk to tap groundwater, many of which remain operational. However, the aquifers in the old crystalline rocks are small and discontinuous, and in fairly large areas of the central and western parts of the city the yield is poor (Tomlinson and Wurzel 1977).

In 1913, in the first attempt to supplement groundwater, Cleveland Dam was built to the east, on the headwaters of the Mukuvisi River, with a loan from the British South Africa Company. Although a cheap site, it was also a poor site and in 1923 the dam was breached. Since 1974 it has been retained solely as a recreational feature (Figure 2.4). Following several years of water shortage, a second dam, the Seke (Prince Edward) Dam, was built in 1928 on the main Manyame River. After the Second World War, increased population, together with a succession of poor rainy seasons, resulted in a water crisis. Residential development went ahead in the areas where groundwater was available, but was held up elsewhere, and many of the former areas were not connected to the city supply until much later. By 1977, 4000 wells and boreholes were still in use, accounting for between 15% and 30% of total consumption. As a result, the water table began to sink. By the 1950s, it was clear that a more radical solution was needed and in 1954 Lake Chivero (McIlwaine) was built where the Manyame River breaches the hills to the southwest (Figure 2.4). In the 1970s, 95% of Salisbury's water supply came from this dam and its associated treatment works (Tomlinson and Wurzel, 1977). In 1976 the Manyame (Darwendale) Dam was built, downstream of Lake Chivero and holding two and a half times the volume.

Water quantity has generally been sufficient since the construction of Lake Chivero, except in drought years such as 1983/4 and 1991/2, when water restrictions and rationing were in force. The dams and treatment works were able to supply more water than was needed in the late 1980s and very beginning of the 1990s. Nevertheless, restrictions on filling swimming pools and watering gardens using mains water are a frequent conservation measure during the dry season (HCMPPA 1989: 17). At the time studies for the revised plan were being carried out, current provisions were expected to be adequate until about the end of the century, but the 11% per annum increase in demand in the later 1980s led to forecasts that capacity would be fully utilised by 1995 (Musandu-Nyamayaro 1992). The supply of treated water is sufficient to serve an area within a radius of 22.5 kilometres from the central area (the existing network serves an area within a radius of 15 kilometres), but further major expansion of supply is then expected to be needed and debate over the options available is well underway, with potential dam sites on the Mabvinzi and Nyagui Rivers to the northwest being considered (HCMPPA 1989). Harare's water supply has thus remained relatively secure. The inherited tradition of strategic planning of supply has been maintained since 1980, even though it is now the responsibility of central government, and the undertaking has a sound financial base. In addition, Harare City Council's relationships with central government have been unproblematic, unlike those of Bulawayo, which for physical and financial reasons has experienced severe water supply problems (Musandu-Nyamayaro 1992).

Water quality, however, has become an increasing problem. The level of pollution has gradually increased in Lake Chivero, due both to its being downstream from the city's sewerage works and to agricultural runoff. Although sewage is treated reasonably adequately before discharge into the rivers (see below), it is, particularly during the dry season, rich in potash, nitrogen and phosphorus. As a result, plant and algal blooms occur in the lake, especially in years of low rainfall. Water hyacinth has been a problem since the 1960s and the choice between

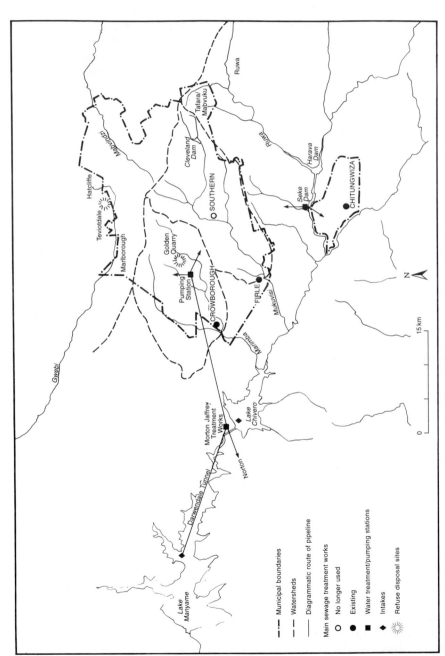

Figure 2.4 Water supply and sewage disposal. After Surveyor General 1985; HCC Department of Works 1984

mechanical and chemical clearing has been controversial. In addition to domestic and agricultural pollution, more recently there have also been signs of industrial pollution (lead, arsenic, cadmium), as a result of illegal discharges of industrial waste to stormwater drains and watercourses (Choto 1991).

Sewage collection and disposal

Much of the early development of the city and much low density development today has been based on septic tank sanitation, though in the centre an early bucket-latrine system was replaced by waterborne sanitation in the 1930s. Except in the extreme northeast of the built up area, where septic tank sanitation is necessary for topographical reasons, the conventional waterborne sanitation system has been extended, though the location of the city on several watersheds complicates the planning of the system. Thus all the high density residential and industrial areas are served by waterborne sanitation, together with about 20% of the low density area. Most of the sewage is discharged into the water catchment area, so that about 85% of the water supplied to Harare is recycled.

Currently, the western part of the city is served by the Crowborough works and the southern part by the main Firle works (Figure 2.4). Chitungwiza's works cannot cope, and domestic and industrial effluent, including arsenic and lead, is discharged into the Nyatsime River to the south before it is fully treated. The Chitungwiza Town Council is refusing to take the works over from Harare, as it does not have the resources either to run or to expand it. Harare's Director of Works started to purchase land around the city in 1972, when five farms were bought. By 1981 nearly 7000 cattle were being run on pasture irrigated by effluent from sewage ponds and it was noted that the profit from this operation was nearly sufficient to cover pollution control expenditure. Since then, farms west of Hatcliffe, outside the northern boundary, have also been brought into use (HCC, Department of Works, various years) (see Figure 2.2).

Solid waste management

In 1986/7 45% of Harare's refuse was collected from the low density residential areas which contained only a third of the city's population, while a similar proportion of refuse was collected from high density areas, despite their housing two-thirds of the population (HCMPPA 1987: 21). Two-thirds of the waste is domestic and commercial, for the collection and disposal of which the city council is responsible, despite its chronic lack of vehicles. Metal bins are only provided to industrial users; domestic users are issued with reusable plastic bags. However, bags in high density residential areas are restricted to one per house and collections are only weekly, giving rise to widespread illegal dumping around the areas, with problems of flies, rats and smells (Tevera 1991). Waste is disposed of mainly by sanitary landfill methods at two sites: Golden Quarry, an old gold mine, which currently takes 90% of the city's waste, and Teviotdale, an old brick pit (Figure 2.4). Lack of compacting equipment hinders tip management, gives rise to problems of fires, dust and methane emissions, and increases the danger of leaching from potentially toxic waste into the groundwater (Tevera 1991). Contracts are awarded to salvaging and waste recycling companies, who issue permits to and purchase material from scavengers at the tips (Tevera 1993).

Land use patterns in contemporary Harare

Harare today is a sprawling city covering 570 square kilometres in all directions from the core of the original settlement. The CBD of the city is based on this original core, and will be discussed first. The development of industrial areas and the pattern of residential development, with its accompanying uses, will be described in the remainder of the section.

The city centre

In the late 1920s and 1930s, central Manica Road was the main shopping area, with two- and three-storey buildings of plastered brick with iron roofs. Roofs and balconies overhung the pavements and were supported by iron pillars and decorated with wrought iron (Figure 2.5). Facades were higher than the buildings themselves, to give an imposing street view and conceal the ugly iron roofs (Smout 1977b): 'parapets of confidence' (Jackson 1986: 16). Some of the original buildings were replaced by larger buildings of three storeys or more, with flat or pitched clay tile roofs, in the 1930s and 1940s, but by then the centre of gravity of the main commercial area had begun to shift eastwards. Retailing, including large department stores, developed, until the end of the 1970s mainly to serve the European community, within an area of about ten blocks (between Angwa and Second Streets running north–south and Samora Machel Avenue and Forbes Avenue running east–west) (Figure 2.1). Imported architectural influences that can be

Figure 2.5 The central business district. Typical buildings from the beginning of the twentieth century: CT stores (1908) and Standard Chartered Bank (1911), Manica Road

discerned in this more recent development include classical styles and, less frequently, art deco buildings (Jackson 1986).

By the mid-1970s, the central area was judged by Smout (1977b) to cover an area of 263 hectares, of which a quarter was the CBD proper. Within the CBD, 72% of the area was used for 'central uses' (defined to include retailing, services and offices). In the rest of the central area only 7% was used for these purposes, and other uses included residential, public buildings, industrial and wholesaling. Office uses are also concentrated in two areas outside the CBD, to the east up to Fourth Street, where many are government buildings, and to the northwest of the retail area. The central part of the Kopje area remains in commercial use, but little renewal has occurred and the buildings remain small and often in poor condition (Figure 2.6). Zoning restrictions which limit the floorspace that can be developed, as well as the area's location on the side of the central area nearest to the main low income residential areas and near the city bus station, have discouraged redevelopment and encouraged owners to hold on to property for speculative purposes (Tekere 1993). In much of the Kopje area to the south of these shopping streets, a mixture of small scale land uses prevails, including commercial, residential, industrial and wholesaling. It is a low rent area with a largely transient population and a deteriorating environment. The latter is due both to unauthorised use of premises and to poorly

Figure 2.6 The Kopje area of the central business district: small buildings in poor condition, with narrow, congested streets

maintained buildings. The need for regeneration and environmental improvement increased in urgency during the 1980s, especially with the development of large imposing public and private buildings including an international hotel and conference centre on the old race course to the northwest. Relaxation of the zoning restrictions to allow more office and shop uses and higher density development will, it is hoped, provide sufficient incentive for private investors to revitalise the area (Tekere 1993).

Today the city's central area is marked by a transition from the Kopje area in the west, through an area of mixed public and private office and retailing development to the more densely developed CBD between the Town House and Africa Unity Square. The first area, as described above, is characterised by small buildings along narrow and crowded streets, many of them the original colonial buildings. The transitional zone includes early buildings along Manica Road in the south and the Town House, built in the early 1930s and today home of the Town Clerk's department. While more densely developed, the CBD is nevertheless characterised by a mixture of original colonial buildings of architectural and heritage value; early buildings of no particular conservation value; retail and office buildings, especially those of financial institutions, dating from the 1960s and 1970s; and a number of large post-independence commercial redevelopments sporting the

Figure 2.7 The central business district: low rise retail use juxtaposed with modern office and commercial development, Samora Machel Avenue

ubiquitous styles of 'international architecture' (Figures 2.7 and 2.8). As yet low density, clean and uncrowded by comparison with most larger cities, Harare's city centre is dominated by formal sector activities. Hawkers, newspaper sellers, beggars and the small flower market are restricted in number by a vigorously enforced licensing system. The parks and gardens are scrupulously maintained, and although car theft and pickpocketing is on the increase, the centre is relatively safe for pedestrians.

Although the need for conservation of many older buildings is now officially recognised, little action has been taken (Jackson 1993). Many CBD sites that do not contain buildings of any particular interest are 'underdeveloped', in the sense that more intensive development would be expected in market terms and permitted in planning terms. That such redevelopment has not taken place is largely explained by the pattern of land ownership. Many of the buildings are reputed to be owned by white Zimbabweans who emigrated around 1980, but who would have to invest the proceeds of sales in government bonds and are only permitted to export a small proportion. Instead, they prefer to wait and see what happens, receiving minimal rents which have to stay in the country in the meantime.

The few large high rise developments which occurred in the early 1980s and the more extensive developments underway today have been

Figure 2.8 The modern central business district: office development underway adjacent to Meikles Hotel on Jason Moyo Avenue (formerly Stanley Avenue)

financed by the large financial institutions, mainly pension funds and insurance houses, but also commercial banks, which experienced considerable asset growth in the 1980s. These institutions appear to have a strong preference for central area commercial development over housing or investment in directly productive enterprises (Bond 1991). As a result, they have bid up central property prices while industry stagnates (Bond 1992). Central area office and shop rents reached Z$25 per square metre and Z$50–100 per square metre respectively in 1991, driven up both by shortages, especially of new shopping floor area, and by competition between financial institutions. Transnational capital is not directly involved, but the concentration of transnational manufacturing and financial interests in the city has triggered investment by domestic capital, some of it with transnational connections, for which the returns generated by investment in the productive sectors are unattractive. Such investment is characterised by international standards and styles of architecture, producing office, commercial and hotel buildings similar to those which can be seen in cities anywhere else in the world. The property press regarded early 1990s investment in prestige buildings as an exciting and positive development, a response to buoyant demand that was expected to result in increasing yields to investors from rents (*Financial Gazette*, 9 May 1991). To others, the operations of these large scale financial investors and developers, typical of financial capital in capitalist economic systems worldwide, exacerbate boom and bust patterns in the economy and property (Bond 1992) or make life difficult for those trying to plan the development of the city. The developers and investors benefit from the certainty of the planning and development control systems, but complain about the rigidity of these systems if the market for commercial floorspace changes (Wekwete 1989b).

The central area is being expanded westwards, where the ugly yellow international conference centre and hotel vies for attention with ZANU's new party headquarters, nicknamed 'Shake-shake' because of its resemblance to the shape of the packs in which local opaque beer is sold. Around the central area, transitional zones have emerged from areas which in the early years were residential, to the northwest of the Kopje area, north of the Town Park and to the east of the CBD. In these areas, pressure for expansion of the CBD, together with high rents, has led to the conversion of houses to offices, sometimes without planning permission, a pressure so extensive that the city council has had to yield to it, despite the zoning incorporated in the relevant town planning schemes.

Industrial areas

Planned industrial areas were set out along the railway running to the south of the central area (Figure 2.9). The earliest and largest industrial areas, Workington and Southerton, lie to the southwest of the city centre, and were developed, along with Graniteside to the south, in the 1950s. In the late 1950s the Ardbennie and Lochinvar extensions of Southerton, and Beverly (to the east and at that time in Greendale Township) were developed, and in the late 1960s, Willowvale, further to the southwest, was laid out. More recently, some industrial development has occurred in small centres outside the city, including Norton, Mount Hampden (HCMPPA 1984a) and, even more recently, Ruwa (Trinder 1977). By 1984, Southerton and Workington were fully developed, while land was still available in the other areas (HCMPPA 1984a). A large proportion of Harare's substantial employment in the manufacturing sector is located in these formal industrial areas: licensing and planning restrictions have limited the growth of small scale enterprises in vacant and residential areas. It was estimated in 1984 that 143 000 people from both Harare and Chitungwiza worked in the industrial zones, many making long daily journeys to work despite earlier attempts to locate high density housing areas within easy reach of the industrial areas.

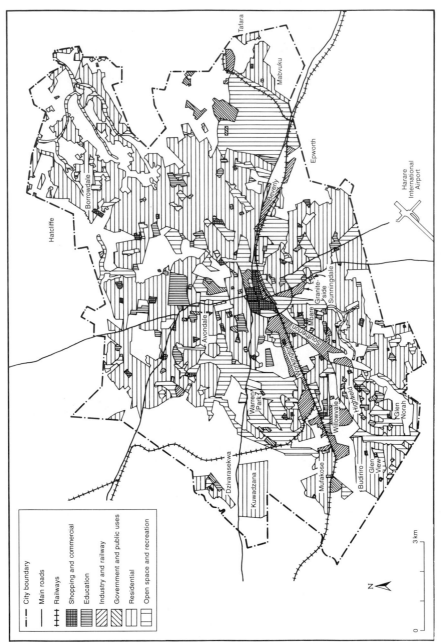

Figure 2.9 Land uses in present day Harare

Housing the urban workforce

As described above, a belt of high density housing areas was initially developed to the southwest of the city centre, north and south of the industrial areas, and to the east of the city at Tafara and Mabvuku within reach of Beverly. In the 1970s, this pattern of development, rational in planning terms if highly segregated, was displaced by ideology, leading to the development of major new housing in Chitungwiza, to the south (see above). Although, since independence, Chitungwiza residents' dependence on employment in Harare and the segregated pattern of residential development have been seen as problematic, efforts to reform the overall urban development pattern have been limited. The location of new low income residential development has been shaped primarily by land availability and also by the constraints on infrastructure extension. Areas around existing housing areas already in council ownership have been developed, for example in Dzivarasekwa, Warren Park, Glen Norah and Budiriro, while the location of the largest new development, at Kuwadzana, appears to have largely been determined by the offer of two farms to the city council (Figure 2.9). A more detailed analysis of the housing provided in these areas will be given in Chapter 6—here our concern is with the overall pattern of development and its physical character. The overwhelming concentration of new development to the southwest and west of the city has reinforced the existing pattern of segregation. The small scale of low income development elsewhere (for example, in Sunningdale to the south of Graniteside, or Hatcliffe in the extreme north) is insufficient to break this pattern.

Low income residential areas are typically areas of small plots (by Zimbabwean standards), with uniform houses, especially in the former municipal rented housing and new tightly controlled sites and services areas (see Chapter 6). The standard plot size in the 1980s was 324 square metres, though some earlier schemes utilised smaller plots, and smaller plots are to be permitted in future schemes. The standard of physical infrastructure is uniformly high in relation to average income levels, with road access to every plot, individual water supply and waterborne sanitation, and street (often tower) lighting, though often individual house electricity connections are not available. By comparison with many other developing countries, these areas are low density, with their overgenerous road allocations, single-storey houses and relatively large plots. However, the large plots and 'overdesigned' physical infra-structure have enabled many of the areas to absorb large additional renter populations without undue strain. Pressure on space and utilities is greatest in Mbare, which contains nearly sixty hostel blocks as well as houses. The rooms in the former were originally designed for single migrants, but today are often occupied by many more people. The houses in this area are of varying sizes. Some are owner-occupied, but some were considered unsuitable for sale to their occupiers and are still rented from the city council. In this area, not only are many rooms sublet, but wooden shacks for rent have been erected in backyards. In 1982, the population of the area was said to be about 28 000, but this was widely considered to be an underestimate. In 1988, 1713 temporary shacks were counted, nearly a fifth of all those in the city at the time (Harare City Council, Department of Housing and Community Services 1988). The number has increased since then, with the average number of shacks per plot variously estimated at between three and six. Many of the permanent buildings are old and in poor condition, and the utilities are under strain (*Herald*, 23 August 1991). In Highfield, the second African township to be built, local plan surveys revealed a total of 15 230 residential structures, of which nearly half had been built without permission. Of the population of nearly 100 000, more than a third were lodgers, and more than two-thirds of the latter lived in illegal out-buildings (*Herald*, 28 January 1991). Other older house ownership areas, such as Glen View, also have high occupancy rates per plot. In newer serviced plot areas and former municipal rented housing areas this process of house extension is still underway (see Chapter 6). Such house extension and renting is, however, limited in some of the latter by the small size of plots.

The high income population and its needs

In the remaining townland area, to the west, north and southeast of the central area, public uses such as hospitals, offices, schools, police camps, the Botanical Gardens and sports clubs predominate, giving rise to low development densities close to the CBD, despite later replacement of some uses with flats of up to four storeys. To the south and east, land was allocated to the armed forces and for European housing during the rapid post-1945 expansion period. Perhaps a fifth of this area is still undeveloped. Low density residential areas sprawl to the east, northeast, north and northwest. Early houses of sun-dried brick with thatch and corrugated iron roofs were gradually replaced by more substantial structures, mostly bungalows, often with verandas, the ubiquitous architectural form of the British empire (King 1990). Other houses illustrate the features of Cape Dutch architecture or London stockbroker belt 'chocolate box lid' houses (Jackson 1986) (Figure 2.10). Much of the land has been subdivided, mostly into plots of 4000 square metres in individual ownership. However, many of these plots have not been

Figure 2.10 A typical house in a low density residential area

developed, and considerable areas have still not been subdivided, even within the outer boundaries of the built-up area (see Chapter 5).

The low density residential areas are served by a series of small neighbourhood shopping centres developed by private capital. Few in number before 1950, by the mid-1960s these areas, which had a population of only 120 000, were served by a hierarchy of 67 shopping centres (Smout 1977d). Only the largest were considered to be centres which could satisfy the whole range of daily needs. They often contained suburban branches of city centre stores, services such as building societies, some specialist shops, and administrative buildings. Most of these larger centres were located about 12 kilometres from the CBD to the northwest and northeast. Nevertheless, suburban residents made a large proportion even of their daily and weekly purchases in the city centre (Smout 1977c).

A contemporary survey of residents in Mbare and Highfield showed that the most common shops were butchers, general food shops and general dealers, reflecting the low purchasing power of residents, though clothes, bicycle, shoe and secondhand goods retailers and repair and personal services were also to be found. The pattern of retail uses differed in the two areas: in Mbare, neighbourhood shops were more common, whereas in Highfield, more were concentrated in the Machipisa shopping centre. Residents bought daily purchases, meat and vegetables locally, but nearly half the Mbare residents questioned and

Figure 2.11   A typical neighbourhood shopping centre in a low density residential area: Mount Pleasant

29% in Highfield bought their groceries in the city centre and most other goods were also bought there, by residents from both areas. While most residents of low density areas considered the shopping facilities adequate, most people in high density areas thought them inadequate and highly priced (Smout 1977c).

The situation had changed little by the 1980s (HCMPPA 1984b; Mutizwa-Mangiza 1991d). Prominent early shopping centres in low density areas (Avonlea, Newlands and Parktown) have given way to other more important ones (for example Avondale, Groombridge, Borrowdale) (Figure 2.11) and vacant premises in the smaller centres indicate a continued competitive disadvantage. In 1981, despite their much larger share of the city's population, there were only 38 shopping centres in the high density residential areas and they were still dominated by general dealers and food shops, while shopping centres in high income areas were dominated by specialist retailers and well served by financial institutions. The best served high density residential areas were the oldest (Mbare and Highfield), while in others many shopping centres are not fully developed and walking distances to them may be considerable, so that informal sector development of markets and stalls (tuckshops) as well as street selling has resulted, despite periodic attempts by the city council to clamp down on it by the use of both licensing and development control powers (Figure 2.12). Even

Figure 2.12 'Tuckshops' in Kuwadzana

within the centres, informal sector entrepreneurs compete successfully with formal establishments. In Mbare, for example, informal furniture manufacturers and retailers squeezed out formal businesses in the 1970s. Less than a fifth of households in the high density areas owned refrigerators or cars at the beginning of the 1980s, so perishable foods are bought locally at least once a day. Despite this local shopping for daily purchases, the inadequacy of shopping facilities in the less well served areas leads to widespread use of CBD shops for groceries and almost universal use for purchases of shoes and clothing (Mutizwa-Mangiza 1991d). In Chitungwiza the district centres are better developed than the town centre or neighbourhood shops, again leading to a proliferation of tuckshops and street vendors in more accessible locations. This has led the town council, on the one hand, as I have noted above, to develop the town centre, and on the other to encourage some development of local shops (HCMPPA 1984b).

The discrepancy in levels of service between high and low density areas prevails in other respects, for example recreational provision. While in the low density areas, which arguably need it least, formal open space allocation averages 1.64 square metres per person, in the high density areas the average is 0.21 square metres per person. Public parks and sports areas are supplemented by private clubs, which also cater for the better off and are located in the higher income areas of the city (HCMPPA 1989).

The fate of squatters

Illegal development has been strictly controlled, in accordance with a series of town planning schemes and, more recently, local plans. Although, in the late 1970s, extensive squatter areas developed, these were all cleared with the exception of Epworth. More recently, small squatter areas have been cleared soon after they developed. This reaction is expected and there is little public support for any alternative policy. Residents are restricted to those who cannot afford even to rent a room, and the shelter they erect is of temporary materials, mainly plastic sheets. These areas develop both in the interstices of urban development, where residents hope (usually unsuccessfully) to keep out of public sight, and near the city centre, especially near the long distance bus terminus at Mbare. For example, on 16 July 1990 over 150 squatters from two sites were rounded up by 100 government and municipal police, who burnt their shacks and belongings (*Herald*, 18 April 1991).

Soon, more cardboard and plastic shacks had developed in two areas called Tashinga and Norton near the Mbare Musika bus station. The city council, in mid-May 1991, notified these squatters by means of an inappropriately wordy newspaper advertisement (Figure 2.13) that their huts would be demolished, justifying this on the basis of the danger of cholera. The council applied for a High Court order, the Town Clerk rather rashly referring to the imminence of a visit from Queen Elizabeth and her expressed wish to visit the Mbare Musika market. On 7 October 1991 more than 1500 people were resettled at Porta Farm, 40 kilometres to the west of the city centre and near Lake Chivero. A furore followed, the President trying to counteract the adverse publicity by asserting that squatters had to be moved because they were trespassers, posed a health hazard to themselves and others, and made government planning of social services more difficult (*Herald*, 10 October 1991) (Figure 2.13).

At Porta Farm, temporary timber frame shelters with sackcloth walls and polythene sheet roofs were provided. Those residents with jobs or informal sector occupations in the city found it almost impossible to get to them, while the remainder depended on food handouts from the Salvation Army and World Vision (*Herald*, 16 December 1991). By 1993, residents had resorted to doing odd jobs on nearby farms, scavenging, producing illegal alcohol or prostitution, while some had moved into new squatter areas nearer town. Those households with a member in work are, in theory, moved to temporary two room wooden houses on an isolated site near Dzivarasekwa (Figure 2.14), from where they have to be bused to school, work or clinic. By December 1992 300 families had been permanently resettled in serviced plot schemes, and houses were soon to be made available to another 750 (*Herald*, 30 December 1992 and

Figure 2.13 Squatters in 1991: attitudes and actions

Figure 2.14 Temporary squatter resettlement, 1990s style: two room wooden houses with communal washing slabs, awaiting resettled squatters from Porta Farm in 1992

8 January 1993). It is intended to send others back to the rural areas, though welfare workers at the camp consider that many have medical or psychological problems. Evictions from Epworth added to the number of people at Porta Farm, so that in February 1993 there were still 3000 people living there. These unfortunate people share 40 latrines, live in shelters which are totally inadequate for the rainy season, have no schools, telephone, mail or recreation facilities, and have insufficient access to health care services. Being forbidden to leave until they have an alternative place to live gives residents the feeling of being confined to a camp, a feeling that is reinforced by the municipal police post at the gate (*Horizon*, February 1992; *Moto*, 121/2, February/March 1993).

Epworth

Epworth, in contrast to the small squatter areas in the city, is a well established area 10 kilometres to the southeast of the city centre. It is situated on land granted to the Methodist Mission Trust in 1900 by Cecil Rhodes, to which adjacent farms were added, giving a total area of nearly 4000 hectares. By 1950, the mission had allowed 500 families to build huts and settle on the land, issuing them with annual leases. The large (4–6000 square metres) early plots were clustered in four villages. In 1957 the area was zoned for 'mission purposes' (Murongazvombo 1989). The settlement, which continued to grow as additional households settled on smaller stands, was estimated in 1987 to contain 35 000 people, and today covers 1500 hectares. Much of the area is rocky or poorly drained. Water supply has been from wells and, more recently, boreholes, and sanitation is based on pit latrines. With extreme reluctance on the part of government, upgrading was proposed for the area in 1983 (Butcher 1986). Most of the land was granted by the mission to the state. Initial surveys have been succeeded by a long and problematic implementation process.

Ninety per cent of the 4300 plots are considered by the main occupying household to be 'owned' and the remainder to be tenanted. An Urban Development Corporation survey showed that 80% were occupied by more than one household, on average by four families containing 13 people in total. The population was mostly young, a fifth of the households were headed by women, over half of those working were wage employees, and incomes were very low (Epworth Local Government Board 1989; Butcher 1993). Lack of experience in handling the upgrading of an existing residential area and inappropriate standards for infrastructure have given rise to long drawn out and sometimes heated consultations.

By-laws to prohibit further squatting were not introduced until 1989, leaving plenty of scope for disagreement over which households are legal settlers entitled to plots in the upgraded settlement. Those with houses considered illegal by the Board were issued with eviction notices at the end of 1990, but managed to get the High Court to uphold their rights. Again, in February 1992, demolition orders were issued for illegal outbuildings and unauthorised extensions, leaving tenants unsure of their position (*Herald*, 20 February 1992). Another appeal to the High Court halted demolitions. Those who had been living in the area before 1990 requested compensation; tenants wanted to be provided with alternative accommodation and insisted that landlords/builders who had knowingly constructed buildings illegally should be fined rather than the tenants, who had rented rooms in good faith, be penalised. Nevertheless, the council succeeded in evicting a number of residents, who were also temporarily settled at Porta Farm. Since 1983 the population has increased to perhaps 48 000 (Epworth Local Government Board 1989), the area has suffered from increasingly severe water shortages (*Herald*, 4 May 1991), and upgrading is said to be threatened by the illegal digging of pitsand for sale by the lorryload (*Sunday Mail*, 19 January 1992).

Getting around: the transport system in Harare

Providing for the car

The initial settlement layouts, as described in the second section of this chapter, were grids. Radial routes developed, connecting the centre with the surrounding farms and townships and with the rest of the country. These also form the main urban roads, resulting in a high quality road network with poor lateral links. A very large proportion of roads in the city are paved (Urban Transport Unit, nd). The city developed on the basis of universal car ownership among Europeans, but assumed that Africans would rely on walking, cycling or public transport. As a result, there was, and still is to a very large extent, a dual journey to work pattern with spatially distinct flows. In the low density residential areas, transport is very car-orientated, for all types of trips, and development of public transport has been limited, especially before independence: 'Wide roads, low population densities, a dearth of public transport and a tropical climate combine to make the average European dependent on his [sic] car' (Hardwick 1977: 96). In 1948 there was already one car for every three Europeans, while by the mid-1970s car ownership had grown to 1.99 cars per European household (or a car for every 1.8 persons) in the most affluent northeastern suburbs (Hardwick 1977).

In the early 1980s car ownership increased by 4% per annum (Brokonsult 1985), but then slowed as foreign exchange shortages limited the number of new vehicles imported (HCMPPA 1988a: 18, 21). Vehicle ownership is closely related to income, and distribution is uneven: 85% of the vehicles were registered in the low density and central areas, giving an ownership rate of approximately 400 vehicles (commercial and private) per 1000 population. Although the rate of growth in vehicle ownership was much greater in the high density parts of the city, the proportion of all vehicles in these areas reached only 15% by the mid-1980s, an ownership rate of perhaps 32 vehicles per 1000 (Brokonsult 1985). The overall figure in 1988 was 38 vehicles per 1000 population, twice that in many other African cities (Mutizwa-Mangiza 1993: 104), reflecting both the relatively large size of the upper income group and the gross inequalities that have accompanied the city's inherited socio-economic structure.

From most of the low density residential areas, especially to the northeast of the city, all journeys to work in the industrial areas to the southwest have to go through the central area, which is itself the main employment centre for workers from these areas. Traffic (especially at peak hours) and parking problems gradually increased in the central

Figure 2.15   Pedestrianisation of First Street in the central business district was implemented in 1974

area as a result. Nevertheless, the effect of this 'congestion' in 1972 was to add only 4.2 minutes on average journey times from the centre to the city boundary, representing a decrease in mean travel speed from 55 kph to 44 kph (Hardwick 1973, 1977). In response, parking meters were installed and a multi-storey car park built.

A 1969 study led to proposals (see also below) to build more multi-storey car parks in the CBD; to develop transport corridors with freeways to the northeast, northwest, south and southwest; to limit the density of development in the CBD; to pedestrianise First Street in the centre of the retail area; and to develop suburban shopping centres to relieve the CBD. The proposals were heavily biased towards the private car (Salisbury 1973). The pedestrianisation was implemented in 1974 (Figure 2.15), a multi-storey car park was built and land for the proposed transport corridors has been safeguarded, though little progress has been made with any of the road construction (see below and Figure 2.19). Long-standing proposals to develop Harare Drive as a major ring route have still only been partially realised, with sections completed in the west but not in the east.

A diagnostic study of Harare's transport problems was commissioned by the World Bank in 1981 and recommended the implementation of a new traffic-responsive traffic signal control system for the central area in order to improve traffic flows (Harare City Council, Department of

Works 1981, 1983/4). This was implemented in the late 1980s, at considerable and unjustifiable expense (Colquhoun 1993). The ending of fuel rationing in 1980 led to a considerable increase in traffic volumes and the emergence of some peak hour congestion (World Bank 1985). However, the problems of congestion are still minor in comparison to most other cities worldwide, and limited mainly to peak hour delays at a few junctions in the central area. The road system is considered to have sufficient capacity to deal with future growth in traffic, with the exception of a few road links in the central area, the road from Chitungwiza to the central area, and some roads leading to high density areas. In addition, there is seen to be a need for routes for heavy vehicle traffic which bypass the central area. The political influence of business and domestic vehicle owners and the relatively sound local financial system have ensured that levels of maintenance have been maintained and capital loans repaid. Although the income from vehicle licences is sufficient to meet only half the recurrent costs, the remainder is made up from rates revenue (HCMPPA 1988a).

Public transport: efficient or struggling on?

The residents of the high density residential areas have always been dependent on public transport, cycling or walking. Of the journey to work trips made from African townships in 1969, a third were made on foot and a fifth by bicycle, compared with a third by bus. From more distant areas such as Tafara and Mabvuku, two-thirds of trips were made by bus, while from Mbare only 10% travelled to work by bus and two-thirds used bicycles. In 1970, 44% of urban African households had bicycles (Hardwick 1973: 27). A survey in 1983 showed that just over a fifth of all trips of over 1 kilometre were work-related, a similar pro-portion were school trips, and over half were shopping trips. Overall, nearly two-thirds of trips were made on foot, especially those to schools and shops, while the rest were equally divided between cars and buses. Journey to work on foot had become less common (17% of work trips from all areas, but 45% from Harare high density areas in 1983) and use of bicycles for all trips had declined to almost nothing (Brokonsult 1985: 11). However, in the 1970s, even from Mbare—closest, at 4 kilometres, to the city centre—poor bus services resulted in the average total journey time to the CBD being 50 minutes, while from more distant areas it was often over an hour (Hardwick 1977).

As a result, increasing numbers of unlicensed taxis began to operate, mainly along the bus routes. In spite of the illegal nature of their business, pirate taxi operators became highly organised among themselves. Through their 'underground' organisations, they liaised on fare levels, route allocation, avoidance of traffic checkpoints by the police, and so on (Mutizwa-Mangiza 1993: 98). In 1981, over half of low income workers were still making their journeys to work by bus, but about a fifth were using pirate taxis. The proportion using buses increased with distance, rising to 80% from Chitungwiza. In theory in 1983, service frequencies to most high density areas were between 3 and 8 minutes during the peak hour and between 7.5 and 20 minutes off-peak. However, total travel times (including walking, waiting and riding) were 50–60 minutes from most high density areas in Harare, and more than 75 minutes for a significant minority. From Chitungwiza, as expected, few residents were able to complete their journeys to work in under an hour and for many, the journey took over 75 minutes (Brokonsult 1985: 54, 60).

The contribution made by 'emergency' taxis in the face of inadequate bus services was recognised in 1983 and licences were introduced for them on 13 routes, compared to 91 bus routes. The aim was to increase control over taxi operators and to restrict competition with the bus services (minibuses were outlawed). It was intended that the recognition of 'emergency' taxis, which were generally station wagons permitted to carry up to seven passengers, would only be needed temporarily, while problems with the main public transport services were sorted out. However, operating an emergency or pirate taxi continues to be a profitable business and in 1988 they continued to provide over a quarter of all public transport person trips, or 7% of all trips (Mutizwa-Mangiza 1993: 104). Over half the operators were owner-drivers and none possessed more than two vehicles. Despite higher fares, the taxis appeal to people who would otherwise use buses, because of their greater journey speed and ability to stop on demand. In addition to the approximately 250 emergency taxis there are at least as many unlicensed pirate taxis, and more and more operators are going 'pirate' to avoid the additional cost of complying with regulations and being registered for tax purposes. While the taxis are very important as a supplement to bus services, users considered them to have a number of shortcomings: poor roadworthiness of vehicles due to old age and disrepair; overloading; the flat fare system which discriminates against shorter journeys; and speeding (Brokonsult 1985; Mutizwa-Mangiza 1993). Nevertheless, to eliminate them as was originally intended is neither practicable nor desirable.

Zimbabwean local authorities became involved in the provision of public transport in the 1930s, since when two aspects of this provision, monopoly and subsidy, have been subject to repeated debate. In 1942 the council itself began to operate a service, but by the end of the 1940s it was in competition with private operators. Acrimonious exchanges led the council to consider operating its own monopoly service. In the end, in 1953, an exclusive franchise was issued to a private company, subject to council regulation. Fare increases in 1956 were followed by a bus boycott and rioting, leading to a revised fare structure which gave preferential treatment to 'second-class' or African services. Although African usage was increasing, the new fare structure led to an operating deficit for the company. After a few years of argument between central and local government, the basis for funding the subsidy was agreed, with the passing in 1960 of the Services Levy Act, which empowered the council to collect a levy from employers of non-domestic workers for subsidy of transport and low cost housing. New exclusive franchises were issued for the operation of the within-Harare bus service for the period 1974–87, and by the Minister of Local Government and Housing in 1977 for the Harare–Chitungwiza bus service. The central government's refusal to permit fare increases in 1980 led to a new request for subsidy. This the council was able to pay initially from the accumulated proceeds of the Services Levy, which had been phased out in the late 1970s (Jordan 1984). In the early 1980s the total number of passengers carried by buses each year in the whole Master Plan area (see below) increased by almost double the rate of both the urban population and the bus fleet (HCMPPA 1988a). Until 1984, good maintenance ensured that despite the increasing age of the fleet, a high proportion of buses were operational (Brokonsult 1985). Since then, foreign exchange shortages have had an adverse effect on the availability of new buses and spare parts. Nevertheless, in the mid-1980s the bus services were considered to be good in relation to those in other Third World cities (World Bank 1985).

Services, however, became more and more inadequate as the 1980s progressed and the operators struggled with shortage of foreign exchange, escalating costs and fares held below the rate of inflation to match limited wage increases (Situma 1987). In 1988 central government acquired 51% of the Zimbabwe United Passenger Company, the Harare Division of which held the monopoly franchise in the city. Central government took over responsibility for agreeing franchises and setting fares from local authorities, leaving the latter responsible only for determining routes and providing bus stops and shelters. A new franchise was agreed in Harare, the operating area was extended to reflect the growth of the city, and greater emphasis was placed on making foreign exchange available for new buses and spare parts. Since then, more new buses have been purchased, though the ground lost in the mid-1980s has not yet been made up. Costs have increased faster than revenue, despite increases in productivity, because of high inflation and the approval of only limited fare increases by government. The replacement of old by new buses has improved their reliability, and service levels have improved, but the financial health of the company is threatened by increased borrowing and the lag of revenue behind costs (Maunder et al 1993). The possibility of allowing other private providers to operate had been discussed for years. In 1993, as part of the current structural adjustment programme, ZUPCO's monopoly was abolished and the urban public transport sector liberalised, allowing privately owned minibuses to operate in competition with the existing services.

Harare is also an important destination on regional public transport routes. Peak patterns of use at weekends, month ends and holidays give rise to congestion at the main regional bus terminus at Mbare, which is separate from the city bus terminals in the CBD. As well as several termini, city buses use kerb-side loading. Neither the long distance nor the city terminals are located adjacent to the railway station and the lack of convenient interchanges causes difficulties for users.

Railways are important for freight, and many industrial firms have their own sidings. However, they are utilised only for inter-urban passenger movements. In the mid-1980s there were two trains a day to and from Bulawayo and one to and from Mutare (HCMPPA 1988a). It has been suggested that routes within the city be used for suburban trains in conjunction with the construction of a new line to Chitungwiza. Although there is considerable doubt as to whether the latter line is necessary or economically sensible, it has been included in the new plan proposals for the city. However, resources to commence its construction have not been available to date.

The public transport system in Harare has suffered from the disproportionate influence of the car-owning European population on investment decisions before independence and the continued influence of car owners since. It continues to suffer from a lack of coordination in the planning of different public transport modes and a failure to integrate public transport planning with new urban development. There is a need to reconsider, at the national level, the priority given to the transport sector, among others, for example with respect to the allocation of foreign exchange. Delays, long waiting times, breakdowns, and fares that increase more rapidly than incomes have typified the bus system since 1980. Open urban dissent is rare, but deficiencies in the public transport system have been one of the few irritants which have provoked occasional outbursts from the city's low income population. Improvements have been achieved since 1988 but these have been limited. The inherited segregated and inegalitarian nature of the city's built environment underlies both the inherited transport system and many of its continuing problems. Because of the cost of providing public transport to the low density residential areas, the majority of their residents will continue to rely on private cars while a minority will continue to be disadvantaged. The elimination of monopolies in the public transport sector is likely to benefit the residents of high density residential areas, provided that it is possible to maintain an effective planning and regulatory system, but the needs of pedestrians and cyclists are neglected. In plans, lip service is paid to the needs of pedestrians and cyclists. However, few provisions are made for pedestrians, despite the continued importance of walking as a way of getting around, and equally few for cyclists. The decline of bicycle use seems to have passed almost without comment: given its earlier importance in the transport system and the resource and foreign exchange advantages of bicycles over cars, this is surprising.

Planning the city of Harare

Like many colonial settlements in eastern, central and southern Africa, Zimbabwe's urban centres were all newly established; none was grafted onto pre-existing settlements. They were laid out from the outset, therefore, in line with the prevailing skills, ideologies and preoccupations of their administrators. The British South Africa Company employed engineers and surveyors to set out townships, which were developed with gridiron layouts and main streets wide enough to turn teams of oxen. The preoccupation of local administrations was with environmental health, and early local government was concerned with infrastructure provision, environmental sanitation and the survey and regulation of land subdivisions, in order to maintain control over the disposal of land in their ownership and to provide a basis for revenue generation from property tax. Imported town planning ideas and skills were added to this from the 1930s on, just as they were in Kenya, Zambia and South Africa, for example; and as urban development spread beyond the commonage, the regulation of private sector activity became increasingly important.

The urban administrative system developed in the context of a particular national government structure and set of ideologies, which were also embodied in the physical and spatial structure of urban areas and the planning process that governed this. Because of the overwhelming dominance established by settlers over indigenous people by the end of the nineteenth century, the extensive reorganisation of landholding and the establishment of an urban system from scratch, a very strong planning tradition and capacity was established:

with the privatisation and racial apportionment of land, a wide range of legislative (statutory) controls were devised in order to perpetuate and maintain the prevailing system. Physical planning emerged as an important means for the state to control and manage land and the fabric of the built environment. (Wekwete 1989a)

In addition, planning formed a framework and provided a mechanism for social control. Colonial states used physical planning to achieve specific goals (King 1990; Simon 1992). Wekwete divides his historical overview of the development of colonial planning in Zimbabwe into three periods: 1890 to 1946, 'characterised by land alienation, infrastructure development and the establishment of what can be termed the colonial spatial structure' (Wekwete 1989a: 51); 1946 to 1964, 'the consolidation period' characterised by major investments in all the economic sectors, especially manufacturing, with a consequent increase in urbanisation; and the UDI period from 1965 to 1979.

During the first period, powers for urban planning were vested initially in Sanitary Boards and then, from 1897 on, in municipalities. Physical planning was achieved mainly through by-laws and public health ordinances (Underwood 1986). The 1933 Town Planning Act (based on the British 1932 Act) formalised town planning and incorporated powers to prepare development schemes (Wekwete 1989a). The prime purpose of the Act was to regulate periurban sprawl, and the five municipalities were required to prepare town planning schemes to control and direct development in their areas (Hosford and Whittle 1979; Underwood 1986). The Act was superseded in 1945 by a second Town and Country Planning Act, which widened the application of town planning schemes to include some periurban areas and contained additional provisions (Underwood 1986; Wekwete 1989a). Town planning schemes incorporated a map and printed document 'which together were designed to give local authorities enforceable powers to control in very great detail various types of development which could be permitted in the different areas shown on the map' (Sparrow 1979: 256). These included the width and alignment of streets, the number, spacing, design and external appearance of buildings, and the use to which they were put. They were effectively zoning schemes, which suited the ideology of strict control.

Early plans

In 1946 the Municipality of Salisbury appointed its own town planning officer and prepared schemes for the Highlands and central areas.

Postwar immigration and investment in manufacturing resulted in pressures for urban development, especially in areas surrounding the original local authority areas or commonages. Attention focused, therefore, on control of land *subdivision* in peripheral areas and it was not until the mid-1950s that it became mandatory to seek permission for *development*. Because of the preoccupation with controlling subdivision between 1945 and 1960, progress with the preparation of schemes was slow, but it speeded up thereafter (Sparrow 1979). The Salisbury Rural Town Planning Scheme was prepared in 1957, in six sections, to ensure infrastructure provision and related services in subdivisions of more than 20 hectares (Wekwete 1989b). By the 1950s, therefore, a strong development control system had been instituted in the industrial, commercial and European housing areas; but, as I have discussed above, residential areas for the growing black labour force were planned and administered separately. The power to undertake low income housing projects is conferred by the Urban Councils Act, which gives the local authority power to prepare layouts for and develop its own land (Underwood 1986). Racial segregation was accompanied by the imposition of different tenure systems, differently organised housing production and different standards (see Chapters 5 and 6). While standards in African areas were geared to achieving environmental health goals (individual water supply and waterborne sanitation), they were much lower than in European areas and governed by different sets of by-laws. African townships were located away from European housing areas, ostensibly to permit journey to work on foot, but in practice to prevent disease transmission, and to maintain cultural separation and social control. Strict use separation was practised, partly reflecting British town planning ideas of the time, and partly to minimise the movement of blacks to work, especially in the industrial areas, through white areas. In the 1950s, layouts were prepared for the townships of Highfield, Glen Norah, Mufakose, Mabvuku and Tafara.

At the beginning of the 1970s, a review of the Outline Plan (for the previous municipal area) and of the scheme for the CBD (Phase 1) were undertaken, and a regional land use and traffic plan and draft schemes for Phases 2, 3, and 4 (the remainder of the old municipal area) prepared. Following a public inquiry, these were approved in 1973 (Sparrow 1979). The Outline and regional plans were land use / traffic plans, influenced in their approach by new British–American developments in large scale land use / traffic modelling (Chadwick 1987) and not unlike those produced, usually by expatriate consultants, for many developing country cities. However, the assumptions on which the population and employment projections were based were peculiarly Rhodesian. Forecasts for European workers, based on the share of national employment in the city, were scaled up by ratios of 2.5:1 in 1973 increasing to 3.6:1 in the year 2000, to give forecasts of the number of African workers, to which were added domestic servants estimated as a proportion of the European, Asian and Coloured population. A population projection was carried out for Europeans and the African population derived from this. Migration was considered only incidentally.

The Outline Plan focused on the future road network and land use zoning for industrial, business, residential, social facility and open space use. On an ordnance survey base, it allocated broad areas of land according to ten use categories, symbolically indicated the location of administrative and social facilities, and showed the existing and proposed major road network (Figure 2.16). It recognised the limitations of planning the road network and land use pattern for only part of the built-up area (and, indeed, by the time the plan was approved, administrative area) and urged the early preparation of a plan for the city as a whole (Salisbury 1973). Superimposed above an existing network of primary and district distributor roads were proposed freeways, as noted in the previous section, running northwest, northeast, south and west from the city centre and intended to provide rapid access to the central and industrial areas, mostly from the European housing areas. Public transport was not mentioned. The open space allocation was based on a standard of 6.6 hectares per 1000 population, which was acknowledged to be generous but was felt to be partly driven by the city's topography, and aimed at 'an interlacing network of open space covering the whole urban region' (Salisbury 1973: 5). However, many of the spaces were simply poorly drained river valleys and vleis and, except for large formal sites such as the Botanical Gardens, resources were insufficient to develop most of the land allocated.

The Outline Plan was accompanied by a regional Land Use / Traffic Plan, which included road proposals for the area within the extended city boundary. The schemes specified land use zoning in more detail, including the boundaries of most sites for institutional and social facilities, different types and densities of residential use and the width of many road reserves. Each was accompanied by a document setting out the scheme clauses or detailed regulations to guide development.

By the 1970s, shortcomings with the Planning Act were evident: large parts of the country were excluded from some or all of its provisions, in particular the areas immediately outside urban council boundaries. In addition, the procedures specified in the Act were cumbersome (Hosford and Whittle, 1979). It was replaced in 1976 by the Regional, Town and Country Planning Act, and policy, under the influence of South African ideas, shifted to favour the location of African housing in or close to the TTLs rather than near the main urban areas.

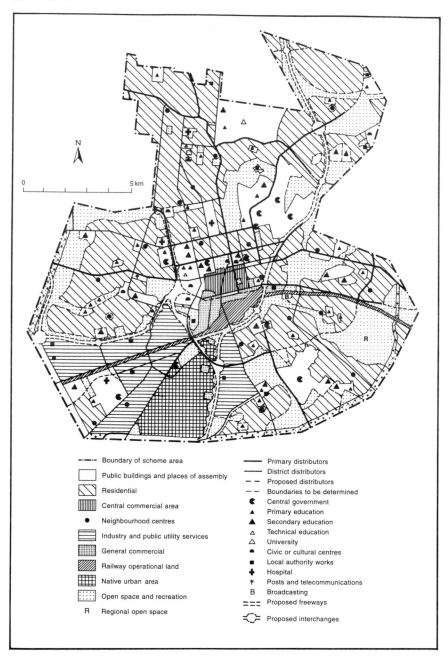

Figure 2.16   The City of Salisbury Outline Plan proposals, 1973

Salisbury's plan was reviewed again in 1975. Foreign consultants developed six alternative strategies (Patel and Adams 1981):

1   non-interference (that is, maintain and enlarge the existing structure);
2   similar to (i) but with a greater increase in the area allocated for residential use;
3   growth to the west, with commercial and industrial growth points as countermagnets;
4   development of Seki TTL for housing, with a commercial/industrial area near the airport;
5   an employment corridor, with residential areas on either side;
6   establishment of towns in the TTLs, at a distance of up to 150 kilometres from Salisbury, starting with Seki, even though the consultants recognised the problems.

The third, fourth and sixth strategies were further investigated, and the last was adopted, despite adverse professional opinion. The development of Seki (Chitungwiza), which has been described in a previous section, was the only element of the strategy that was implemented.

Although the 1976 Act introduced provisions for regional planning for the first time, the basic nature, assumptions, procedures and mechanisms of the planning system remained unchanged. The Act ostensibly introduced new imported ideas and attempted to solve the problems being experienced with the earlier Act, but the functions and practice of planning in a racially segregated system changed little. It introduced a two tier system of plans, as had the 1971 Act in the UK. In Zimbabwe, these were called Master and Local Plans. Master Plans were intended to be strategic guidelines for development over a 20 year time horizon. They have to take into account broad policy issues and the economic development of the urban area concerned. The proposals are to be shown on a diagrammatic map and accompanied by a Written Statement. Local Plans are more detailed, are intended to provide a guideline for development control, and are to be prepared after the Master Plan is adopted. They include measures to regulate land use, construction and use of buildings. Again, a Written Statement is accompanied by maps and diagrams. In both cases, the Written Statement is supposed to state goals and objectives, put forward and justify proposals, examine constraints on implementation and resources available, and suggest phasing. While supposedly modelled on changes in the British planning system, Local Plans continue to be detailed zoning plans because this suits the Zimbabwean view of planning. Experience with this type of physical planning in developing countries has been far from positive, and in accounts of other low income cities the ineffectiveness of land use planning and development control makes extensive consideration of the plans prepared irrelevant. In Harare, in contrast, despite the lack of connections between land use planning and the resource allocation process, the relatively developed financial capacity of the city council and the efficacy of the development control system mean that plan preparation is by no means irrelevant to the development process.

By the early 1980s, the planning framework for the Harare city region was extremely fragmented. Within the city's own boundaries, development was governed by the 1973 Outline Plan for the pre-1971 municipal area, eight Schemes, and eight Local Plans prepared between 1978 and 1984. Outside the city boundary, the Harare Rural Town Planning Scheme was still operative, in addition to the plan for Chitungwiza, seven new district development plans, and statutory layouts for five smaller centres. There was an obvious need to update and replace the older plans, many of which applied to areas under considerable pressure for new development, such as Kopje, Avenues, Hatfield and Waterfalls.

Planning for future development: the Harare Combination Master Plan

In 1983/4 work on local plans halted in favour of the preparation of a new master plan for the city region, for which studies were completed on population, commercial and shopping development, employment, transport infrastructure and natural resources (Harare City Council, Department of Works 1983/4). The boundary of the combination plan area (Figure 2.17), which included parts of a number of local authority areas, was chosen with Harare's future expansion in mind, as well as existing and potential future water supply areas and the need to incorporate areas with economic or other strategic relationships with the city (HCMPPA 1987), and certainly not for administrative convenience. The plan preparation technical team was made up of planners from the Department of Physical Planning and Harare's Department of Works (the only departments with planners to spare). It reported to a coordinating team on which Chitungwiza was represented in addition to these organisations. By 1985 all the reports of study for the Combination Master Plan area had been completed, except for Traffic and Transportation, which was not finished until 1988, and Financial Resources. Considerable delays followed. A city-wide household survey was undertaken in 1987, few of whose results have ever been published.

In 1988/9 the Harare Combination Master Plan Authority was formally inaugurated, covering an area of 4571 square kilometres and

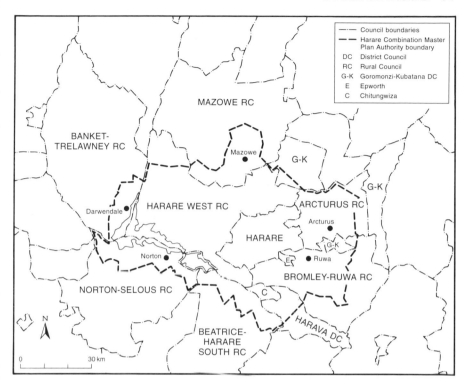

Figure 2.17 The Harare Combination Master Plan area. Council boundaries from Surveyor General 1988

including representatives of the two relevant ministries (Local Government and Rural and Urban Development, and Natural Resources and Tourism) and eleven local authorities. The individual reports of study were updated and consolidated into a single report (HCMPPA 1987), and a further report on sectoral issues and recommendations was prepared (HCMPPA 1989). The plan aimed to provide 'a meaningful strategic policy framework for the coordinated and contained development and control of the physical environment in the interests of the Community' (HCMPPA 1989: 5). It was also intended to provide a framework for local plan preparation and to set out policies on major issues of national and regional importance, strategic development control policies, and a strategy on phasing, implementation and monitoring of development proposals, including allocation of resources. Some confusion over the desirable plan period, which varied from ten to twenty years, was evident in the various reports. A major planning effort, potentially of considerable significance for the city, it is worth considering both the process of plan preparation and its outcomes, in terms of proposals for future development.

The eight main issues identified in the reports (HCMPPA 1987, 1989) of the study were as follows:

1 *Rapid population growth*: The population of the plan area was projected to increase from 1.52 million to 2.34 million by the year 2020.

2 *Infrastructure and land development potential*: While it was recognised that there was considerable potential for infill development, areas suitable for accommodating further population growth were also investigated. The main constraints on potential were considered to be water supply and sewerage, but also considered were minimising journeys to work, avoiding river banks, and the airport height limitation zone. Five areas of high and medium potential were identified (see Figure 2.18): A Darwendale and Muzururu drainage area; B Waterfalls area South; C Gwebi drainage area; D Mabvinzi drainage area; E adjacent to Chitungwiza. It was considered that the water resources in the planning area could support a population of between 4 and 5 million, but only at the considerable cost of developing two new dams. Typical of the worldwide adoption of supply-led planning for water supply, the potential for water conservation does not appear to have been considered (Swedeplan 1988).

3 *Transport*: Few problems were identified with the existing road network, other than the need for some missing links to be completed, though some doubt was cast on the freeway reservations because of the lack of recent traffic survey data, the cost of constructing major roads, the shift of emphasis in transport planning to traffic management, the suitability of the routes being safeguarded, and the blighting effect of the undeveloped roads. Problems with the public transport system were recognised to be more severe, but were given little attention in the planning process (however, see the previous section).

4 *Housing*: The inherited pattern of residential development was seen as creating a number of problems, mainly because of the low densities of former European housing areas (estimated at about 9 persons per hectare, compared to 110 per hectare in Harare's high density areas and 152 per hectare in Chitungwiza). Finding ways of increasing densities within the existing urban area and setting aside and servicing housing land for the anticipated, largely low income, increase in population, were seen as the main requirements.

5 *Employment and industry*: The increased lag between the number of

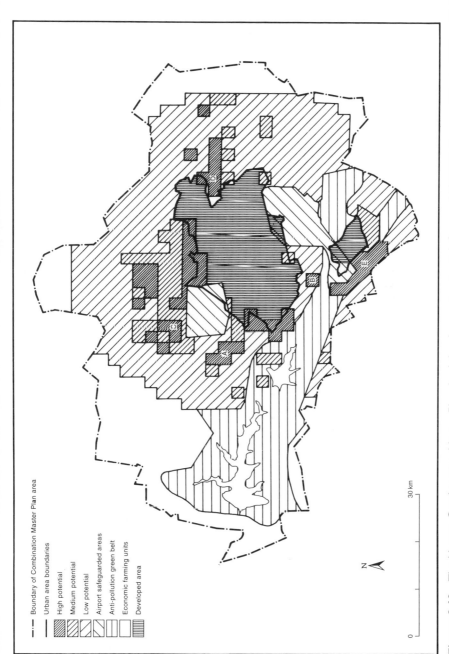

Figure 2.18 The Harare Combination Master Plan: land development potential. Source: HCMPPA Report of Study 1989, p. 18. A Darwendale and Muzururu drainage area; B Waterfalls South; C Gwebi drainage area; D Mabvinzi drainage area; E Chitungwiza

available jobs and population growth was identified as a problem. However, it was not considered that the plan could do anything to influence economic performance other than set aside appropriate areas of land. Just over a fifth of the land in the six main industrial areas was still undeveloped, but the task of the Combination Master Plan was seen as to identify sufficient additional land for all types of industrial use.

6   *Commercial facilities*: The existing provision of land for commercial facilities in the central area and high income residential areas was seen as unproblematic, and the main issue in low income areas was identified as mediation in conflicts between formal and informal sector retailers in their shopping centres and how to accommodate the latter appropriately.

7   *Community and recreational facilities*: Existing and increased pressure on education and health facilities was identified as a major problem, as was the imbalance between recreational open space provision in low and high density areas (1.64 and 0.21 square metres of formal open space per person respectively, exacerbated by the tendency of larger facilities such as clubs and golf courses to cater for the better off). High quality hotel beds were considered to be overprovided, while there was underprovision of more modest tourist accommodation. Finally, 70% of the space in the area's six cemeteries was found to have been used, and a need for new cemetery sites was identified. More appropriate planning standards to ensure economic land utilisation were felt to be needed.

8   *Environment*: A variety of issues was considered under the heading of 'environment', ranging from the need for a positive conservation policy for the city's townscape, to the need to identify new sites for refuse disposal.

The draft Written Statement was then prepared (HCMPPA 1991). It contained a brief summary of the main problems, constraints and opportunities and the broad preferred land use strategy, and then proceeded to set out goals, objectives, policies and proposals for each sectoral area of concern, and proposals for implementation and monitoring, indicating the location of the proposals on two very poorly reproduced key diagrams or proposals plans. No explicit reference was made to any of the earlier documents and, as a result, the proposals were presented in an extremely user-unfriendly fashion, deterring any form of public discussion. The proposals are an odd mixture: some refer to national goals and objectives and suggest policies and proposals for agencies other than those involved in the planning process, while others are detailed local physical objectives, involving specific actions.

Three simplified land use strategies had apparently been considered: concentration, sprawl, or maintaining the status quo. The recommended strategy opted for concentration of growth within the existing boundaries on vacant land and at higher densities, in addition to controlled growth of Harare and Chitungwiza. However, it was recognised that the expansion of these settlements would eventually be limited both by infrastructure considerations and the need to safeguard land of high agricultural potential, so there was also a recognition of the need and potential for developing smaller centres such as Mazowe, Norton, Ruwa, Arcturus and Darwendale (Figure 2.17). This strategy, it is thought, will encourage the best use of existing land and facilities, gradually increase the integration of the urban form, and enable planning ahead for new development.

With respect to *population*, the confusion of the plan preparation team about the functions and scope of a master plan is evident. The first goal is to 'Evolve a national population growth and control policy in line with overall national goals', which hardly seems appropriate for the plan for a particular city region. The second goal, to match population distribution within the region to economic opportunities, is perhaps legitimate, though the means of achieving this, rather oddly for a master plan, include the recommendations that health facilities should provide birth control on demand, that population control [sic] should be included in school curricula, and that local *land use planning* authorities should advocate smaller families. Population resettlement strategies for homeless migrants are to be based on the creation of institutions for those unable to look after themselves, and reception centres from which the able-bodied 'destitute' can be resettled; but who is going to undertake these actions is not specified, with the exception of a local authority role in the identification of sites.

Many of the goals, objectives, policies and proposals with respect to *infrastructure and land development* are, in contrast, within the scope of the statutory planning and local authority land development system. Realistic proposals include the intention to economise on land by allowing smaller plots, especially in low density areas; to develop all areas from which sewage can be collected for treatment using existing facilities; and to encourage local authority land banking and forward planning for new investment. Immediate development is thus expected to occur to the west and northwest of the existing built-up area in Tynwald and Bluff Hill, and by densification south and east of the centre in Hatfield, Waterfalls and Greendale (Figure 2.19). There is a proposal for feasibility studies to establish the potential for developing the area between Harare and Chitungwiza. Further, it is intended to construct a tunnel to the south of the Firle and Chitungwiza sewage

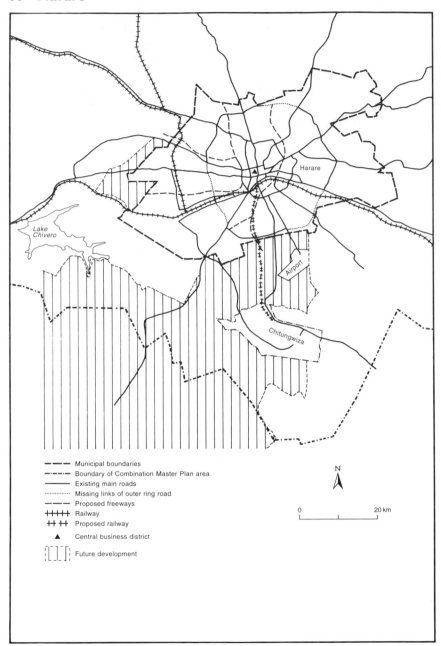

Figure 2.19   The Harare Combination Master Plan: key proposals. Source: HCMPPA 1991

disposal works, to enable discharge to the Mupfuri river, to the south of Chitungwiza, which would open up areas to the west, south and east of the town for development.

High sounding goals are stated with respect to development of the *transport* network, though the resource implications of the proposals are not considered: to proceed with the construction of missing links in order to produce an integrated road hierarchy; to provide alternative routes for heavy vehicles which bypass the CBD; to develop inner and outer ring roads; to reassess the proposed freeway routes with respect to their appropriateness and the cost of construction (the possibility that they may not be needed appears to have been dropped); to implement a proposed suburban rail network, especially a link to Chitungwiza; to allocate resources to public transport (though the source of these resources is unclear); and to develop cycle routes.

With respect to *housing*, the plan proposes to encourage more socially mixed housing, allowing higher densities and developing new house designs suitable for higher density development; public sector provision of rental housing to complement that provided for purchase (which goes against recent trends in housing policy and practice and has considerable but unexplored resource implications); and the setting aside of 'planned self-sustaining transient settlements for homeless migrants or displaced people to avoid squatter settlements'. What is meant by self-sustaining in this context is not clarified.

Specific policies for *industry and employment* are limited to providing sites for large and small scale enterprises, the former in industrial areas and the latter in residential areas. Even approval of small scale enterprises on residential plots is signalled by the plan, representing a change of heart from existing policy. Only a couple of years earlier, in 1990, when councillors resisted the issue of enforcement orders for unauthorised business uses on residential plots, the 'sound town planning principles' advocated by officials were said to have won the day, and enforcement orders continued to be issued (*Sunday Mail*, 1 July 1990). Other ways of achieving economic growth and diversification suggested in the plan include encouraging business initiatives, identifying scenic areas with potential for tourism, and the development of raw materials based industries. Finally, the planners have leapt on the bandwagon of the latest imported planning ideas (simplified planning zones, office and technology parks), with little critical analysis of their use and outcome elsewhere or of the real constraints on economic development in Zimbabwe.

As noted above, few problems were identified with respect to *commercial facilities* (though the residents of many high density areas might not agree with this diagnosis), so the plan confines itself to advocating the development of a hierarchy of facilities with good access, realisation of the full floor area potential of the CBD as defined at present, and measures to accommodate informal sector activities in all shopping centres by designating appropriate areas for their use. In the section on *community and recreational facilities*, the need for appropriate standards and a programme of provision that keeps pace with population growth and new residential development cannot be disputed. The plan then moves outside the land use planning sphere, without presenting a rationale or justification for its proposals, to advocate encouragement of the voluntary sector, of marriage guidance counselling services to minimise the need for child welfare, and of churches in order to meet the spiritual as well as physical needs of urban residents. The aim is to achieve an accessible range of recreational and sports facilities and to develop a coordinated regional open space system for tourism, in part by the development of the Mukuvisi and Manyame River corridors with an appropriate mixture of residential, commercial and recreational uses, and also by the purchase and development of Mermaid's Pool, in the extreme east of the Combination Master Plan area, as a national recreational area.

Environmental goals are to be achieved by the use of environmental impact assessments of major development proposals; the maintenance of buffer zones along rivers and around areas of ecological value; the development of procedures for conservation of buildings of architectural or historic value; plans for waste disposal (including use of brickfields at Mount Hampden for tipping and the incineration of toxic waste); developing a work programme for the development of open space; and strengthening of pollution control agencies. The recommendation that land be zoned for allotments within the urban area is positive, as long as the administration escapes the usual stranglehold of excessive bureaucracy, but is somewhat counteracted by the determination to enforce controls, the need for which is not clearly proven, over streambank cultivation. Finally, the plan includes a proposal to designate a green belt to contain urban sprawl, without any evaluation of the potentially positive or negative outcomes of such a designation or of the results of green belt policies elsewhere.

The section on *implementation* is very brief, merely listing the 57 main proposals, specifying whether they are to be implemented by the government, local authority and/or private sector, and giving a rough time frame (short, medium or long term). The intention to monitor progress is stated, but no guidance is given on what should be monitored or how. There is no section on resource allocation.

Further delays occurred in the consideration of the plan proposals. Eventually, officials of the local and central authorities considered them first. At this stage, the apparent lack of involvement of local authorities not represented on the Technical and Coordination teams gave rise to some difficulties, for example the initial expression of opposition to proposals for expansion to the southeast of Chitungwiza by Harava District Council (*Herald*, 16 July 1991). The proposals were then revised and circulated for consultation and exhibition. Theoretically, plan proposals are subject to decision making by elected councillors at local level. The central Department of Physical Planning maintains control by approving Master Plans, as well as layouts prepared under the Urban Councils Act. The Planning Act requires local authorities to consult widely during the process of plan preparation. The draft plan (or layout) is then exhibited, and objections received must be forwarded with comments by the local planning authority to the Minister of Local Government and Rural and Urban Development in the case of Master Plans and layouts prepared outside the framework of a statutory plan, and to the Administrative Court in the case of Local Plans. 'It is apparent that public participation is very much a passive requirement and centers more on providing opportunities to object to the proposals than requiring that the public participate in the plan preparation process' (Underwood 1986: 200).

This procedure reflects practice as embodied in the 1947 Planning Act in Britain and exported to the colonies, rather than current British practice, which provides more extensive opportunities for public participation. It also fails to incorporate experience gained through the involvement of local people in decision making and implementation in developing countries. 'Exhibition' of plan proposals seems deliberately geared to minimise public input and restrict it to knowledgeable and better educated urban residents. Unsurprisingly, in the case of the Combination Master Plan, formal public exhibition of the Written Statement and Proposals Map produced little feedback, although there was some criticism of the plan for concentrating on Harare and neglecting the outlying areas, and paying insufficient attention to transport and too much to the preservation of historic buildings (*Financial Gazette*, 30 January 1992). The final revised version was forwarded to the minister, who finally approved it later in 1992.

While many of the proposals are sound, if insufficiently justified and poorly presented, in other cases, the arguments for and against alternatives (if alternatives have been considered, which is often unclear) are not presented in the published documents, and the reasons for advocating certain ways forward are far from self-evident. Some planning concepts have been adopted from overseas (mostly from the UK), apparently without critical review. However, the main problem is likely to stem from the confused concept of the purpose and function of a Master Plan. This seems to stem from the nature of the statutory land use planning system, its existence in parallel with other planning systems (with which its relationship is unclear), and the absence of any corporate strategy for either of the two large local authorities. A few of the proposals can be implemented by the planning sections and departments of the local authorities concerned; more can be implemented by other departments of the same councils, subject to agreement from those departments and resource availability; but many cannot be implemented at the local level, as they involve central government policies and resources (and not just those of the Ministry of Local Government and Rural and Urban Development) and actions to be taken by private sector enterprises. Local authorities are given scope by the Act to do anything necessary to implement plan proposals, but their specific powers are limited to control over development; and the prevalent conception of planning tends to equate it with control over land use and physical development, reinforced by its relegation to a subsection of the Works department. This is by no means atypical of the model of planning exported to the British colonies, in which it continues to have this limited role today, despite the obvious inability of most urban local authorities to exercise effective control over development, and the need for a more action-orientated and managerial approach to planning (Devas and Rakodi 1993). The underlying weakness of this type of physical planning system is that it is not tied into resource allocation procedures, and to a large extent it can only respond to private sector initiative rather than take a proactive role in achieving development goals.

Simultaneously with preparation of the Master Plan, the local planning process proceeded in fits and starts, as urgency of need vied with the desire to ensure compatibility with Master Plan proposals. By 1989, seven Local Plans had been approved, including plans for the Kopje area and Highfield, and seven were in preparation but had been deferred pending completion of the Master Plan (HCMPPA 1989). One was for the Mukuvisi Corridor and was completed the following year: it contained proposals for recreational, social and community facilities, flats, and other uses not considered detrimental to the open space designation of the area, for which the council then invited proposals from developers. In 1993 a draft Local Plan for the CBD was prepared, which proposed higher permitted densities for development and a new road bypassing the centre to the south of the railway (*Herald*, 17 March 1993).

The old Outline Plan and town planning schemes provided the basis for an effective, if rigid, development control system, which has produced a high quality urban environment in formerly 'European' parts of the city. Although standards were lower in the former African housing areas, the high degree of municipal control and investment again ensured controlled investment to relatively high standards. The very rigidity and effectiveness of the system has, however, inhibited the development of innovative responses to the rapidly changing national and urban situations. Recognition of the need to update plans and increase the responsiveness of the system to change competes with the desire to maintain standards and control over development. The attempt to produce a revised strategic plan without using external resources is commendable, but the process of plan preparation has been problematic and long drawn out because of the absence of a strong city-regional planning body and lack of resources. The test of the plan which has now been approved will be in its implementation, but continuing political rivalries and resource shortages, as well as the nature of some of the proposals, do not encourage optimism. The decision making process will deal with urgent issues (for example future water supply for the city), and the local planning process seems to be progressing fairly satis-factorily, if local plans are regarded primarily as guides to development control; but planning for the future of the city requires a more radical administrative rearrangement and a more coherent conception of the purpose and nature of a strategic plan than have been demonstrated to date.

3

The city's economy

Africa was integrated into the world economic system, through the mercantile and colonial periods, as a supplier of primary commodities and importer of manufactured goods. In some pre-existing urban centres, indigenous modes of production based on trade and artisanal manufacturing survived, modified to a greater or lesser extent by incorporation into colonial economic systems. In most of eastern, central and southern Africa, however, as has already been described, the indigenous economy was based on subsistence agriculture with a limited amount of trade and metal-working. In the new colonial settlements, including Harare, the organisation of production from the outset was capitalist. International commerce was dominated by trading companies based in the European colonial countries, while intermediary functions and domestic commerce provided opportunities for indigenous traders where these existed, Asian, Lebanese or Syrian immigrants, or (especially in the case of the settler societies) European immigrants. Since the 1960s, often with help from national governments, indigenous people have increased their involvement in trade and commerce, in state marketing boards, in trading companies and the retail sector and, above all, in petty trade. Vendors and traders congregate on the streets, in the markets and in the city centres of Africa cheek by jowl with department stores, supermarkets and luxury shops.

Another significant employment sector in urban settlements has arisen from their administrative role, initially in colonial administration, later in the growing civil services of newly independent countries and their proliferating parastatal sectors. The job opportunities in this sector, as in others, were predominantly for men, reflecting both colonial and indigenous ideologies and the pragmatic value of relying on women's traditional role in food production both to keep wages down and to ensure male compliance in migrant labour practices. Important in itself in employment terms, the steady wage employment in bureaucracies generates a demand for goods and services provided by the commercial and personal services sectors. Not the least important of these services was and remains domestic service.

In the capitalist economic systems of Europe, the raw materials imported in the course of and surpluses generated by mercantile trade were invested in industry. Older craft industries were displaced or transformed, and employment in the manufacturing sector became the main dynamic behind the growth of great industrial cities. In Africa, industrialisation was not part of the colonial design for the continent. While urban and rural craft industries survived in some places, especially in west Africa, elsewhere they could not compete with cheap manufactured goods from Europe and they declined, with extensive loss of skills. Where urban and European populations were small, there was little scope for the development of manufacturing, even to satisfy domestic demand, and it was limited to elementary food processing or the production of basic consumer goods such as kitchen utensils and hand tools. Agricultural and mining products destined for European markets were not processed, as such manufactured exports would have competed with European industries.

At independence, countries inherited economies based on primary products, with underdeveloped manufacturing sectors. Despite determined attempts to start processing and other manufacturing industries, in sub-Saharan Africa as a whole they accounted for only 24% of exports in 1992. Even in those countries which had been most successful, manufactures constituted less than 40% of exports, compared to 71% of India's or 73% of the Philippines' exports. Only 4% of the total value added in manufacturing in low and middle income countries in 1991 was generated in Africa (World Bank 1994). Such training as was provided and any jobs generated were again mainly for men.

> Under these conditions, commerce remains more important than manufacturing, in terms both of value added and employment, in most African cities. The commercial sector comprises a varied mixture of local and foreign private and state capital, varying in scale from small businesses to large TNC operations. The evolution of such a spectrum is mainly a postcolonial feature, consequent upon greater involvement of local capital and the growth of indigenous capitalist classes. Previously there had frequently been a sharp contrast between large, state-owned or foreign companies and small, local enterprises. . . . The continued relatively greater importance of commerce transcends individual states' official ideology and development strategy. (Simon 1992: 75–6).

Although the capitalist mode of production has become dominant in manufacturing and services, the forms of production and their relationship with non-capitalist modes of production vary from place to place, depending on the pre-existence of extensive organised craft sectors and trading systems, the extent to which the resources available are of interest to transnational corporations (TNCs), the degree of success in fostering an indigenous capitalist class, the extent and efficiency of state capitalist production, and the implementation of regulatory policies by central and local governments. In countries where foreign direct investment in manufacturing has occurred, this may have an influence on the capital intensity of the technology installed, and thus the number of jobs generated, wages paid, tolerance of trade unions and scope for development of industry by domestic capital. Although foreign direct investment in Africa has been very limited in world terms, it is often important for particular economies, not only because of the employment it generates but also because of the specialised business and financial services for which it generates demand and which are invariably located in the largest cities, which are the fulcrums of flows of international banking, commercial and industrial capital, travel and communications (Thrift 1987; Simon 1992). Foreign direct investment is even more concentrated than domestic investment in the largest cities, because of its executives' greater knowledge of the local economic environment, and the presence of commercial facilities to intermediate between extraction/production and the international market where these are not contained within a TNC itself (Sit 1993). The locational attractions of the city are often magnified by policy with respect, for example, to transport tariffs, energy and service policies, and incentives for industrial development. Official policies to encourage decentralisation are often counteracted by the spatial effects of non-spatial policies: Oberai (1993) quotes the example of Nigeria where over 90% of total net subsidies granted to industries benefited those located in Lagos.

In some countries, the virtual absence of a domestic bourgeoisie at independence led the state to adopt a significant role not only in marketing but also in production and in the regulation of capital markets, to extend economic diversification, achieve developmental goals and ensure indigenous control. The failure to achieve efficiency in these extensive parastatal sectors in situations of limited skills, bureaucratic control and political manipulation is now recognised, though the World Bank / IMF prescription of privatisation is not necessarily going to be any more successful where supply constraints on inputs, including capital and skills, and lack of entrepreneurial experience continue to inhibit the development of the domestic capitalist sector. The relative absence of indigenous capitalism is by no means universal, however. Access to the state by virtue of bureaucratic position or political office, or the windfall profits from natural resource bonanzas such as oil in

Nigeria, has given local entrepreneurs access to opportunities for capital accumulation, though they are just as likely—or even more likely—to invest in property or trade as in the productive sectors. State action to reserve certain sectors of economic activity (for example public transport or retailing) for local people, via the issue of licences, has made opportunities available to those with less capital.

Although not all the activity in the capitalist sectors that I have discussed so far is legal, it mostly falls within the purview of state regulation both at the national and local levels, including controls over access to foreign exchange or import licences, taxation, wage and employment legislation, company registration, planning, and pollution control. It comprises those enterprises that are enumerated in national statistics and the output of which is reflected in national indicators of economic growth: the formal sector. Although not all enumerated enterprises are large scale, many are, and it tends to be these enterprises that can gain access to both public and private sector institutional credit. However, they are only part of the urban economy. Alongside, linked to and dependent on the large and medium scale formal sector, is an extensive small scale or petty commodity production sector. Always extensive in some African cities, in others, especially those founded by the colonial powers, it was frowned upon and restricted in order to curb unwanted migration. Nevertheless, opportunities existed in the inter-stices of the colonial wage labour system for small scale services, including retailing, brewing, repairs, personal services, rental accom-modation and the provision of domestic and sexual services to male migrants. With the advent of independence, and the end of migration controls, the scope for further development of the small scale sector widened. The growth of wage jobs in administration and manufacturing succeeded in some countries, for example Zambia, in absorbing many additions to the urban wage labour force in the 1960s. By the mid-1970s, however, the demand for wage labour was stagnating or falling. In countries with a tradition of entrepreneurship and trading, or with an urban labour force with craft or manufacturing skills, the informal sector grew rapidly, expanding both to exploit the new markets generated by rapid population and economic growth and to absorb those members of the labour force who could not find wage jobs. As real wages and jobs in the formal economy declined still further in the 1980s under the impact of the debt crisis and structural adjustment programmes, the informal, parallel economy expanded still further, in some cities accounting for between one- and two-thirds of those working. An amorphous sector, its boundaries are unclear: the boundary between formal and informal varies with the nature and efficiency of enumeration and regulation; that between legal and illegal depends on the scope and temptations for activities such as smuggling, and the vagaries of national and local regulations; that between large and small scale depends on the size and structure of the economy; and that between productive and reproductive depends, for example, on whether demand exists and a surplus for sale can be produced from self-provisioning activities such as cultivation. Marxist analysis would distinguish between the social relations of production in the capitalist and petty commodity production sectors, but it is acknowledged that within the latter there is a wide range of organisational forms, degrees of subordination to the large scale sector, and conditions of employment (Bromley and Gerry 1979). The understanding of the nature of the urban economy in African cities has typically been shaky, analysis often gender-blind, and policies towards both the large and small scale sectors contradictory and inconsistent.

The connections between cities and the global economy have traditionally involved the capitalist sector, through trade, foreign ownership of capital, relations with other states, and relations between states and trading blocs or international institutions. However, the non-capitalist sector within the city is linked to the capitalist sector in 'a complex and changing set of relationships' (Simon 1992: 83) and, as trade is liberalised, even, on a small scale, with neighbouring national economies.

It is within this general discussion of the nature of urban economies in Africa that our analysis of Harare's economy has to be situated. The economic structure of urban areas in Zimbabwe ranges from smaller settlements dominated by a single sector, such as the mining centres; to agricultural service centres, often with some agro-processing industry; to the larger regional and national centres with diversified economies and significant manufacturing sectors. In 1980, 68% of wage employment and 82% of GDP was non-agricultural and mostly urban; of wage employees, 45% were in the eight major towns, earning 70% of all wage incomes (World Bank 1985: 13). As the largest city, Harare has a diversified economic structure with a significant manufacturing sector. Economic structure, employment, wages, the position of women in the labour force, and the informal sector are discussed in this chapter.

Employment

In contrast to most other developing countries, and because of Zimbabwe's recent colonial urban and economic history, as outlined in Chapter 1, the urban workforce is overwhelmingly in formal sector wage employment. Most of the available information relates to this sector, which probably accounts for 80–90% of all employment. Reasons for the relative unimportance of the informal sector will be explored later in the chapter. Because of its significance, the characteristics of the formal economy will first be examined in some detail.

By the end of 1992, half of all formal sector employment was in the nine largest urban centres, reflecting the declining importance of agricultural employment (CSO 1993). Manufacturing employment in particular is overwhelmingly concentrated in the seven main industrial centres. Already by the 1950s, the smaller urban centres were less attractive to industrialists than the large centres, because they lacked engineering, technical and repair facilities, social and recreational facilities, and housing for skilled white employees. Despite decentralisation being considered desirable, it has not proved possible to persuade industry, which tends to be dominated by large firms, to invest outside the three or four largest centres (Zinyama 1987). Harare increasingly dominates both total and manufacturing employment and output. Over half of all urban employment is in the city, just as at least half of Kenya's urban wage employment is in Nairobi (Simon 1992). From 39% of manufacturing employees in 1969, Harare increased its share to 45% in 1985, while Bulawayo had 28%. The two cities' relative shares of output are similar (Zimbabwe nda: 95–6). In 1969, a quarter of the employees in Harare were white (Whitsun Foundation 1980: 50–1) but more recent figures are not broken down by race.

Responses to census questions about participation in economic activity are intended to reveal the size and demographic characteristics of the labour force, and the proportion of those who regard themselves as economically active but who cannot get work. Even in developed countries with benefits systems for the unemployed such data are not wholly reliable and may, in particular, underestimate the number of those who would like to work but have been discouraged from actively seeking work by the lack of opportunity. In developing countries, the absence of social security or a formal registration system for the unemployed, and the resulting need of those with dependants to earn money in casual work or self-employment, however sporadically, make it even more difficult to arrive at estimates of economic activity rates, and unemployment figures are particularly unreliable. Nevertheless, the 1982 census in Zimbabwe gives some indication of both these dimensions of the urban labour force. The participation rate in Harare and Chitungwiza in 1982 was similar to the national urban average (58% and 63%, compared to 62% nationally). The figures for the city are not broken down by gender, but those for all urban areas indicate significant gender differences: the labour force participation rate for men was 82% but for women appeared to be less than half that (37%). This was similar to the rural areas for men but considerably lower than for women in rural areas (52%). Although only a third of young men and women (aged 15–19) were economically active, the vast majority of older men were working. Women in a wide range of age groups were involved in the labour force, but invariably the participation rate was less than half that for men (Zimbabwe 1985a: 112–14).

That the female participation rates should be regarded with some suspicion is borne out by figures from an early 1980s survey in Glen View, Mbare and Mabelreign, which showed that overall about 70% of women were working (Drakakis-Smith 1985: 1288). While similar proportions of Harare's and Chitungwiza's adult population in 1982 regarded themselves as economically active, the unemployment rate varied greatly between the two settlements, being much higher in Chitungwiza (53%) than in Harare (9%), though because of Harare's greater population size it was only 18% overall (CSO 1989). Already in the 1970s, job generation was not keeping pace with labour force growth in urban centres. Investment in urban economic sectors was adversely affected by the war, while in-migration from rural to urban areas increased for the same reason. Thus the ratio of population to employment in Harare deteriorated from 2.17 in 1969 to 2.55 in 1978 (Whitsun Foundation 1980: 57). Since 1978 there has been an upward trend in employment in most sectors, interrupted by decreases in years of particular economic difficulty, for example 1982/3, but it has continued to fail to keep pace with labour force growth (HCMPPA 1988b). By 1991, when an intensified economic structural adjustment programme was introduced, unemployment nationally was officially estimated at 26% and unofficially at even more. Measures to slim down the civil service and parastatals, and short term job losses in the private sector, exacerbated by the effects of the severe drought in 1991/2, have certainly resulted in increased unemployment rates. The unemployed are predominantly young and educated (over a third to secondary school level), and are comprised of equal numbers of men and women (Zimbabwe 1991a).

In the account of Chitungwiza's development in the previous chapter, the settlement's dependence on Harare for employment was noted. A survey in 1987 showed only 10 114 employees in Chitungwiza, of which nearly half worked in the industrial estate, compared to nearly 300 000 in Harare (HCMPPA 1988b: 11). The most recent figures available for people in work in Harare at the time of the research on which this book is based were, for 1989, based on Central Statistical Office employment and earnings surveys of formal sector employers. Because these are workplace-based surveys, many workers from Chitungwiza are included in the returns. The survey results will be used to examine the structure and characteristics of Harare's economy.

The structure of employment in Harare

In 1989, a total of 4691 firms were surveyed in the employees and earnings surveys in Harare (unpublished returns) (Table 3.1). These employed a total of over 300 000 workers, of whom less than a fifth were women. The growth of total employment in the three subsequent years was only 8% (CSO 1993). The great majority of these employees were full-time and only a tiny minority were designated as casual or part-time workers. According to the classification used in Table 3.1, the largest single sector was manufacturing, employing nearly a third of all workers and concentrated in the industrial areas. It is seen as the basic sector in the economy of the city and the key sector for policy attention. It demonstrated a steady though limited absolute and relative increase in employment between 1978 and 1989, with the exception of 1982/3. Employment in 1989 was 150% of the 1978 level compared to 131% for formal sector jobs as a whole (Figure 3.1), but it is likely that the years from 1992 have been marked by a downturn. In the mid-1980s it was forecast that at the national level, manufacturing output was only likely to grow at between 2 and 3% per annum and employment at not more than two-thirds of this, because of the continuing deterrents to foreign and domestic investment in manufacturing (World Bank 1985). The ultimate aim of the structural adjustment programme is to encourage investment and employment creation, but hoped-for gains in the later 1990s will first have to offset current job losses. The structure of the manufacturing sector will be considered in more detail below.

Domestic service is second only to manufacturing in importance in the urban employment structure, and in 1989 still employed half as many people as the entire manufacturing sector. Again this reflects the legacy of a settler economy with a substantial relatively wealthy European population, who were able to maintain living standards higher than those they would have enjoyed in their countries of origin by ensuring the availability of cheap black labour. Although the upper income groups are no longer solely white, cheap labour, the need for assistance to run large houses with extensive gardens, and the social tradition of employing domestic help continue, if on a reduced scale. Even this sector is dominated by male employment (73%), though not to the same extent as manufacturing (91%). Although a slight upturn in employment occurred in the mid-1980s, following several years of decline related especially to white emigration, the HCMPPA's hope of future growth appears unrealistic, and continued stagnation or decline seems more likely (World Bank 1985). The distribution, restaurants and hotels sector is of the same size as the domestic service sector, and is considered in

Table 3.1 Employees and earnings in Harare, 1989

	National[a]			Harare[b]								
	Employees		Average monthly earnings (Z$)	No. of firms	Employees							Average monthly earnings (Z$)
					Male		Female		Total			
	No.	%			No.	%	No.	%	No.	%		
Agriculture, forestry and fishing	284 600	24.4	151	32	1 680	0.6	430	0.8	2 110	0.7		450
Mining and quarrying	55 700	4.8	513	5	258	0.1	5	–	263	0.1		583
Manufacturing	195 300	16.7	666	967	85 186	32.7	8 332	14.8	93 518	29.5		735
Electricity and water	8 800	0.8	903	2	1 696	0.7	145	0.3	1 841	0.6		1 635
Construction	66 600	5.7	385	65	8 684	3.3	481	0.8	9 165	2.9		500
Finance, insurance and real estate	17 100	1.5	1 434	227	8 807	3.4	3 739	6.6	12 546	4.0		1 371
Distribution, restaurants and hotels	91 900	7.9	591	2 042	39 263	15.1	6 802	12.1	46 065	14.5		720
Transport and communications	51 800	4.4	909	208	19 979	7.6	2 027	3.6	22 006	6.9		831
Public administration	93 500	8.0	581	70	20 811	8.0	4 369	7.7	25 180	7.9		774
Education	104 200	8.9	775	78	11 083	4.2	7 224	12.8	18 307	5.8		756
Health	23 600	2.0	694	102	2 982	1.1	4 876	8.6	7 858	2.5		666
Private domestic	102 400	8.8	135	6	33 866	13.0	12 635	22.4	46 501	14.6		140
Other	71 200	6.1	497	887	26 559	10.2	5 350	9.5	31 909	10.0		644
Total	1 166 700	100.0	481	4 691	260 854	100.0	56 415	100.0	317 269	100.0		648

Source: [a] CSO Dec. 1991: employees working 31 hours or more, domestic servants projected from the 1969 census, though earnings are based on six-monthly sample surveys. [b] CSO Employment and Earnings Survey, unpublished returns.

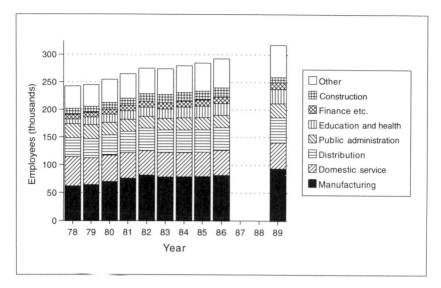

Figure 3.1   Employment in Harare, 1978–1989. Sources: HCMPPA 1988b, Table 1A;
Employment and Earnings Survey unpublished returns 1989

more detail below (Table 3.1 and Figure 3.1). Public administration and
education are also significant sectors. While employment in public sector
administration had stayed steady since 1978 (despite the need for new
and reformed institutions after independence), employment in education
and health had more than doubled as a result of the priority attached to
these sectors in government policy (HCMPPA 1988b: Table 1A). Finance,
insurance and real estate, though smaller, had also exhibited significant
growth, as expected. The sectors considered in this paragraph are often
grouped together as 'services'. Overall, with two-thirds of employment,
they dominate the urban economy, as is common in both developing
and developed country cities. However, employment growth in this
sector as a whole (25% between 1978 and 1989) was less than in
manufacturing (50%) or in the city as a whole (31%), held back by the
decline in domestic service and stagnation in public sector employment.
Prospects, at least in the short term, are no brighter, as liberalisation
measures have adverse effects, exacerbated by the 1991/2 drought, on
public and private formal sectors alike.

Only in health, domestic service, education, and finance, insurance
and real estate do women make up more than a quarter of the
workforce (Table 3.1). Nationally, including agriculture, nearly half of
the workforce was female in 1986/7. However, if agriculture is
excluded, only 28% of formal sector workers were women. The propor-

tion of the workers who were women was above this average in services, sales, clerical and professional, technical and related workers, while women were under-represented among administrative and managerial and production workers (Zimbabwe 1989: 60, based on the 1986/7 Labour Force Survey). Women are concentrated in certain occupations and employment sectors. Their labour force situation will be discussed in more detail in a later section of this chapter.

Manufacturing

Harare's industrial structure is similar to that of the country as a whole, the main differences being in the greater relative significance of chemicals and plastics and, to a lesser extent, clothing, and the less important role of basic metals production and metal fabrication. Bulawayo, in contrast, has an economic structure more dominated by heavy industry: a result both of its geographical situation and past government policy (Zimbabwe nda: 92–5). Sectors that have grown in importance since the 1970s are represented to a greater extent in Harare's economy than in Bulawayo's (drink and tobacco manu-facturing, chemicals and plastics), while the opposite is true of sectors that have declined in relative importance (basic metals and metal fabrication) (Zimbabwe nda). Food processing is, overall, the largest subsector. Other important subsectors in employment terms were metal fabrication, clothing, and chemicals and plastics, each employing between 10 000 and 15 000 people and accounting for between 11 and 16% of manufacturing employment (Table 3.2). However, if the figures for employment in 1989 are compared with those for output in 1985, different degrees of capital intensity in manufacturing are revealed. Most capital intensive are chemicals and plastics, food and beverages and tobacco, while the metals industry (basic metals and fabrication), in contrast, is relatively labour intensive, as is clothing and footwear. Although Harare has a large and diversified manufacturing sector in which high-potential industries are well represented, these also tend to be relatively capital intensive, which may have implications for their future capacity to absorb labour force growth.

Despite being cut off from international markets during the period of sanctions, and government attempts to increase local ownership since 1980, foreign owned industry is, as noted in Chapter 1, important in Zimbabwe. In addition, the need to gain access to export markets is seen as crucial to national and urban economic development. Some progress was made in the mid-1980s in response to a package of incentives and efforts to find new markets (Riddell 1992). However, Africa as a whole

Table 3.2 Industrial production and employment in Harare

| | Industrial production | | Employees[b] | | Male | Female | |
	Z$ '000	%	Total no.	%	no.	no.	% of total
Food products	801 925	21.0	14 376	15.4	13 882	494	3.4
Drink and tobacco	454 437	11.9	7 971	8.5	7 582	389	4.9
Cotton ginning and textiles	272 401	7.2	7 690	8.2	7 175	515	6.7
Clothing and footwear	253 958	6.7	12 627	13.5	9 992	2 635	20.9
Wood products and furniture	92 381	2.4	4 593	4.9	4 451	142	3.1
Paper and printing	212 098	5.6	6 103	6.5	5 248	855	14.0
Chemicals and petroleum products	853 106	22.4	10 653	11.4	8 659	1 994	18.7
Non-metallic mineral products	111 164	2.9	2 453	2.6	2 305	148	6.0
Basic metal industries	⎫		1 454	1.6	1 430	24	1.7
Metal products and machinery	391 129 ⎬	10.3	14 814	15.8	14 423	391	2.6
Electrical machinery, equipment and supplies	138 562	3.6	4 236	4.5	3 981	255	6.0
Transport and equipment	187 391	4.9	4 481	4.8	4 307	174	3.9
Other manufacturing	41 891	1.1	2 067	2.3	1 751	316	15.3
Total	3 810 443	100.0	93 518	100.0	85 186	8 332	8.9

Source: Central Statistical Office: [a] Census of Production 1988/9. pp. 51–5, gross output. [b] Employment and Earnings survey, 1989, unpublished returns.

is marginal to the interests of manufacturing capital. Zimbabwe's government is ambivalent towards attracting more foreign direct investment, because of its concern over external control of the economy. Even where it has tried to do so, despite its good infrastructure and political stability, it has found it difficult to attract new investment. In addition, increasing exports to protectionist northern markets or impoverished African countries is slow and problematic and is expected, in view of South African competition, to become more so. The future of the leading functions in the city's economy, especially its manufacturing base and related economic activities, while not dismal, is uncertain, especially given the scepticism with which the World Bank's approach to industrialisation has been greeted (Riddell 1992).

Trade

In the introduction to this chapter, I noted the importance of commerce in African city economies. Although, because of the developed manufacturing sector in Harare, commerce is relatively less important in that city, it is still a significant economic function. In 1969, the only year for which figures are available, the retail sector was as dominated by Harare as manufacturing, with well over a third of all units in the seven main centres located in the city, compared to under a fifth in Bulawayo. To some extent this was a reflection of population, but Harare also provided (as it still does) higher level retail services. In addition, between 1965 and 1979, retail turnover increased by over 250% in Harare, more rapidly than in any other urban centre in Rhodesia (Whitsun Foundation 1980: 93). In more recent figures, 1980 has replaced 1965 as the base year. Although the index of retail turnover more than doubled in Harare between 1980 and 1988 (from 100 to 256), the rate of growth was higher in some other centres, including Bulawayo, that had maintained less healthy growth in the previous period. Within the distribution, restaurants and hotels category in 1989, formal wholesale and retail trade were of roughly equal importance in employment terms, with just over a fifth of jobs in retailing going to women. Restaurants and hotels employed fewer people and only one in ten of them were women (Table 3.3). These private sector services depend on markets generated by both international tourists and residents. While there are still many rich Zimbabweans and while numbers of tourists visiting Zimbabwe continue to grow, this demand is counterbalanced by the straitened economic circumstances of middle and lower income residents and the newly unemployed.

Table 3.3   Employment in trade, 1989

	Total		Male	Female	
	No.	%	No.	No.	% of Total
Wholesale trade	21 188	46.0	18 872	2 316	10.9
Retail trade	18 374	39.9	14 503	3 871	21.1
Restaurants and hotels	6 500	14.1	5 886	614	9.5
Other	3	–	2	1	–
Total	46 065	100.0	39 263	6 802	14.8

Source: CSO, Employment and earnings survey, 1989, unpublished returns.

The employment situation of low income households

Because of the limited availability of data, the previous section analysed only the formal urban economy, in terms mostly of individual wage employees. This does not, however, tell us much about the part played by wage employment in household incomes. For a view of the urban economy from the point of view of the residential unit or household, we must turn to household surveys. Some information on the employment situation of low income households is available from household surveys carried out in 1982 for a city-wide sample and in 1991 in four typical high density housing areas. Neither of these surveys included areas in Chitungwiza. In 1982, 84% of household heads were in full-time wage employment and 9% were self-employed. Two-thirds of those working were employed in the private sector, and about half as production or transport workers. Only 4% of household heads mentioned a second source of income from work, and few spouses were in wage employment. Although 7% of household heads were unemployed, only 3% of households had no source of income from work. Over 40% of heads worked in the industrial areas and 21% in the city centre (Hoek-Smit 1982: 27–30).

The areas surveyed in 1991 represent a broad range of low income housing areas, but resources were insufficient to permit city-wide sample surveys so generalisations can only be made with care. Typically, three-quarters of households contained only one earner and most of the remainder two. While in 13% of households the head was not working, only 2% had no member in employment. Only in 9% of households was the spouse of the head working. Those containing more than one earner tended to be at a later stage of their life cycles, with adult sons and daughters. Over 80% of those working and 85% of those in full-time regular jobs were men, and relatively few men (4%) worked irregularly and/or part-time compared to a quarter of women. Of those working in formal sector wage employment, a quarter were clerical, sales or secretarial workers, while 18% were skilled blue collar workers, and 13% each semi-skilled and unskilled industrial workers. Other employment categories included supervisory posts, the armed forces and police, and drivers. Only one in twelve considered themselves to be in the professional/managerial category. Although the 1982 and 1991 surveys were not strictly comparable, the results are consistent. The inherited pattern of a low income urban population supported largely by men in stable formal sector wage employment, which originated in the colonial migrant labour system, persisted throughout the 1980s, despite the country's economic difficulties, though it may be under graver threat as the structural adjustment programme proceeds. A similar ability of the formal sector to expand wage employment to absorb the majority of the urban labour force was seen in some other African countries, for example Zambia in the 1960s, but this capacity has long since been exceeded; since the mid-1970s in most, if not all, other African countries, the formal sector has been able to provide jobs for only a minority of labour force entrants.

Figures were also obtained for five middle and higher income areas (Mount Pleasant, Hatfield, Avenues, Mabelreign and Houghton Park), excluding domestic workers. Again, few (10%) household heads were not working, and only in 3% of households was no-one working. However, over half the wives of householders were working and so, in contrast to households in low income areas, over a third of households had one member in employment and half had two. The availability of more than one source of income helps to explain the ability of households in these areas to either maintain their accustomed standard of living or obtain access to scarce and costly private sector housing, an issue which will be taken up again in Chapter 6. The access of women from middle and upper income households to employment will be considered further below.

Wages and incomes

In comparison with the limited change in employment structure, there have been major changes in the wage structure for formal sector employees since independence. Wages constitute a critical, if not the only source of income for households. Before considering changes in wages since 1980, the pre-independence position will be examined.

Wages and incomes in Salisbury

The wage and income structure in Harare before 1980 was a product of the colonial political economy, in which, as described in Chapter 1, access to economic opportunities was biased strongly towards European settlers, and Africans lived in urban areas on sufferance to provide cheap labour. The result was extreme inequality of wages and incomes.

European pre-tax per capita incomes grew in real terms at 4.5% per annum in the prosperous period between 1965 and 1974, at a time of a growing European population. Income sources were diverse, with whites, who accounted for only 5% of the population in 1968, receiving 57% of total personal income (Sutcliffe 1971) (62% of cash wages, 45% of income from unincorporated enterprises and 90% or more of dividends and profits from companies) (Clarke 1977: 14). In 1969–71 in Harare the *average* white household received Z$440 per month— three-quarters from the earnings of household heads and a further 9% from spouses' earnings (Clarke 1977: 17). Inequalities existed within the European population, though these appear to have decreased during the 1960s and 1970s, while there was little material deprivation: by 1969 92% of white households had cars compared to 7% of urban African households, 97% had refrigerators, 68% had televisions and 56% lived in owner-occupied premises.

The wage distribution for black workers in Harare and all urban areas in 1977 is shown in Figure 3.2. The figures used include both wages and the cash value of in-kind incomes in the form of a rent free house and/ or food rations or meals. In Harare 42% of black employees received supplements of this nature, accounting for 5–9% of total earnings in most sectors but 50% in domestic service (Clarke 1977: Table 20). Other income sources, such as property, were insignificant and 92% of the average household income of Z$54 was derived from the household head's earnings (Clarke 1977: 36). All except 14% earned less than Z$90.

The average income of black households was an eighth of the average white household income (see above) and the black population accounted for about 37% of total disposable incomes throughout this period of economic growth, despite making up about 94% of the total population (Clarke 1977: Table 4). Nationally, African per capita incomes increased by about the same rate as European incomes between 1961 and 1974 (Clarke 1977: Table 3) so there was no reduction in the inegalitarian income distribution. In addition, the income distribution for African households was extremely skewed towards the lowest income groups, as borne out by estimates in 1974 and 1978 of the poverty datum line (Whitsun Foundation 1980: 59, 66, 68). In 1974 it was estimated that the poverty datum line in urban areas was above the modal wage income

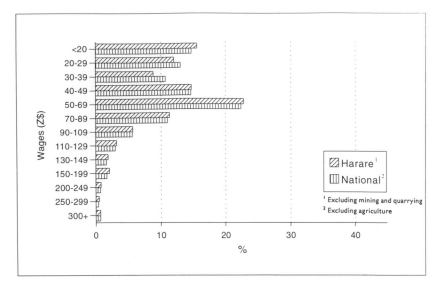

Figure 3.2 Wage distribution of black employees, June 1977. Source: Whitsun Foundation 1980, pp. 66, 68, 69

for a family with three or four children (between Z$58 and Z$74). However, it was not possible, in the absence of income data by household type, to estimate the total proportion of urban households living in poverty (Cubitt and Riddell 1974). The 1960s and 1970s were marked by increased monetisation of earnings and a decline of payments in kind (Clarke 1977).

The urban workforce since 1980: participating in the fruits of independence?

> At independence, capitalists had two main concerns: first, they were fearful about the prospect of expropriation or nationalisation of their assets and, second, they were worried about the loss of control over labour, as this was bound to undercut their profits. (Moyo 1988: 209).

The new government was well aware of these fears and anxious to allay them, which it was able to do relatively quickly with respect to the former. However, independence was followed by a wave of strikes, as workers demanded higher wages, better working conditions and so on (Moyo 1988; see also Astrow 1983). The 1981 National Manpower Survey showed that blacks constituted 90% of the labour force but received only 60% of the wage bill (Raftopoulos 1986: 282). In the same year, it was estimated that 28% of all workers received the lowest possible wage (Z$30) (Herbst 1990). This was estimated in 1978 to be the poverty line for an unmarried man living in single accommodation (still a third of all legal tenants in African housing), while the poverty line for a typical household (a couple with three or four children) was between three and four times this level (Cubitt 1979: 24–5). Because such a large proportion of all workers were at or near the bottom of the wage scale, the minimum wage was significant to many employees. The Riddell Commission recommended a minimum wage based on the poverty line for a family of six and suggested that a target of 90% of this be set, to be achieved within three years. This recommendation would have implied major wage increases and was ignored by government (Herbst 1990).

Nevertheless, action was taken with respect to the setting of minimum wages. These varied by sector, with differentiation based on the perceived ability of the sector to pay. Thus minimum wages for the agriculture and domestic service sectors were set lowest, because of the government perception that disemployment effects were likely to be greatest in these areas, while minimum wages in industry, commerce and mining were set at higher levels, based partly on existing practice. Firms were also allowed to apply for exemption, because of particular economic constraints (Herbst 1990).

Wage increases have occurred in a number of phases. During the immediate post-independence economic boom, significant increases in minimum wages were imposed by government, in response to the pre-independence grievances of black workers and the wave of strikes, rather than as part of an income or employment policy, and with little reference to either employers or the unions. During the wage-regulation period which followed, across-the-board freezes and increases were imposed by government: annual increases continued until July 1987, when a wage freeze was imposed for nine months. This was followed by further increases in 1988 and 1989, favouring low wage workers and sectors over the better paid. The interventionist model adopted by government with respect to wages was accompanied by other actions related to employment practices. Regulations barring employers from dismissing workers except with the approval of the Ministry of Labour were brought in, despite employer opposition, and workers' committees were set up in all industrial establishments. In practice, many employers managed to evade central government controls over dismissal by laying off workers, increasing the capital intensity of their operations or resorting to short time working (Moyo 1988). Despite the attempts to mollify workers, both the government and employers were alarmed at the effect the continuing wave of strikes might have on the economy, so the government inserted itself between management and workers and emphasised discipline and stability in the name of the 'national interest'. Capital 'succeeded in portraying the strikes (sic) as irresponsible, disorganised, unpatriotic and subversive social elements bent on economic sabotage' (Sachikonye 1986: 254).

Even ZANU (PF) instructed workers to submit to the negotiating machinery of the workers' committees (Astrow 1983). The indigenisation of management has occurred in the years since independence, mainly in personnel and industrial relations, rather than in engineering-related areas, but the result has been to substitute black for white managers in an existing hierarchical system, both in the private and public sectors. Workers' committees have resulted in little real transfer of power to employees in what remain top-down management systems (Moyo 1988). The 1981 National Manpower Survey also revealed that black workers were already performing many semi-skilled jobs, if at lower rates of pay than white workers doing equivalent work. Regrading reduced this discrimination.

For a more detailed analysis of incomes and standards of living, wages need to be considered in conjunction with social security arrangements and taxation, as well as in relation to inflation. The latter will be considered first, with respect to both minimum and average wages.

In 1985 the Labour Relations Act consolidated both workers' rights and the framework for wage negotiations. It entitled employees to belong to a union or committee; gave protection against discrimination on the basis of race, tribe, creed or sex; safeguarded rights to basic working conditions, including minimum wages, maximum hours, occupational health and safety; and restated the right to industrial action. However, a very large proportion of the economy was considered to provide essential services, and strikes in these sectors were prohibited, while in other sectors, long negotiating procedures had to be satisfied before a strike would be considered legitimate (Sachikonye 1986). Direct government setting of wages was replaced by what was essentially three-way collective bargaining, with the Employers' Confederation of Zimbabwe (EMCOZ), the Zimbabwe Congress of Trade Unions (ZCTU) and the government agreeing on minimum wages, and the Ministry of Labour regulating wage increases in all except a few firms, where employers began to be allowed to agree wages with their workers within the parameters set by the national negotiations (Herbst 1990).

The initial gains made from the 1981 minimum wage increases were substantial, especially for lower paid workers, including domestic workers. Between 1982 and 1985, however, as described in Chapter 1, the Zimbabwean economy was depressed for a variety of reasons and wage

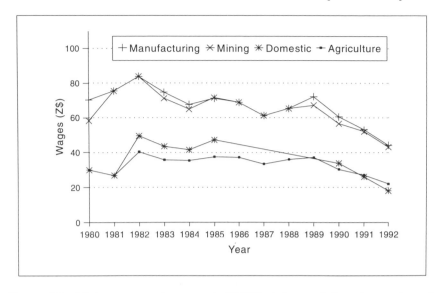

Figure 3.3   Minimum wages by sector in 1980 Zimbabwean dollars. Source: Journal on Social Change and Development 1992, No. 28, p. 18; MacGarry 1993, p. 12

increases were limited, to ensure the continued economic viability of industries and to maintain employment levels (Herbst 1990). The result was that real minimum wages fell below the 1980 level for manu-facturing employees by the mid-1980s, and although real minimum wages for domestic workers stayed above the 1980 level for longer, their gains had also been eliminated by the 1990s (Figure 3.3). IMF pressure and stabilisation measures reinforced the fall in real wages in the mid-1980s, as subsidies began to be reduced (Davies and Sanders 1988).

In practice also, the nature of the minimum wage has changed. Prior to independence, several sectors set wages above the national minimum. Since 1980, however, wage increases have mirrored the rates at which minimum wages have increased, tending to regard the latter as maxima (Davies 1988). The national wage distribution for mining, industrial and commercial workers illustrates this for the early 1980s (Table 3.4): the modal wage band moved from Z$100–149 in 1982 (when the minimum wage was Z$105) to Z$150–249 in 1985 (when the minimum wage increased to Z$143.75). The small proportion of employees earning below Z$100 in 1982 and Z$150 in 1985 illustrates the effectiveness of the minimum wage legislation, at least in these sectors. This is also reflected in responses to a survey of manufacturing firms carried out in the mid-1980s, which showed that over two-thirds set wage levels in relation to the minimum wage, just under a third on the basis of

Table 3.4 National wage distribution (excluding domestic and agricultural workers)

	1982 %	1985 %
<50	0.4	1.2
50–74.99	1.5	0.9
75–99.99	0.6	2.7
100–149.99	43.3	8.6
150–249.99	26.2	41.3
250–499.99	15.4	21.9
500–749.99	5.6	9.5
750–999.99	3.0	4.7
1000–1499.99	2.9	4.4
1500+	1.2	4.8
Total	100.0	100.0
Minimum wage	Z$105	Z$143

Source: Zimbabwe 1989: 58.

comparisons with similar firms, a fifth following negotiations with trade unions, and only 5% after negotiating with workers' committees. Although the actual minimum wage was still important, over three-quarters of the firms reported paying wages at a fifth higher than the minimum (Hawkins et al 1988).

Since independence, average cash wages have increased most in the lowest paid sectors. Thus between 1980 and 1987, nominal wages increased by 150% in agriculture and 217% for domestic servants, compared to less than 100% in public administration, health, transport, education, and finance and real estate (Zimbabwe 1989: 58). Comparisons of changes in average real sectoral wages and employment between 1979 and 1984 show that the government's apprehensions with regard to agriculture were justified: while wages increased by 47%, employment fell by a fifth (Table 3.5). However, employment in manufacturing and distribution increased, despite modest wage increases (Hawkins et al 1988).

Average wages for each sector are given in Table 3.1. The national average wage in 1989 was Z$481, held down by the low average wage in agriculture, in which a quarter of employees worked and, to a lesser extent, in domestic service. The overall average wage in Harare was 135% of the national average, because of the relative absence of agricultural employment and the importance in its economy of relatively high wage employment sectors. In addition, Harare's employment

Table 3.5 Changes in wages and employment, 1979–84

	Change in average real wage (%)	Change in employment (%)
Agriculture	+47	−19.1
Mining	+28	−8.5
Manufacturing	+11	+15.0
Distribution	+1	+18.6
Zimbabwe economy	+13	+5.1

Source: Hawkins et al 1988: 13.

structure is characterised by the presence of relatively large numbers of headquarters and managerial jobs in the private and public sectors, and these influence average wages. However, average earnings have lagged behind inflation just as minimum wages have done. From a 1980 baseline of 100, average earnings in Harare had increased to 227.1 in 1990, but the high income consumer price index had risen to 327.9 (CSO 1987b: 7; December, 1991: 8, 9; year averages).

Gross wages, even if corrected for inflation, do not give the whole picture. As noted in the previous section, before independence a substantial minority of black employees in Harare received part of their income in kind, but earnings had already become increasingly monetised. This trend accelerated after independence. By the late 1980s, payments in kind had become uncommon, with the partial exception of housing, mainly for domestic workers. Further analysis of unpublished tables from the Employment and Earnings survey of 1989 throws light on the significance of social security contributions in wages for urban employees. The returns distinguish between 'salary' and 'earnings', the latter being greater. The difference between the two includes employer contributions to pension and provident funds and medical aid societies, and the current cost to the employer of food, clothing and housing provided free of charge, and can be taken to indicate 'benefits'. Of the earnings figures given in Table 3.1, 12.5% is made up of these benefits. The proportion of earnings made up of benefits is greater in public administration, manufacturing and utilities (about a quarter) and nearer 3% in most of the other sectors, including domestic service. If the market rent of alternative accommodation was reflected in the latter rather than the current cost to employers, it might compensate in part for the lower wages in that sector.

Taxes, especially in an economic system where formal sector employment is predominant, also have an impact on disposable income arising from the tax rate, the incidence of taxes, and the tax structure.

This is especially the case in Zimbabwe, where a major proportion of government revenue has been derived from direct taxes on income and profits: 48% in 1974, 41% in the first half of the 1980s (CSO 1987a: 62; Zimbabwe 1989: 114). The share of direct taxes generated by individual income tax increased from 42% in 1974 to 54% in 1980 and 63% in 1985. Indirect taxes on goods and services, which are also to some extent ultimately borne by households, have been increasingly emphasised by government. Personal income tax as a percentage of earnings has historically been low, though it has increased on average from 7% in 1974 (Clarke 1977: 15) to 10% in 1980 and 18% in 1987 (RAL Merchant Bank, June 1987). However, when estimates of average indirect tax borne by income tax payers are added to this, it was estimated that the total tax burden increased from 24% of average earnings in 1980 to 46% in 1986/7. This level of taxation was considered to be the maximum feasible, especially given the relatively small number in the taxable bracket (perhaps 15% of all non-agricultural employees in 1985/6) (Zimbabwe 1989: 131).

The tax structure is progressive overall, even though indirect tax burdens are regressive (Zimbabwe 1986a: 83). Income tax rates vary (currently from 20% to 60%), increasing with income. The tax threshold was increased to Z$300 in 1991/2, when the minimum wage in industry and commerce was Z$253, to offset price increases induced by the liberalisation policy, while allowances can mean that taxpayers earning up to Z$1000 but with large numbers of dependants may not be liable to tax. At the upper end of the income distribution, the tax burden was estimated in 1989 to be 65–75%. However, it was acknowledged that the progressivity of the tax system is diluted by employers who offer non-cash packages to staff, ostensibly to keep employees with scarce skills, but also clearly to help them avoid high personal taxation (RAL Merchant Bank, March 1989). Nevertheless, the relatively progressive tax system does, to some extent, counteract the extremely unequal income distribution.

Not only are data on wages complicated by the effects of benefits and taxation, but also the use of average wages conceals variations within and between sectors. Rising average wages may be a result of laying off of unskilled workers rather than sector-wide increases. There is evidence that this has occurred in Zimbabwe and it is likely to occur more widely as restrictions on labour shedding are relaxed as part of the liberalisation programme (Zimbabwe 1991a). More detailed wage distribution figures are only available for a limited number of sectors, including manufacturing but excluding much of the services sector. Those figures which are available are given in Table 3.6.

In September 1988 wages grouped dramatically around the category

Table 3.6 Wage distribution by sector in Harare, 1988 (per cent)

Z$ per month	Manufacturing			Wholesale and retail trade			Other services			Total		
	Male	Female	Total	Male	Female	Total	Male	Female	Total	Male	Female	Total
0–50	0.5	2.1	0.6	0.3	0.4	0.3	0.3	0.7	0.4	0.4	0.9	0.4
50–75	2.5	6.0	2.7	0.6	0.3	0.6	1.0	0.6	0.9	1.4	1.9	1.5
75–100	0.2	0.3	0.2	0.4	0.8	0.6	0.6	0.3	0.6	0.5	1.4	0.6
100–150	1.9	1.1	1.8	2.3	4.2	2.6	3.8	5.2	4.0	2.4	4.0	2.6
150–250	32.2	34.4	32.3	30.6	30.8	30.6	56.4	17.2	49.9	32.2	22.4	30.9
250–500	41.3	14.5	39.6	37.1	21.4	34.5	14.2	14.5	14.3	33.4	14.2	30.9
500–750	7.9	8.5	7.9	10.2	12.2	10.5	5.7	14.1	7.1	9.7	13.5	10.2
750–1000	4.2	10.0	4.6	4.5	8.6	5.1	4.0	13.0	5.5	6.1	13.4	7.1
1000–1500	3.5	12.3	4.1	4.8	12.1	6.0	5.2	17.2	7.2	5.2	15.8	6.6
1500+	5.8	10.8	6.2	9.2	9.2	9.2	8.8	17.2	10.1	8.7	12.5	9.2
Total	100.0	100.0	100.0	100.0	100.0	100.0	100.0	100.0	100.0	100.0	100.0	100.0

Source: CSO Employment and earnings survey, 1989, unpublished returns. Excludes agriculture, most education, health and public administration employees, and domestic servants. Three main sectors shown; total includes others.

containing the minimum wage in industry and commerce (Z$187) and also the wider one above. Just under a third of employees in manufacturing and trade earned wages at or near the minimum, but nearly a half in the lower wage sector of the 'other services' category; the wage distribution as a whole is still, as it was at independence, heavily skewed towards the lower end (Table 3.6). Women make up only 13% of the employees covered in these data and so have little effect on the overall distribution. It is not possible to assess the proportion of the workforce earning below the minimum wage or below the eligible household income level for free health services (Z$150 at that time) precisely from these data, though it was clearly very limited. However, the statutory minimum wage has never borne much relation to the poverty line, analysis of which shows a less optimistic picture. A rough adjustment to the 1980/1 poverty line of Z$128 in line with the low income consumer price index would give Z$263 in 1988. If valid, clearly over a third of employees would be considered as living in poverty if they were not able to supplement their wages from other sources.

Typical sources of household income drawn upon by low income households in African cities (other than formal sector wages) include labour force participation by members of the household other than the head (both adults and children), self-employment, gifts or allowances from relatives, and rent from letting residential accommodation. As noted in the previous section, although wages cannot be equated with household incomes, the reliance of low income Zimbabwean urban households on the wages of a single worker resulted in quite a close correspondence prior to independence. If trends prevalent elsewhere in Africa have also affected Harare, a diversification of income sources by low income households might have been expected to have accompanied the post-1982 decline in real wages.

There is a variety of post-independence estimates of household income, none of them fully comparable. In 1982 a household survey was carried out in high density residential areas (1060 households) in Harare, in which the main wage incomes of households were obtained with a reasonable degree of precision. Additional income was considered to have been underestimated, though it was thought to have been relatively unimportant (Hoek-Smit 1982). The survey-based income distribution for low income areas was extended to obtain city-wide estimates by updating 1978 figures for high income households and adding in domestic servants, most of whom earned between Z$50 and Z$70 (Table 3.7). The median income in Harare was estimated to be Z$173 (Z$130 in high density residential areas). Twenty-eight per cent of households had incomes of over Z$600, compared to 3% in the high density residential areas (HDRAs), but about a third, both in HDRAs and in the city as a

Table 3.7   Household income distribution in Harare, 1982

	1982 HDRAs, household income (%)	1982 Harare, household income (%)
<30	5	2
31–50	4	2
51–70	6	25
71–90	3	1
91–110	14	6
111–130	16	
131–150	11	} 20
151–200	15	
201–300	14	6
301–600	9	8
601–900		11
901–1200	} 3	9
>1200		8
Total	100	100

Sources: Hoek-Smit 1982: 33–7 (Percentages do not total 100 in original due to rounding).

HDRAs High density residential areas.

whole, had incomes below Z$110, because of the location of domestic servants within low density areas. The incomes of low income households included not just the wages and benefits of those in employment, but earnings from informal sector activity, gifts from relatives and rent from letting rooms. Rent, received by about a quarter of households, generally added up to Z$50 per month to household incomes. Because of the movement of blacks into former European housing areas and the continued residence of domestic workers there, differences between the two distributions cannot be equated with a black/white distinction, but the persistent differences in household income distributions between types of residential area and racial groups are clearly revealed by Heath's data for the following year (Heath 1986) (Table 3.8).

More recent city-wide income data are not available; the only available up to date figures are from small household sample surveys in selected residential areas in 1991. In these surveys, household income included net earnings from employment or self-employment plus regular income from other sources—for example secondary jobs, pensions, money given by relatives, or rents. Thirty per cent of the owner households interviewed in high density areas and 10% in medium and low density areas rented out rooms in their own houses, but other secondary income sources were probably underestimated. In

Table 3.8 Household income distribution by type of residential area and racial group, 1983 (per cent)

Z$/month	Residential areas				Racial groups			
	High income	Medium income	Low income	Total	Black	White	Coloured	Total
0–300	4	13	69	23	35	4	13	23
301–600	9	26	23	21	25	11	33	21
601–900	17	27	7	20	20	22	20	20
901–1200	27	20	1	19	10	21	19	19
1200+	43	14	–	17	8	37	15	17
Total	100	100	100	100	100	100	100	100

Source: Heath 1986: 50, 66. Heath's sample survey was primarily concerned with recreation, so adopted a sample biased towards medium density areas and excluded the poorest areas because middle income households were considered to be those with the greatest potential to increase their holidays and recreational activity in the future. Although less attention was paid to collecting income information in her survey, it does give a broad idea of the income distribution by type of residential area and, unlike Hoek-Smit's figures, by racial group. Domestic workers in high income areas are excluded.

Percentages have been read off from bar graphs and so are approximate.

addition, while refusals to answer the income-related questions were relatively rare in high density areas (13% of respondents), they were twice as common in medium and low density areas. The data show that over half the households in the four high density areas surveyed earned between Z$201 and Z$600 (Table 3.9). The areas included a suburb of small 1950s former municipal rented housing (Mabvuku), a well established sites and services scheme (Warren Park D), a new sites and services scheme with an income ceiling of Z$650 in 1990 (Budiriro Phase I), and households who had bought houses in a mid-1980s serviced plot scheme (Kuwadzana) (see Chapter 6 for more detail on housing policies). They did not include inner city areas with higher densities, more illegal backyard renting and probably lower incomes, but can, nevertheless, be used in a rough comparison with Hoek-Smit's 1982 figures.

In 1982, just under a third of households in high density residential areas had incomes below the minimum industrial wage, compared to perhaps 10–15% in 1991. However, this illustrates the effectiveness of the minimum wage legislation, and the continued ability of formal sector wage employment to absorb most adult men, rather than a reduction in poverty. In 1982, about 60% of households had incomes below the poverty line for a six person family. Between 25% and 30% of the households in the 1991 sample surveys in high density residential areas had incomes below an updated poverty line (Z$356) (Zimbabwe

Table 3.9   Household incomes in residential areas in Harare, 1991 (per cent)

Z$/month	Mabvuku	Warren Park D	Budiriro I	Kuwadzana[a]	Harare
1–200	6.5	1.2	3.7	6.9	4.6
201–400	25.8	20.0	37.0	23.6	25.7
401–600	18.3	35.2	38.9	23.6	28.0
601–800	20.4	18.8	11.1	19.4	18.1
801–1000	16.1	11.8	3.7	12.5	11.8
1001–1200	4.3	1.2	3.7	5.6	3.6
1201–1400	4.3	3.5	1.9	2.8	3.3
1401–1600	2.1	3.5	–	4.2	2.6
1601–2000	1.1	2.4	–	–	1.0
>2000	1.1	2.4	–	1.4	1.3
Total	100.0	100.0	100.0	100.0	100.0
Average:					
owners	b	892	498	723	
tenants		555	402	413	

Z$/month	Hatfield	Mount Pleasant	Mabelreign	Houghton Park	Avenues	Harare L & MDRAs[c]
<500	9.4	2.9	4.4	–	2.2	4.2
501–1000	17.0	–	15.6	5.1	19.6	12.4
1001–1500	11.3	–	11.1	8.0	17.4	12.0
1501–2000	15.1	20.6	13.3	20.5	15.2	16.6
2001–2500	13.2	17.7	26.8	25.6	15.2	19.4
2501–3000	15.1	17.7	15.6	10.3	15.2	14.7
3001–3500	7.5	5.8	4.4	12.8	6.5	7.4
3501–4000	5.7	14.7	4.4	2.6	6.5	6.4
4001+	5.7	20.6	4.4	5.1	2.2	6.9
Total	100.0	100.0	100.0	100.0	100.0	100.0

[a] Households who have bought plots under the cessions procedure and are higher income on average than original allottees.
[b] The Mabvuku sample includes households in houses being rented to buy (average household income Z$579) and households in ceded houses (owners' average household income Z$699, tenants Z$493).
[c] Excluding domestic workers.

HDRA High density residential area.
L & MDRAs Low and medium density residential areas.

1991a), which reveals an apparent reduction in absolute poverty. However, it must be remembered that the lowest income areas in the city (Mbare, Highfield and Epworth) were excluded from this survey. Even if there had been a reduction in the extent of absolute poverty during the 1980s (and it is not possible to be certain from the inadequate figures available), this is unlikely to have persisted into the 1990s, as it is widely acknowledged that one of the population groups most affected by structural adjustment policies, especially the abolition of subsidies and increase in costs of goods and services, is the urban poor (Kanji and Jazdowska 1993; MacGarry 1993; Rakodi 1994).

Very low income domestic workers are excluded from the figures for low and medium density residential areas. These areas ranged from a high income suburb (Mount Pleasant) through a more mixed area (Hatfield) to middle income neighbourhoods of houses (Mabelreign and Houghton Park) and flats (Avenues) (Table 3.9). The modal income group overall was almost five times that in the HDRAs (Z$2001–2500), and only 17% of households earned under Z$1000 compared to 88% in the HDRAs, while over half had incomes of over Z$2000 compared to only 1% in the HDRAs (Table 3.9). It is apparent that residential segregation by income has largely replaced segregation by race. As in the 1960s and 1970s, the income distribution for the urban population is very skewed, with a large proportion living on incomes close to the minimum wage and below the poverty line, and a long tail of high incomes, mostly, but not all, still earned by whites. The income groups continue to be heavily segregated by area of residence, with the exception of domestic workers.

Despite the minor concessions made to lower paid urban labour in the early 1980s, many analysts see the state, itself occupying an ambiguous class position, as having aligned itself with capital, in order to achieve its immediate aim of not destabilising the economy (Astrow 1983; Sachikonye 1986; Davies 1988). Control was exerted over the unions and they in turn were used as an instrument of control, rather than as a means of advancing the interests of the working class (Davies 1988). Also, workers' committees have been fragmented and, regarded with suspicion by many unions, they have not been able to sustain a radical challenge to management (Wood 1988). The relations of the state with urban workers have, therefore, been difficult and ambiguous since 1980. I have already noted the opposition to government expressed by voting for ZUM in the 1990 elections (see also Quantin 1992). Much of this vote originated in the cities (for example, 30% of the votes in Harare and 21% in Bulawayo, compared to 17% nationally). This can be explained, Sachikonye (1990) suggests, both by the genuine grievances and anxieties of the working class (unemployment, falling incomes, housing and transport crises) and by the greater ease of organisation and access to the media in urban areas. Meanwhile, formal sector wage employment has remained stagnant. What investment has occurred has been relatively capital intensive, while wide income inequalities have preempted a large share of potential investment funds for consumption purposes. As a result, as in other African cities, the sector is unable to employ a large proportion of those entering the labour force, and the growing unemployment further strengthens the bargaining position of capital (Stoneman 1988).

Herbst attributes the lag of minimum wages behind inflation to the increased influence of employers, who are able to capitalise on IMF/ World Bank pressure for wage restraint. Although minimum wages are effectively enforced, they have lagged so far behind the amount needed for basic subsistence that they do not provide households with an income above the poverty line. The unwillingness or inability of ZANU to advance the interests of urban workers further reduced their bargaining power. Herbst suggests that the government, by its own actions with respect to industrial relations and the institutionalisation of the wage bargaining process, reduced its ability to negotiate from strength with employers. Early gains by workers were obtained by wildcat action outside the formal organisational framework; outlawing such action reduced the power of labour either to oppose or support the state (Herbst 1990).

Women and work

Women, as I have noted, are under-represented in the urban formal sector labour force. At independence, they made up only 13% of the formal workforce and were particularly under-represented in the professional, skilled and semi-skilled categories. However, there were marked differences between the races: a much larger proportion of white than black women were in formal sector employment, and only 39% of the trained female workforce were black. Even within formal employment, as I have noted above, women were concentrated in relatively few industries and occupations, such as teaching, nursing, clerical work and a few in unskilled manufacturing jobs (Batezal et al 1988). Women were discriminated against in law, being eligible for lower minimum pay rates than men, for example (Kazembe 1986). Attempts to outlaw discrimination against women in post-independence labour legislation have not greatly improved the situation. Although discriminatory minimum wages were abolished, other safeguards provided by this legislation, particularly provision for maternity leave and time for breastfeeding, have discouraged employers from increasing female employment (Hawkins et al 1988). Women, it is suggested, tend to earn less than men and to be concentrated in lower grades.

In 1988 women made up only 13% of those employees for whom wage figures were available, so their wages made relatively little difference to the overall wage distribution shown in Table 3.6. However, there were marked differences between the wage distributions of men and women: fewer women than men were in the modal groups, double the proportion earned less than Z$150 and, more unexpectedly, double the proportion earned above Z$500. Not all women, therefore, are earning low wages, though it is likely that they are earning less than men in equivalent industries and jobs. However, the ability of nearly half the working women to earn a relatively high wage does not illustrate good conditions for women, but instead reflects the dearth of unskilled and semi-skilled jobs open to them, especially in manufacturing but also in other sectors. Women still only constituted 21% of those earning more than Z$500 in Harare.

The data for the main private employment sectors throw additional light on this picture (Table 3.6). The modal wage for women in manufacturing in Harare was similar to that for men. However, a higher proportion of women earned both less than Z$100 and more than Z$500, illustrating how few unskilled and semi-skilled jobs in this sector are open to women. In the trade sector, there is a smaller concentration of women than men in the modal income band and a higher proportion than men in the higher wage bracket. Women constituted a larger share of the workforce than in manufacturing and were again over-represented in the lowest and highest wage categories compared to the modal groups. Total employment in the 'other services' sector was less than in trade. However, for women, who made up 17% of employees, it was a relatively high paid sector, with over 60% earning more than Z$500 in clerical and secretarial work. In all sectors, a larger proportion of women than men earned over Z$1000.

A variety of explanations can be advanced for these patterns of women's earnings. They are a legacy of colonial policies, especially the discriminatory policy with respect to urban residence of black and white men and women. Unskilled and semi-skilled urban jobs were seen as appropriate for black migrant men, while black women, unlike white women, were prohibited or discouraged from taking up residence in the towns. Those that did were removed from their traditional economic role in food production and became largely dependent on the husband's wage for household maintenance. Black women's lack of access to formal sector jobs is also a result of their disadvantaged access to education and training. Thus in 1985 only 55% of women age 15 or over were literate, compared to 70% of men (UNDP 1991: 129). By 1987/8 access to primary school education had markedly improved for girls as well as boys, but enrolment rates in secondary and tertiary education were still only 70% and 60% respectively of boys' (UNDP 1991: 139). Although the proportion of black women entering the labour force is likely to increase, there seems little likelihood that their access to formal sector jobs, especially semi-skilled and skilled work, will improve, as they will continue to be disadvantaged in educational terms. However, even if this were not the case, cultural attitudes to women's employment, which are reflected in the proportion of women who seek work and the types of occupation which are acceptable for them, are entrenched: 'The idea of skilled industrial work being regarded as men's work, combined with the myth of the male breadwinner, places women in an extremely vulnerable position' (Batezat et al 1988: 162).

Although a relatively large proportion of women in manufacturing industry are trade union members, they are often inactive and the leadership is nearly all male (Wood 1988). Attempts at government level to advance women's economic position have been marginalised (in the Ministry of Community Development and Women's Affairs) and confined to literacy classes and some small scale income generating projects. Ironically, of the few formal sector jobs filled by women, a relatively large proportion are fairly well paid. These are the clerical, secretarial, bookkeeping, teaching and nursing jobs occupied predominantly by white women prior to 1980 and today by residents of medium and low density residential areas.

In most other low income countries, the situation is no different with regard to access to education and training and to formal sector employment. The result is that women are disproportionately represented in the informal sector, whatever the size of that sector in relation to the urban economy as a whole: the most recent estimates available for Zimbabwe suggest that 64% of people engaged in informal sector activities are women, compared to 25% in the formal sector (including agriculture) (Zimbabwe 1991a). In a survey in three medium and low income areas in the early 1980s it was found that 28% of women were involved in formal wage employment (10% in Mbare, 25% in Glen View and 50% in the middle income area of Mabelreign) but many more were involved in informal sector activity (43%). However, the proportion who were self-employed was less in Mabelreign (15%) than in the low income areas (35% in Mbare and 66% in Glen View). The opportunities in Glen View were related in particular to its peripheral location, which provided scope for the production of and trading in food. Moreover, almost half the women were engaged in non-income earning productive activity, such as growing food, gathering fuel or making clothes (40% in Mabelreign, 45% in Mbare and 53% in Glen View) (Drakakis-Smith 1985). Many plots are large enough to be used for vegetable gardening, while rainy season gardening in unused land near residential areas is also common, despite the attempts of the local authority to prevent it. Although men contribute labour to urban food production, when they are in full-time employment this, and the production of crops on rural land to which many urban families have rights, are predominantly the responsibility of women (see Chapter 4).

A small survey of women engaged in informal sector activities in Epworth found that the most common occupations were sewing, knitting and embroidery, followed by vegetable selling, while less common activities included gardening, basket and pottery making, and selling cooked food (Sijaona 1987). For more than a third of the women, these activities provided their sole source of income, and many had been engaged in them for many years. Although 80% considered that they only worked part-time, a typical working day including domestic and income earning activities was fifteen hours long. Most had learnt their skills informally, though some were members of women's clubs or income earning groups. Few had had any start-up capital to speak of, and none was able to get credit from the retailers who supplied their raw materials. Expenditure on inputs and earnings were irregular and varied widely, but maybe 40% made monthly profits of less than Z$200 (well below the poverty line). As in the formal sector, in the informal sector women are typically confined to culturally acceptable occu-pations, which are often extensions of their domestic roles, and are under-represented in the more lucrative activities.

The informal sector in the urban economy

In Zimbabwe, there is little systematic information about the informal or small scale sector. It was underdeveloped at independence because of physical planning practices, which had isolated black housing areas from the city centre; the demand for formal sector employment as a condition of urban residence for Africans; rationing of resources during sanctions in favour of large firms; and the failure to provide much government support (World Bank 1985). Following the 1986/7 Labour Force Survey, it was estimated that 7.7% of the employed population were engaged in informal sector activities, a figure which was probably an underestimate. The Harare Combination Master Plan refers to a national estimate of 10%. A rough count of informal retailing and other employment in and around markets and shopping centres in the mid-1980s revealed 7000 businesses, of which a larger proportion were in Chitungwiza (24%) than its share of formal employment (about 3%) (HCMPPA 1988b: 13). This omitted those who operated from residential premises or who were itinerant. Some of the literature and many policy documents are characterised by unsubstantiated assertions about the character of informal sector enterprises, typified by that in the master plan's study report:

People in this category engage in enterprises requiring little or no capital, no expertise, little or no managerial or accounting skill and in many places only for subsistence. . . . Enterprises in this sector vary from vending of vegetables, small manufactured goods, handcrafts, through shoe repairing to light service and manufacture like carpentry, and very few (in proportion) of operators settle on authorised premises, hence they are generally of a migrant nature. (HCMPPA 1988b: 4–5).

Confusion is evident between what constitutes a small business and what an informal sector enterprise. This issue is taken up by Leiman (1984/5), who identifies both conceptual and local definitional and practical reasons for it. He suggests that, for local use,

It can be assumed that any entrepreneur operating from premises designated 'industrial' or 'commercial' in the city plans, and rented or purchased exclusively for that purpose, falls within the formal sector . . . even though the goods and production techniques involved may not differ from those of the individual operating from home or, as often happens, from beneath a roadside tree. The difference lies in the fact that the former group have incurred costs: rent, licences, and so forth. (Leiman 1984/5: 121–2).

The Transitional National Development Plan noted the existence of a supposedly 'large, vibrant and dynamic informal sector' (Zimbabwe 1982: 14) into which entry was considered to be free despite discrimination against it and which was said to produce competitively priced goods and services. However, no evidence was produced to support these supposed characteristics and no policies towards the sector were developed in the plan. Empirical evidence on the characteristics of the sector is scarce, but what is available will be presented in the next subsection. In conclusion, policies towards the sector will be reviewed.

Informal sector entrepreneurs at work

The most revealing published surveys have been a detailed study of a particular (anonymous but fairly centrally located) area in Harare carried out in 1981 (Brand 1986), and a University of Zimbabwe nationwide survey in 1983, reported by Leiman (1984/5). Brand interviewed 194 informal sector operators, of whom 72% were men. While three-quarters of the men were married, half the women were widows and only a third were married women. Not only are a larger proportion of those engaged in informal sector activities women, therefore, but these activities provide important means of subsistence for women heads of household. Over half were long term (15 years plus)

Figure 3.4   A trader in Mbare Musika, the largest market in the city

urban residents, a finding echoed by Leiman, and only 42% retained rights to rural land. Just over a fifth had never attended school and most of the rest had only primary school education, with very few having had any formal vocational training. Half had learned the necessary skills from friends within Harare. Eighty-seven per cent of the men and 55% of the women had had formal sector experience (another parallel finding with the wider survey reported by Leiman), half leaving because their employment was terminated by their employers, a quarter because of dissatisfaction and the remainder because of family or personal problems.

Within the area surveyed, a fifth of the enterprises were vegetable vendors operating from stalls in the market for which they had to pay a small weekly fee (Figure 3.4); just under a fifth operated from shop pavements, paying 'rent' to the shopowner in return for the pitch and night-time storage for their equipment for production (of canvas bags, belts etc.) or repair work (such as watch repairing); a quarter operated at the roadside selling vegetables or cooked food, or doing simple production and repair work; and the remaining 38% traded alongside the footpaths traversing the open space and used by many workers on their way to work. All except the market traders were unlicensed. Of the entrepreneurs 39% were engaged in a limited range of productive activities (tailoring, carpentry, leather work, making sandals from car tyres, and metal work), a quarter in repairs (mostly shoe repairs), and the remainder were in petty trade, mostly in food and provisions, but also including a number of herbalists. Almost all worked alone, generally by preference; very few had employees, and few cooperated with each other. Where they did cooperate, it was mostly for materials purchase. Most materials were obtained from formal sector companies, while fruit and vegetables for sale were purchased in Mbare market. Most worked regularly for six or seven days per week.

The great majority of entrepreneurs were experiencing difficulties, varying with the type of workplace. Brand categorised these into

- environmental: lack of shelter and exposure to weather conditions, linked to problems of storage and security (though security problems were also experienced by marketeers);
- economic: lack of demand, especially for shoe repairs;
- lack of capital;
- delayed payments from customers;
- high rents, complained of by the storefront workers; and
- personal: inadequate transport and sanitary provisions, poor health or disability, harassment by the police.

Few complained of lack of skills, and most gave priority to shelter, storage, security, credit and cheaper inputs, when those interviewed were asked to suggest improvements.

Estimating turnover and profits, as expected from work in other countries on informal sector activities, proved difficult because of the lack of written accounts, the need to consume earnings on a daily basis, fluctuations in takings, and a failure to distinguish between turnover and profits. Incomes ranged widely, with just over a fifth claiming to earn more than the minimum industrial wage and over two-thirds above the minimum wage for domestic service. Higher incomes were earned from productive activities rather than from repair or trade, by Zimbabweans rather than non-Zimbabweans, by men rather than women, and by storefront workers and marketeers rather than roadside operators. The majority depended solely on their informal sector earnings for their livelihoods. Greater security of workplace was associated with higher earnings and an ability to save. Half the stallholders and storefront workers were happy to remain in their current informal occupations, whereas 69% of fringe workers wished to change and over a half wanted to find formal industrial wage jobs. The entrepreneurs mostly lived in the nearby Mbare hostels (26%) or high density areas (66%), some coming a considerable distance to this area of operation, with its large passing trade (Brand 1986).

Informal sector enterprises thus vary from microenterprises that barely enable survival, such as recycling plastic bags and other refuse (Tevera 1993, see Chapter 2) or unlicensed hawking, to small industries, such as those in Mbare or Highfield. In the latter, mechanics expected in 1991 to realise a monthly profit of Z$150–300, and some vehicle repairers, metal fabricators and carpenters expected much more (*Weekend Gazette*, 3 May 1991). Market activities have always been focused primarily on the Mbare Musika market near the long distance bus terminal, but in the early 1990s they extended to a large vacant site between Mbare and the city centre. Trade liberalisation and economic difficulties have increased the importance of informal trade with neighbouring countries, involving the export of crocheted goods and other women's handicrafts, and the import of clothes (often secondhand) and consumer goods. Traders in Harare deal in both Botswana and South Africa to the south and Zambia to the north.

Brand's detailed study, along with other available information, clearly illustrates the heterogeneity of informal sector enterprises and entre-preneurs. These sources provide evidence of the nature of the sector as a provider not only of last resort economic activities but also of oppor-tunities to earn a reasonable income. Entry, far from being free, requires knowledge, contacts, skills and often capital, especially for the more lucrative activities, and is therefore open predominantly to established urban residents. Lack of these assets confines some operators, especially women, foreigners and the disabled, to oversubscribed and less profitable activities. It is a competitive sector, in which cooperation and organisation are rare, and in which few businesses grow beyond a one-person concern.

At the beginning of this section, we noted the factors which had constrained the development of small enterprises in the 1970s. Little changed during the 1980s. The 1991 Framework for Economic Reform suggested that 'The growth of the small scale sector has been inhibited by the availability and cost of finance, land and basic utilities, as well as numerous licensing and other regulations' (Zimbabwe 1991a: 19). It has been suggested elsewhere that the sector has also remained undeveloped because of the dominance of large manufacturers in the production of wage goods and its inability to compete with the extensive, well established and diversified large scale sector. Leiman's aim (1984/5) was to examine whether the informal sector was complementary to or in competition with the formal sector. He concluded that there was little intersectoral competition for factors of production, including labour (given high unemployment), capital and raw materials. Inputs are mostly obtained from the formal sector, either by direct purchase from wholesalers or retailers, or by use of offcuts too small for efficient use by larger scale producers. Competition for markets is more complex. Most overt resentment is expressed by formal sector retailers in both low and high density areas, who mobilise public sector support to enforce licensing regulations, but Leiman concluded that in other respects there was little competition, as the informal sector was thought to serve different markets.

Policy and prospects

Government policy, first stated in 1983, has been to support the informal sector as a source of employment, income and low cost goods and services (Leiman 1984/5). In the early years this took the form of attempting to bring informal sector enterprises into the formal sector by a system of licensing and registration (ZANU (PF) 1985). There were frequent crackdowns on those operating without licences, and sometimes on those operating in unauthorised premises such as tuckshops (kiosks), especially in the more formal areas of the cities.

Since independence there have been various policies and programmes to support cooperatives and small scale enterprises, but they have been small in relation to demand and have had little impact, especially on informal sector microenterprises (Davies 1988). In addition to credit programmes operated by national level organisations, there have been a limited number of training courses. These include those run by Harare City Council at Mbare Vocational Training Centre (welding and carpentry); courses for women in sewing, other crafts and sericulture, for example at Chinembiri Training Centre; and, more recently, courses for young people in Budiriro (workshops in screen printing, tie-dye, Vaseline and soap manufacturing, paper technology and stone carving). The city council also provides support to community (especially women's) income generating projects, and to agricultural and industrial cooperatives, of which there were nearly 300 in 1989. In 1988 the 91 small (10–20 or so members) periurban agricultural cooperatives had ploughed on average about 4 hectares each. Many of the 189 industrial cooperatives were operating on 'home industries stands' in the HDRAs, and the city council was considering starting a revolving loans fund to provide them with credit (Harare City Council, Department of Housing and Community Services, 1985–9). However, no evaluation is available of the effectiveness of the council's training or support programmes.

The Government anticipates that small scale enterprises will benefit from the improved investment climate hoped for in the 1990s, and also that subcontracting by the large scale sector will increase, with a view to creating between 25 000 and 35 000 jobs in the small scale sector between 1991 and 1995 (Zimbabwe 1991a). However, Imani

Development Consultants criticised continuing policy which insists upon all enterprises occupying premises formally allocated for industrial and commercial use in development plans, paying 50% corporate tax, abiding by labour regulations intended for larger enterprises, and providing collateral for loans. Meanwhile, the constraints experienced by small scale enterprises (lack of transport, technology, support, skills and access to credit) are not addressed (*Herald*, 25 March 1991). The desire to regularise and keep control of the sector still dominates official attitudes, despite lip service to the contrary. Both officials and politicians use the sector's untidiness and the apparent unfairness of its competition with large scale enterprises to justify repressive measures, while attempts to assist enterprises have often displayed little understanding of the way in which they operate.

The stagnation and decline in formal sector employment which has occurred in Zimbabwe since the beginning of the 1990s as a result of liberalisation measures has not only eliminated most of the gains made by low paid urban workers, in terms of minimum wage increases, greater employment security and improved conditions of service, in the years after independence; it is also threatening the viability of a manufacturing base which despite its problems is more diversified and efficient than its counterparts in most other African countries. Experience elsewhere has shown that rapid economic liberalisation gives existing enterprises too little time to adjust to increased competition from imports and higher costs of capital, especially where shortages of inputs constrain the industry's ability to increase production; or where public sector purchases are reduced as budgets are cut, and declining real wages constrain effective demand. Despite the evidence from countries that implemented structural adjustment programmes in the 1980s, the IMF and World Bank have imposed, and Zimbabwe has accepted, liberalisation measures which look set to cause the same problems, despite some phasing of trade liberalisation. Rapid increases in interest rates have had a particularly bad effect on companies which embarked upon retooling and other capital investment programmes following import liberalisation, and are deterring other companies from making necessary investments. Export markets are difficult to break into, especially given northern protectionism, competition from the newly industrialised countries of Asia, and the end of sanctions against South Africa. At the same time, domestic demand has been badly hit by declining real wages and increasing unemployment, exacerbated by the drought which had at least a temporarily devastating effect on rural incomes. The role of the informal sector as a means of supplementing inadequate wage incomes, or as a substitute for them following redundancy or failure to find a job, may grow in the years to come, and it may spread beyond its carefully controlled locations to become an omnipresent feature of the street scene, as it has in other African countries. However, the informal sector is also adversely affected by declining domestic demand for goods and services. For it to constitute a 'large' and 'dynamic' sector, not only does discrimination against it have to be replaced by understanding and effective support, but also there must inevitably be a period during which entrepreneurs learn to identify potential opportunities, obtain supplies, manage their businesses, and market their products. Newly redundant civil servants and wage workers do not necessarily have the appropriate skills, nor are profitable opportunities easy to identify. Although the economy of the city of Harare is still prosperous compared to that of many African cities, the policies of the World Bank and central and local government are fraught with contradictions which, given the interests involved, will be hard to resolve.

4

Social characteristics of Harare's population

The recency of urban growth in Africa, its origins in colonial labour processes and its interconnection with factors influencing birth and death rates combine to shape both the changing demographic composition of urban populations and the lives of urban residents. The migratory trends to which colonial labour needs gave rise determined the direction and composition of migration streams, and thus which urban settlements grew, their rate of growth, and social characteristics of their populations. The relationship between colonialism and urbanisation in Africa as a whole and Zimbabwe in particular has been discussed in Chapter 1 and will be further developed in this chapter, as the demographic characteristics of the urban population, its spatial distribution within the city, the characteristics of migrants and aspects of the lives of the city's inhabitants are explored in more detail. Although the colonial period has left a social as well as an economic legacy everywhere in Africa, other factors came into play at independence. In most other countries, these trends have now influenced the social characteristics of urban populations for thirty years, and we might expect the imprints of colonial policies to have become less distinct compared to Zimbabwe, where the strength and recency of the settler-colonial legacy is very apparent. The extent to which this is the case will be assessed as recent demographic trends, changes in the spatial distribution of population groups, the migration patterns of modern residents, the social characteristics of households, and features of the lives of men and women are analysed.

The history of urban development in Zimbabwe has been described in Chapter 1, both in terms of the labour policies which underlay urban growth and overall levels and patterns of urbanisation. Harare's population, we noted, grew from about 310 000 in 1962 to 373 000 in

Table 4.1 Population of Harare in 1962 and 1969

	1962	1969
African		
African housing areas	143 030	168 520
Rest of city	72 780	98 410
Total	215 810	266 930
Non-African		
European		96 764
Asian		4 055
Coloured		5 131
Total non-African	94 548	105 950
Total	310 358	372 880

Source: HCMPPA, 1988d: 2. Excludes St. Mary's.

1969 (3.2% per annum) (Table 4.1), and then more rapidly to nearly 660 000 by 1982 (6% per annum). However, if Chitungwiza's population is added to that of the original city, the conurbation's population in 1982 had reached 850 000, representing an average annual growth rate of 5.7%. In the absence of recent census results, in 1987 the Harare Combination Master Plan technical team carried out a household survey and used the results to estimate the population of the master plan study area. Harare and Chitungwiza were thought to have grown at approximately equal rates of about 10% between 1982 and 1987, when the population was estimated to have reached 1.26 million (Table 4.2). Provisional figures from the 1992 census showed that Harare's population (including Epworth) was 1.18 million and Chitungwiza's 274 000, representing growth rates of 6.1% and 4.7% respectively since the previous census in 1982. If the figures are confirmed, the total population of the conurbation was 1.46 million and it had grown, overall, at 5.8% per annum during the previous decade (Zimbabwe 1992).

Some aspects of these overall demographic trends will now be explored in more detail, including the age and gender structure of the population and its racial composition. Spatial variations in demographic characteristics and trends will be examined in the subsequent section. Crucial to the social structure of the city are patterns of migration and the changing influence that these have had on household characteristics and urban lives.

Table 4.2 Harare's population, 1969–1992

	1969	1982	1969–82 (% p.a.)	1987	1982–7 (% p.a.)	1992	1982–92 (% p.a.)
Harare Municipality							
LDRAs	179 690	218 604	1.7	291 588	6.7	} 356 230	4.5
MDRAs	9295	11 542	1.9	15 581	7.0		6.4
HDRAs	168 220	412 045	11.2	634 044	10.8	765 238[c]	
Other	12 195	16 173	2.5	20 258	5.1	–	
Total	369 400	658 364	6.0	961 471	9.2	1 121 468	5.5
Chitungwiza							
St Mary's	13 160	36 126	13.4	41 241	2.8	47 503	2.8
Zengeza	–	24 394		72 078	39.1[b]	75 700	12.0
Seke	–	111 936		150 071	6.8	150 832	3.0
Total	13 160	172 456	93.1	263 390	10.6[b]	274 035	4.7
Epworth	3480	18 000[a]	32.1	32 250[a]	15.8	62 701	12.6[d]
Total	386 040	848 820	5.7	1 257 111		1 458 204	5.6

Source: HCMPPA 1988d: Tables 3.3 and 3.4; Zimbabwe 1992.

There are discrepancies in figures given in different sources, and the figures given in the table may not be identical to figures from other sources quoted elsewhere in the text.

LDRAs Low density residential areas. MDRAs Medium density residential areas. HDRAs High density residential areas.

[a] Undercount in 1982; 1987 figure projected from 1985 census in the area showing 27 400 residents.
[b] In 1982 there were 8454 houses in Zengeza, so the 1982 census population for Zengeza is considered to be an undercount and the 1982–7 rate of growth for Chitungwiza is therefore overstated.
[c] See Table 4.3; low and medium density areas grouped because of difficulty in ensuring compatible definitions.
[d] 1985–1992.

Demographic trends

The age and gender structures of urban populations reflect changing migration patterns. In Figure 4.1 the age–sex structure of the population of Harare is compared with that of the population as a whole for 1969, and of Harare/Chitungwiza with the national population for 1982. In 1969 the national population showed a slight preponderance of men over women, but a ratio of 142 men for every 100 women in the main urban areas and 150:100 in Harare. At the national level this was accounted for by the sex ratio among people, 64% of them men, born outside Zimbabwe, who comprised about 10% of the population (Zimbabwe 1985a: 17). The labour migration policies of the colonial and settler governments, which have been discussed in Chapter 1, account for the dominance of men in the urban population, a pattern found to a greater or lesser extent elsewhere in colonial Africa. By 1982, the ratio of men to women in the national population had already reached a more typical 97:100 and by 1992 95:100 (Zimbabwe 1985a: 16, 24; Zimbabwe 1992). This is to be expected, given the greater life expectancy of women (UNDP 1991: 139). Increased rates of rural–urban migration during the 1970s had already led to a similar change in urban areas by 1982, as more women joined the migration stream, leading to a sex ratio of 115:100, and a continued trend towards parity is expected to have occurred in the most recent intercensal period, though figures for all urban areas are not yet available (Zimbabwe 1992). Similar changes in the gender composition of migration streams and the resulting urban populations were observed in the 1960s and 1970s in other African countries, as women and children joined male migrants and some women migrated in their own right.

The sex ratio varied with age: in 1969, in all except the 5–9 age group males exceeded females, and this ratio increased with age, so that in the main working age group, there were twice as many men as women in the urban population as a whole (Figure 4.1). In 1982 slightly more boys were born in Harare/Chitungwiza than girls. In the 0–14 age group, however, there were fewer boys than girls, perhaps illustrating both the higher survival rates of girls and a greater propensity to send boys to the rural areas to be cared for or to attend school. This was particularly marked in the 15–19 age group. Although in some age groups there were fewer boys than girls in 1969, the low sex ratio in the 15–19 age group was not present. Among working age groups, men continued to predominate, but it was only in the older working age groups, incorporating many with a long history of urban work, that there were more than twice as many men as women. Above the age of 60 in Harare, women had by 1982 begun to exceed the numbers of men,

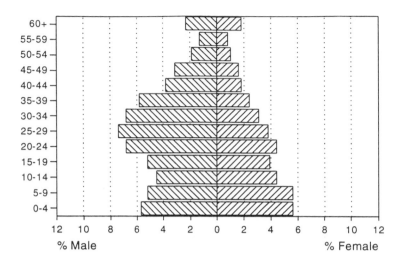

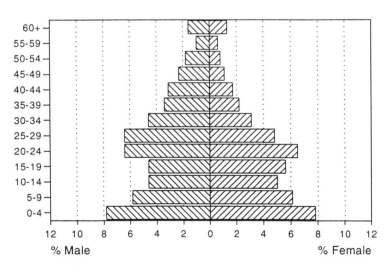

Figure 4.1 Age–sex structure of the population. Sources: CSO 1989; Whitsun Foundation 1980; Zimbabwe 1989

National
1969

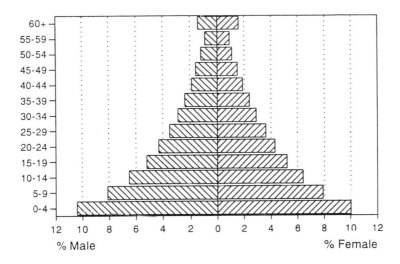

National
1982

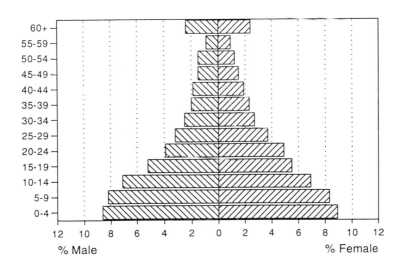

unlike in 1969. This change was probably partly because of the tendency of widows to live with their sons and partly because of the difficulties faced by women heads of household in returning to the rural areas on retirement. Overall, the male:female ratio had decreased by 1982 to 112:100 in Harare (CSO 1989) and even further, to 108:100 by 1992 (Zimbabwe 1992). A breakdown of the 1992 population by age is not yet available.

In 1969 children under 14 already formed nearly a third of the population in Harare, but by 1982 this had increased to 37%. Nevertheless, in both years this was less than in the national population (nearly half in each case). In the urban areas, as might be expected, a larger proportion of the population were in the working age groups in 1969 than might have been expected from the national age distribution, but by 1982 this had evened out, with the main working age group (25–54) containing just over a third of the population in both cases.

The proportion of non-Africans in Harare's population, which was large compared to cities in non-settler economies, stayed fairly steady during the 1960s (31% in 1962, 28% in 1969). Most of these were Europeans, with Asians and Coloureds constituting only 2.5% of the population in 1969, a smaller proportion than in countries such as South Africa, Zambia, Kenya and Uganda (Table 4.1). Of the African population in the 1960s, two-thirds lived in African housing areas, where the male:female ratio was 150:100 in 1969, compared to 152:100 for the population of the city as a whole. Many of the rest were dispersed throughout the European housing areas as domestic servants, giving rise to a total African population in which the male:female ratio was 269:100. Except for child care, house and garden work 'became constructed predominantly in African male gender terms' (Hansen 1989: 30), partly because many of the early European migrants were men and partly because of colonial migrant labour policies. Colonial households were hierarchical, paternalistic and characterised by relations of domination and subservience. Households were generally run by European women, and servants were regarded as household commodities (Hansen 1989). The juxtaposition of predominantly male domestic workers with white women fuelled difficult and sexually loaded relationships and periodic, often almost hysterical allegations: the 'black peril', in which blame invariably rested on black workers. The ability of white employers to impose a requirement for sexual favours on black women domestic workers rarely got the same attention. Although African women later became domestic servants in eastern and southern Africa and parts of Francophone Africa, private household service in Northern and Southern Rhodesia remained predominantly male. The growth of the black population in European housing areas led in 1969 to expressions of alarm that in some areas the number of black people had exceeded the white population. Regulations were introduced forbidding white residents to house anyone not in their employment, and a policy was formulated that eventually servants' accommodation would be eliminated and domestic workers relocated in African townships (HCMPPA 1988c). Little progress was made in implementing either objective. After 1969, data are presented by residential area rather than race, and information on the racial composition of the population becomes scarce and patchy.

Spatial distribution of the urban population

Access to urban land and housing, which is determined by its cost in relation to income, the relative locational attractiveness of different areas, the way in which housing production is organised, and the assumptions on which planning and development control is based, varies between different groups within an urban population. The interrelationship between these factors produces a built environment which, because it is enduring, influences the distribution of social groups over time. However, changes in economic, social and political conditions, and improvements or deterioration in the physical condition of housing, may give rise to changes in the spatial distribution of the urban population over a shorter time scale than changes in the pattern of urban land use and building.

Population in the low and medium density residential areas in which European residents lived grew very slowly between 1969 and 1982, as earlier growth was offset by white emigration around independence. Between 1982 and 1987, however, population in these areas grew at almost 7% per annum (Table 4.2). This, as we will see later, was associated with very little new residential building and thus occurred largely within the existing housing stock. Four factors are relevant: the movement of black families into formerly white housing areas, relaxation of controls on the accommodation of domestic workers' families, slowing down and halting of European emigration, and letting out of servants' quarters to tenants.

The movement of black families into former white residential areas has been studied by Sioux Cumming (Harvey). Between February 1978 and July 1979, a net in-movement of 1560 black households into formerly white areas was detected using surnames in the electricity account records of the city council, though this was outbalanced by a net out-movement of 2880 white households. In most areas, with the exception of those in the east and northeast of the city, out-movement of

Table 4.3 The population of high density and other areas in 1969, 1982 and 1992

	1969		1982		1992	
	No.	%	No.	%	No.	%
Mbare	58 010		59 767		97 078	
Dzivarasekwa	6 440		22 749		44 946	
Highfield	52 560		73 651		101 134	
Kambuzuma	9 510		23 548		40 558	
Mabvuku	6 900		39 032		47 471	
Mufakose	20 620		44 717		61 846	
Rugare	8 140		8 362		a	
Tafara	6 030		21 069		30 693	
Glen Norah	–		45 687		42 529	
Glen View	–		59 791		109 704	
Warren Park	–		13 672		52 663	
Budiriro	–		–		34 542	
Kuwadzana	–		–		75 080	
Hatcliffe	–		–		8 161	
Sunningdale	–		–		18 833	
All high density areas	168 210[b]	45.1	412 045	62.6	765 238	68.2
City centre / Avenues	n.a.		26 019		n.a.	
Mabelreign / Haig Park / Meyrick Park	n.a.		17 427		n.a.	
All medium and low density areas	204 670	54.9	246 319	37.4	356 230	31.8
Total	372 880	100.0	658 364	100.0	1 121 468	100.0

Sources: HCMPPA 1988d; Central Statistical Office printout from 1982 census; Zimbabwe 1992.

n.a. not available
[a] No map of ward boundaries is provided in Zimbabwe 1992, so it is unclear if and where Rugare has been included.
[b] Excluding Marimba Park, then an African area but medium density.

whites was accompanied by a gain in numbers of black households. Black in-movement was concentrated in areas in the west and south and around the city centre, including Waterfalls and Houghton Park, relatively near former African areas, suggesting that 'proximity to former residence and familiarity with the new area of residence are important factors when first moving into former white suburbs' (Harvey 1987: 182), while the same factors help to account for the white out-movement which resulted in high vacancy rates (Cumming 1993). These are also areas with lower priced houses, though plots vary in size, and are located close to the main areas of industrial and commercial employment. A more detailed case study of Mabelreign, a suburb built in the 1950s by the national government to provide housing for white immigrants, mostly artisans, is described in Cumming 1990. In-movement by black families started in about 1979, as the repeal of the 1969 Land Tenure Act became imminent, but the main changes did not occur until after independence in 1980, when black households moved in first to the parts of the area with smaller and cheaper houses and later to the remaining areas. The in-movement of black households levelled off after 1985, as the number of sales decreased when remaining whites, often elderly, found that they could not afford to purchase elsewhere in the city because prices of houses in low density residential areas had started to rise (see Chapter 6).

A survey in 1983 bore out Cumming's findings (which were based on 1978–81 data) and echoed her explanations. Thus in six high income residential areas 80% of respondent households were white, compared with 32% in twelve middle income areas. Suburbs to the south and west of the city showed significantly greater racial mixing than did those to the north and east (Heath 1986: 44).

As black households were, on average, larger than the previous households, some increase in population in these areas occurred. This is illustrated by information collected in 1991, which reveals another trend occasioned by pressures in the housing market. Surveys showed that while in Mount Pleasant, a prosperous area in north Harare, servants' quarters on each plot were still almost entirely used for domestic workers, in Hatfield and Mabelreign the situation was quite different. In Hatfield, two of the 52 stands included in the survey had 'guest cottages' and both were occupied by tenants. In addition to this, almost all the stands in both Hatfield and Mabelreign had servants' quarters, of which a quarter or more were occupied by tenants and a few by adult members of the main household.

Despite the increase in numbers of people living in low and medium density areas, and the doubling of densities which resulted, by international standards densities remained extremely low: they ranged from 1.08 people per hectare in Borrowdale to 9.12 in Mabelreign in 1969 (overall average 5.26 people per hectare) compared to 2.4 and 20 people per hectare respectively in the same areas in 1987 (HCMPPA 1988c). There has been little expansion of low density housing areas since the mid-1970s; what new development has occurred has mostly been infill and limited in scale. The reasons for this will be explored in Chapter 6.

High density residential areas, in contrast, have expanded in area to accommodate a growing black population. The largest areas in 1969, with populations of more than 50 000 each, were Mbare and Highfield (Table 4.3). By 1982 Mbare's population had increased relatively little, while Highfield's had reached nearly 74 000 and Glen View also had a population of over 50 000. In the 1980s, Mbare's population increased, in part due to the proliferation of illegal backyard shacks, Dzivarasekwa and Warren Park were extended, and several new areas were developed (see Chapter 6). In addition, the population in existing areas had, in many cases, continued to increase. As a result of this differential growth, the proportion of Harare's population which lived in high density residential areas had increased from 45% in 1969 to 68% in 1992 (Table 4.3), a proportion which would have been 76% if Chitungwiza and Epworth were included. Because of the large remaining employment in domestic service, the population of low density residential areas cannot be equated to those with high incomes, while a proportion of middle income families live in high density residential areas.

St Mary's, in what was later to become Chitungwiza, accommodated 13 000 people in 1969. Massive population growth has occurred in this area and in Zengeza and Seke since the mid-1970s, and although population underestimates for Zengeza in 1982 make it difficult to estimate a rate of growth, population in this predominantly high density town was thought to have increased at about 10% per annum between 1982 and 1987. The discrepancy between this figure and the rate of growth shown by the census data (4.7% per annum) is very wide, and the latter is surprisingly low compared to Harare (6.1% per annum), though the census figures have apparently been accepted. Because of the high planning standards adopted for plot size, road access and social facility provision, and the relative absence of unauthorised development, densities in 'high density' areas are still low by the standards of most Third World cities, reaching a maximum of only 87 people per hectare in Seke and 150 people per hectare in Mbare in 1987 (the latter an increase from 129 people per hectare in 1969). That such low densities do not necessarily imply generous standards of available living space will be demonstrated in Chapter 6.

The difficulty of knowing the extent to which the 1982 census counts of the African population in Harare and Chitungwiza were under-estimates and the sample nature of the 1987 data made projections of population a hazardous undertaking. No explicit attention was paid to the possible impact of AIDS. In the earlier 1980s, growth rates of between 7 and 8% per annum tended to be assumed. The Harare Combination Master Plan Preparation Authority (HCMPPA) carried out projections from 1987 to 2000 using the population estimates derived from its 1987 sample survey and an age–sex structure identical to that revealed by the 1982 census. It assumed declining fertility and increasing life expectancy and a pretty arbitrary 1.6% per annum rate of growth from in-migration. These assumptions gave rise to annual rates of growth of 4% per annum for Harare and 7.33% per annum for Chitungwiza at the beginning of the plan period, declining to 2.9% and 4.66% per annum by the year 2000, or averages of 3.41% and 5.88% over the whole period. An increase in Harare's population from just under one million to nearly one and a half million, and in Chitungwiza's population from 263 300 to 553 000 was thus expected. These projections were unrealistically low given the growth rates of around 10% per annum between 1982 and 1987 revealed by the Authority's own figures (HCMPPA 1988d). However, as the actual population growth rate seems to have been less than expected, the projections may not be altogether unrealistic. The uncertainties involved in population projects for rapidly growing cities throw considerable doubt on the use of traditional blueprint approaches as a basis for planning their future development (Devas and Rakodi 1993) and on the master plan estimates of land requirements used in Harare (see Chapter 2).

Migration and mobility

The establishment of urban areas to serve European needs and the colonial and settler labour policy which followed meant that African in-migration has always been a major preoccupation of white policymakers and analysts: initially, how to encourage it and, later, how to exercise control, both with respect to migration flows and over the urban African population which resulted. Labour policy and social control were discussed in Chapter 1.

The increased volumes of rural–urban migration which occurred in the 1960s attracted the attention of researchers, who suggested that the volume of migration was related to urban–rural income differentials. Faced with continued rapid migration in the face of increasing un-employment and the inability of formal sector job creation to keep up with the growth of the urban labour force, the model was modified to consider not only urban wages but also the problem of obtaining a formal sector job. Todaro's theory underlay the belief that urban bias in investment and policy, backed by a politically powerful elite and a wage labour force paid above market wages, discriminated against agriculture and rural areas, thus encouraging out-migration (Lipton 1977; Todaro 1994: 264–9). The assumptions underlying these theories have been subjected to serious criticism by Jamal and Weeks (1993), among others.

In particular, the continued high levels of migration, despite the reduction of urban–rural differentials in income and investment in the 1980s, are not explained by either the Todaro model or the urban bias hypothesis.

Migration is an extremely complex process, comprising a variety of different patterns of migration movement and the influence of underlying structural causes, immediate explanations for household and individual behaviour, and the presence of facilitating conditions. Any explanation of continued rural–urban migration must take into account not only the colonial roots of peasant incorporation into the international and national cash economies, but also post-independence trends. Governments continue to rely on both extraction of foreign exchange and revenue from cash crop exports and a supply of food for their urban populations from food crop surpluses. Farmers also long ago became used to and dependent upon cash purchases. The role of subsistence agriculture in meeting part of the costs of reproduction, as a way of maintaining low wages for colonial enterprises, has already been mentioned. As long as migrants retain rural ties, they can remain permanently in the rural areas, but the effect, it is suggested, is to withdraw surplus from the rural economy to maintain the urban labour force. Eventually, the effect is to reduce rural incomes to the point that out-migration occurs despite a lack of urban opportunities (Standing 1984). In some areas, population growth and environmental deterioration place pressure on land and other means of production, while increasing life expectancy and larger families reduce the prospects of access to land. Although migration is not the only response, it is a common one (Gugler and Flanagan 1978; Standing 1984). Out-migration may have an impact on the productivity of the household unit, even giving rise to a labour shortage which may or may not be met by recruiting wage labour. In addition, government reductions of producer prices in the interests of exporting and cheap food reduce the returns to agriculture.

Other factors which often increase the relative attractiveness of urban areas, in addition to the availability of wage jobs, include, in some places, the better access to social and educational facilities in town. Transport improvements, and greater awareness of opportunities because of better access to education and the media, facilitate the process. However, remittances and return migration to rural areas are significant, and complicate the relatively simple picture portrayed by Todaro and Lipton.

In this section, a considerable tradition of work on the urban migrant population will be analysed, with respect both to the changing theoretical and policy preoccupations of analysts and what studies have to say about the changing nature of the migration process. This will lead into a discussion of urban life for households and their wider social networks.

The migrants of the late 1960s and early 1970s

Studies of rural to urban migrants in Harare in the late 1960s and early 1970s were concerned with:

- the rural links of urban residents and the changing nature of kinship ties;
- 'modernisation' of attitudes and lifestyles; and
- the emergence of an African 'elite'.

The ambivalent attitudes of the time towards stabilisation of the African urban population have been explored in Chapter 1. As a result of those attitudes and the legislative and housing policies which resulted, the population in the late 1960s can basically be divided into 'stabilised urban Africans' living with their families as municipal tenants in areas such as Mufakose, and circular migrants (almost entirely men) living primarily in hostels for single people (Moller 1974). At that time, half of all legal occupants in African housing areas were living in married units, 38% were in hostels and the remainder were registered lodgers (Cubitt and Riddell 1974: 42).

Although almost all of the household heads in Moller's 1973/4 sample in Mufakose were married, and more than three-quarters of their wives normally lived in Harare, his analysis of 'townsmen' concentrated on the former and ignored the latter. These male heads of households were mostly first-generation migrants, but long term urban residents (average 20 year residence as adults) with stable wage employment (half the sample had had only two jobs). They lived in municipal rented housing and the majority were in nuclear households, though 14% of the households contained members who normally lived in the rural areas. Most residents in Moller's sample of hostels were also married, but either chose not to bring their families to live in Harare or could not, because of house rules. They had a higher turnover of jobs than the men in Mufakose, but Moller's data did not reveal whether this was by choice, with a view to spending time with their rural-based families, or whether instability of employment made it more difficult for many of these men to make their way to the top of the housing waiting list and thus obtain the family accommodation needed to settle more permanently in town.

Bourdillon's 1972/3 survey of labour migrants from the remote area of Korekore in the northeast of the country throws further light on the nature of the migration process. He notes the institutionalisation of circular labour migration, both as an economic and social phenomenon. Adult men went to work in urban areas (or, less commonly, on commercial farms) to raise money for general household needs: marriage payments, education, clothes, agricultural equipment and consumer goods. An economic imperative had become socially accepted and it was expected that all men would leave to work at some time. Jobs tended to last between three and seven years, but migrant careers were very varied: while many chose to return home for prolonged periods between spells of work, some settled permanently in town. Despite the economic need to work, most migrants complained that the cost of urban living made it difficult to live comfortably, remit money or save. That over half sought domestic work, with its very low pay and accommodation to which in many cases they were not permitted to bring their families, served to reinforce the circular nature of migration and to perpetuate the need to continue working, given the limited scope for saving. Of the few reliable informants on remittances, Bourdillon found that those with wives at home sent, on average, 22% of their annual cash earnings to sustain the rural household (Bourdillon 1977).

Although women's migration was discouraged, divorced and deserted women lost their rights to land, to which they had access only through their husbands (see below). If land was in short supply in the village of their birth, migration was one way of ensuring survival. Often migrant women left their children behind in the rural areas while retaining financial responsibility for them. Divorce or widowhood in town left women with a similar lack of options. Difficulty in obtaining access to formal employment prevented women from becoming municipal tenants and even from registering as legal urban dwellers. Without registration, children could not be enrolled in school (May 1979). To survive, women engaged in informal sector activities, including the provision of domestic and sexual services for men.

On arrival in town, young first-time migrants were given accommodation and helped to find employment by relatives. Thus the choice of destination was primarily influenced by the prior residence of kin, especially for those seeking domestic service: 62% of the labour migrants from Korekore had obtained their jobs through a friend or relative from home (Bourdillon 1977: 15). In the absence of many close relatives, the migrant's social network widened to include wider kin and friends from his or her area of origin. These contacts provided not only the practical assistance referred to above, but also a social network for leisure time visiting and drinking, and a communications network through which

Table 4.4   Visits to rural areas by African men in the early 1970s (per cent)

	Non-visitor	Occasional visitor (1+ p.a.)	Regular visitor (weekly, fortnightly, monthly)
Mufakose townsmen	33	42	25
Hostel residents	10	48	42

Source: Moller 1974: 27.

news spread. This network was important because of low levels of literacy, the unreliable postal service and the infrequent nature of visits home to such a remote area. Thus although many key kinspeople were absent from the urban network, reliance on kin persisted for those aspects of life where such reliance was traditional (for example the safeguarding of property, and help in sickness or emergencies such as job loss) (Stopforth 1972). Researchers disagreed, however, on the *extent* to which such reliance was continuing to be the basis for urban networks: Bourdillon (1977) stressed the wider kinship network, while Stopforth (1972) noted the replacement of support from kin by support from urban friends, neighbours, co-workers and employers. In addition, Stopforth emphasised that only half of his respondents wanted to live near relatives in town, and noted that women were even more reluctant to do so than men. Obligations to kin, it was clear, while they had to be fulfilled to ensure reciprocity in an insecure situation, were also burdens which many low wage urban households could ill afford.

Links between migrants and their areas of origin were also explored. Moller (1974) looked in detail at visiting patterns, noting that two-thirds of 'stabilised' urban men continued to visit their homes, while almost all the circular migrants in his sample did so, though less than half of them were married (Table 4.4). These regular or occasional visits, he asserted, achieved 'family unity' and showed the persisting importance of such ties for the great majority of urban households. However, his evidence also showed, he suggested, the gradual detachment from rural ties of nuclear households committed to urban life. Men, he found, tended to make short frequent visits, especially at public holiday times and during their annual leave, the frequency being greater if and when their wives were living in the rural areas, which applied to a quarter of the Mufakose married men and almost all the married men living in hostels. It must be remembered that these responses from men may portray a degree of commitment to their wives that exceeded their practice. Anecdotal evidence from women and research in the rural areas revealed significant problems of men failing to maintain contact with and support for rural-based wives and children, perhaps taking 'urban wives'. The result was that the family left behind fell into poverty.

Given the prevailing pattern whereby women's predominant means of obtaining access to land is through their husbands (May 1983; Seidman 1984), women's visits were mainly to their husbands' area of origin.

> Under customary law, women had no land-use rights in their individual capacity. Land was allocated to the head (who was always a man) of the family by the chief, sub-chief or headman. He, head of the family in turn, gave portions of the land to his wife or wives for their subsistence production, while he worked (with the help of his wives) on the larger portion and claimed the produce. (Kazembe 1986: 382)

Women's visits to the rural areas tended to be longer than those of men. They were seasonal, peaking in December and January, when the need for labour on the land is greatest, and fewer in the dry season, as were those of children, though some of the latter were accounted for by children attending school outside Harare.

> Short-term mobility [Moller asserted] provided an opportunity for combining the benefit drawn from continuous employment in the urban economic sector during a working lifetime with the benefit of a rural society and economic security upon retirement. (Moller 1974: 31)

However, the system of rural–urban migration has been widely criticised for enabling the payment of urban wages which were insufficient to meet the full reproductive costs of households individually and the labour force in general, and for its social costs. In rural areas, Moller's sanguine appraisal ignores the adverse impact of the removal of husbands' labour power on agricultural production and the women responsible for it (see also Seidman 1984), the difficulties caused for women by the irregularity and sometimes absence of remittance flows, and the social and family tensions caused by separation and reunification. In urban areas, as a result of settler urban policy, the population was vulnerable to a life of constant insecurity and intimidation (Potts and Mutambirwa 1990).

Colonial policy had always intended that urban African workers return home on their retirement. The studies all noted that the great majority of their respondents wished to do so, understandably in the absence of anything approaching a comprehensive welfare/pension system. This desire was in part economic (the ability of older people to support themselves on a subsistence basis without the need for much of a cash income) and in part social. The continued effort to visit rural areas of origin therefore served the very necessary and practical purpose of maintaining rights to land and property. Although these writers did not analyse rural property in any detail, use rights to land, ownership of cattle and the construction of a house are all important. Cattle were regarded as the main source of wealth and social status. They were a source of food and other materials, a form of currency and a repository of savings, as well as having important roles in life cycle ceremonies, including their use for marriage payments (*roora, lobola*) (Makamure 1970). Older women could acquire cattle (or goats) as gifts from their husbands on their daughters' or granddaughters' marriages and pregnancies, but the great majority of cattle were owned by men (May 1983). However, Moller (1974) noted that some households who intended to retire to their villages of origin were not in practice maintaining their rural ties and that this might affect their ability to take up residence there on their retirement.

The pressures for change in this 'quasi-stabilised' urban labour supply identified by Stopforth (1972) were changes to the nature of kinship relations and changing behaviour and attitudes on the part of children born and brought up in urban areas. Residents' ambivalence about such changes is clearly revealed. Ambivalence about kinship claims and obligations has been noted above. While complaining about low wages and poor living conditions, parents saw the solution for their children as better education leading to a better job. This strategy was pursued despite the perceived impact of education and urban life on children's willingness to observe and practice customary behaviour, especially that concerned with deference to elders, and to support their parents in old age (Stopforth 1972).

A further pressure for change stemmed from the deliberate policy to promote the emergence of an African 'elite' or middle class. This elite was studied in 1968/9 in Marimba and Westwood, the only areas where Africans were permitted to own houses (on plots of 1000 square metres or more) at that time (Kileff 1975). The study sat squarely in the modernisation tradition, judging middle class characteristics in terms of how they differed from what were considered to be the traditional characteristics and behaviour of urban Africans. It was noted that these higher income urban residents maintained fewer kinship ties, especially with their extended families in the rural areas, and they preferred urban to rural life, desired a pension on retirement rather than the security represented by cattle ownership, were much more likely to listen to the radio or read a newspaper, and preferred modern over traditional courts, when compared to Highfield residents (Stopforth 1977: 38). Kileff noted distinctions between the businessmen and professionals in his sample, the latter tending to be better educated, and, although lower income than the businessmen, able to afford an owner-occupied house at a younger age. In the absence of credit facilities for African entrepreneurs, the businessmen had accumulated wealth gradually, depending on business opportunities, acumen and luck. They performed 'chiefly' roles by providing support and mediation for kin and contacts. The social networks of these middle income residents were not primarily based on ethnic ties, though parents shared the ambivalence of lower income families about the impact of the declining importance of kinship ties on children's behaviour (Kileff 1975).

The term 'quasi-stabilisation' thus covered a situation in which some families were divided permanently, but almost all maintained rural ties, at least in part in order to retire to their rural homes on retirement. This pattern, it was once thought, would be transitional between a migrant labour situation and a fully stabilised urban population which would give up its claims to rural land and become proletarianised. Comparisons between the results of surveys in 1973/4, the mid-1980s and 1991 enable us to examine whether such a trend is discernible.

An urbanised present day population?

Migration controls were abolished at independence, despite periodic ineffectual attempts to return the 'able-bodied indigent' to rural areas. Mazur's study of selected rural areas in the early 1980s showed that out-migration of men was selective by education level, level of prosperity of the area of origin, area of land held by the farm household, and cattle ownership. Men with a higher level of education showed a greater propensity to migrate, as did men from wealthier and poorer areas rather than those with a middle level of resources. Migration rates were also found to be greatest among those with the largest and smallest landholdings, though this was affected by control over other productive resources. Thus members of households with little land tended to migrate primarily because the land area was inadequate, but this was exacerbated if cattle and equipment ownership was inadequate to work the land and mitigated if these resources were available. Similarly, migration was greatest from households with much land who could not work it effectively because of undercapitalisation. Little evidence was found that remittances received or brought back by migrants were used to improve agriculture. Instead, the need to hire labour in the absence of male household members precluded saving for cattle and equipment purchase and so perpetuated the need to continue hiring labour even when the migrant returned. The returned migrant sometimes then needed to turn to non-agricultural supplementary jobs to earn cash income (Mazur 1986/7).

The links between urban family members and their rural relatives perform complex economic and social functions. Before examining the lives of urban households, including their social characteristics and ties with the rural areas, the data available from Potts and Mutambirwa's surveys in the 1980s and our 1991 surveys (Rakodi with Withers 1993) in low income areas will be examined to see what light they throw on migration patterns from the urban end in recent years.

The 1991 surveys showed that, while the majority of household heads in the high density residential areas had lived in the rural areas prior to coming to Harare, 8% had been born in Harare, 21% had come from other urban areas and 8% from outside Zimbabwe. However, of the migrant heads, more than two-thirds had come to Harare before independence and a third had lived in the city for more than twenty years. These long term migrants are excluded from Potts and Mutambirwa's survey, which included only households whose head had migrated to Harare during or since 1980 (Potts and Mutambirwa 1990). A smaller proportion of the recent migrant heads in their sample were married (74%) than of the wider sample (81%). A slightly smaller proportion of households in their survey were divided: 23% had wives and/or children who normally lived in the rural areas compared to 27% in the 1991 survey. They also noted that a large proportion of the households in their surveys were landless, and they considered this to demonstrate that land shortage is a push factor in migration. However, in both the 1991 survey and Potts and Mutambirwa's survey in Glen Norah sites and services area, nearly a fifth of the household heads' wives lived in the rural areas for six months or more out of the year. The extent to which 'permanently' separated families choose or are forced into this pattern of living was addressed by Potts and Mutambirwa by asking whether those with absent family members wanted them to join the respondent in Harare. Two-thirds wished for this, which was considered by the authors to prove how drastically the circular migration of men diverged from people's preferences, but explanations for why they did not then live together were not explored.

Although neither of these surveys is directly comparable with the 1970s surveys, it is clear that male migration and family separation have not ended with independence. Among the factors that might influence the choice of such household strategies is access to housing in the city. Potts and Mutambirwa did not distinguish between households who owned their own houses and those who were tenants. In the 1991 survey it became clear that tenure was related to both age and migration history, but that the relationship was complicated by other factors. The great majority of adults marry and it is with marriage that most men are eligible to seek home ownership. Almost all the owner households in the sample were or had been married. Just over a quarter of tenant households had never married: these were young single people, mostly men, who preferred to rent. Some of these were recent migrants: the proportion of tenants who had migrated to Harare since 1980 was many times that of owners (63% compared to 14%). While, inevitably, owners in the older housing areas had lived in the city for a long time, even in the newer areas the housing allocation system favoured long-established urban residents. In Warren Park D, for example, nearly two-thirds of tenant households had moved to Harare since independence and a third in the five years prior to the survey, while 93% of owners had lived in the city before 1980. Only in the newest area of Budiriro were a significant proportion of allottees (26%) recent migrants, and only 4% had moved into the city in the previous five years.

While most married heads of household aspire to home ownership, therefore, not all of them, even those who have lived in the city for many years, succeed in obtaining a house of their own. The primary reason for this is the increasing lag of the supply of new housing for low income households behind demand (see Chapter 6). This shortfall is compounded by the cost of housing in relation to incomes. Most tenants rent one room, and their inability to gain access to a larger house may deter them from bringing their families to town: the proportion of tenant households with married heads who had wives who normally lived in the rural areas was double that of owners (30% compared to 16%). That such a decision may be partly but not solely due to housing conditions is demonstrated by the responses, but the data still do not allow us to assess what proportion of tenant households deliberately maintain living patterns for their families in which some members live in the rural areas, and what proportion are forced into such a strategy for economic or housing reasons.

Even among households in which the wives normally lived in the urban area, cultivation of rural land continues to be common (see below). The male low income population, once established in urban employment, tends to become urban, at least for the duration of a normal working life. That is not to say that no men are circular migrants—some still are, from preference or because of the obstacles to bringing their families to the urban areas. However, circular migration seems to have been maintained as a more widespread pattern for married women, who are less able to obtain access to urban wage or self-employment than men are, via traditional systems of rights to rural land for cultivation. It is also still the case that many men, on losing their jobs, have no choice but to return to the rural areas, and that many choose to do so on retirement (see below).

Although the concerns of earlier migration studies with the

'modernisation' of attitudes and lifestyles and the emergence of an African 'elite' reflected settler ideology and policy and have been of less interest to recent analysts, the migration process and the nature of urban–rural ties, as well as the implications of these for urban household characteristics and lifestyles, continue to fascinate.

Urban lives

The lives and livelihoods of urban households are, however, not just conditioned by their migration history, but by their opportunities for access to work, housing and facilities, which may vary by household type, including the gender of the household's head. Household strategies (Grown and Sebstad 1989; Rakodi 1991a) combine attempts to take advantage of urban economic and social activities provided by the formal private and public sectors, selective maintenance of rural and kinship ties, and productive but not necessarily income earning opportunities, especially urban food production. In urban areas, men's extra-domestic economic activity, which has been analysed in the previous chapter, is crucial for family maintenance and social standing. However, unlike agricultural activity, wage employment takes place outside the home, thus marginalising the domestic economy. The productive roles of women are, as described in Chapter 3, limited in town and the status of their reproductive activities reduced, even though they may be crucial to household strategies.

The social characteristics of households

In the dynamic situation produced by changing and gender-specific patterns of migration, analysis of household composition and size is fraught with difficulties. The household size data provided by the censuses are of limited value, and even overall population figures cannot be taken as reliable, especially in the absence of certainty that all households interpreted questions about normally resident household members in the same way. The average household size in Harare in 1982 was relatively small (3.6), reflecting the continued importance of single male migrants and the presence of smaller European households. In Chitungwiza, the average household size was slightly larger (4.1) (CSO 1989). In both cases the average household size had increased somewhat by 1992 (4.0 in Harare, 4.4 in Chitungwiza). The area breakdown of the 1982 census showed a range of average household sizes for different areas. Most of the high density residential areas had average household sizes of four or more, though those with a considerable number of lodgers had lower average household sizes. However, large average household sizes were by no means confined to the high density residential areas. In 1992 the smallest average household size was in the high income areas of Borrowdale and Highlands, but elsewhere the differences in average household size between low and high income areas appear to have blurred.

Household composition data are not available from the censuses, which may, as Schlyter (1989) notes, have included the members of some lodger or employee households with the main household where they shared a dwelling unit. However, a snapshot of household composition in selected areas during the dry season of 1991 is available from our household sample surveys (Rakodi with Withers 1993) in four low and five middle and high income areas chosen to represent different housing submarkets. Between 50 and 90 households were surveyed in each area, giving a total of 352 households in low income areas and 234 in middle and high income areas (excluding domestic workers). In this analysis, the two subsamples in Mabvuku (one of households renting-to-buy their houses from the city council, and the second of households who had purchased houses through the cessions procedure—see Chapter 6), are analysed separately.

In this survey, the overall average household size in high density residential areas was 4.5, similar to that revealed by the census, with the largest households in Mabvuku rent-to-buy houses. Overall, the average size of owner households (5.4) was twice that of tenants (2.7) (Table 4.5). In part, this difference is a life cycle effect. Over a quarter of tenant household heads had never married, compared to only 3% of owners. Owner household heads therefore tended to be older than tenant heads. The oldest tenant household heads were found in the oldest residential area (Mabvuku rent-to-buy) where many were former municipal tenants, and where three-quarters had lived in Harare for over 21 years, compared to less than half of all owners. The average age of household heads was considerably younger in Budiriro, the newest area, and in the Kuwadzana sample, in which most had bought houses from those to whom the plots were originally allocated. Overall, three-quarters of owners were 35 years old or more compared to only 27% of tenant household heads, 20% of owner heads were between 25 and 34 compared to 63% of tenant heads, and only 3% of owners were 24 years old or less compared to 10% of lodgers.

The characteristics of households in the middle and upper income areas were similar to those in low income areas: owners and the tenants of main houses had, on average, larger households than tenants of flats and domestic workers' houses, and they were generally older, except in

Table 4.5 Household characteristics in Harare residential areas in 1991

	Average household size			Average age of head		Never married	
	Total	Owners	Tenants	Owners	Tenants	Owners (%)	Tenants (%)
Warren Park D	3.9	5.5	2.5	42	31	2	32
Budiriro	4.7	5.1	2.6	38	33	–	18
Kuwadzana	4.1	5.4	2.5	57	30	2	30
Mabvuku rent-to-buy	5.6	5.9	3.9	54	34	2	22
Mabvuku cessions	4.6	5.3	3.1	41	35	9	18
Total	4.5	5.4	2.7	54	37	3	27
Hatfield	4.7	5.6	3.9	42	32	10	14
Mount Pleasant	4.3	4.3	–	48	–	–	–
Mabelreign	4.8	5.1	2.7	41	30	2	9
Houghton Park	4.9	4.9	–	36	–	4	–
Avenues	3.2	–	3.2	–	35	–	29
Total	4.4	5.0	3.0			5	18

Note: Owners and tenants of main houses grouped in Mount Pleasant and Houghton Park; the few owners in the Avenues flats have been grouped with tenants.

the newly developed area of Houghton Park (Table 4.5). As in high density residential areas, this was partly because younger single person households tended to be predominantly tenants.

Household situations and composition are, therefore, complex. Of the great majority of low income household heads who had married by the time of the survey, a third were married under civil law, a third had registered traditional marriages, a quarter had unregistered traditional marriages and the remaining 8% were mainly widowed. Owner households were more likely than married tenant heads to be married under civil law, and those married under traditional law were more likely to have registered marriages, both linked to house and plot allocation policies which required proof of marriage. A similar proportion of high and middle income households had married, but of these by far the majority had civil law marriages and fewer than a third had had traditional marriages. The rest were divorced or widowed. The differences relate both to racial composition and educational level, which in turn is related to income.

The marital status of the head was linked to household composition at the time of the survey, though this changes over time seasonally, during the household life cycle, and according to changes in individual circumstances. Nearly half the urban households were nuclear families (that is, spouses with some but not necessarily all of their children). Although polygamy is permitted, it has only ever been the relatively affluent few who have been able to practise it, and this appears to be still the case. As expected, nuclear households are more common among owners than tenants (Table 4.6). Many households had either more components than the basic nuclear unit or less. The small proportion with more accommodated additional relatives or, less typically, un-related members (9% overall and, as expected, more owners than tenants). Typically, the additional adults were siblings of the head or sometimes of his spouse. As in other central and southern African countries such as Zambia, fixed urban wages and small dwellings encourage households to resist traditional obligations to provide support to kin and to limit their hospitality to close relatives or short visits. Families may also include grandchildren of the head, or a parent of the head or his spouse. Three and four generation households did not occur among tenants, but made up 7% of owner households. Only some of the additional adults had incomes of their own; these may either be choosing to pool their incomes with those of the household on a long term basis or are potential heads of household in their own right, likely to form their own households on marriage or when accommodation becomes available. Other households had fewer components than a nuclear unit: a couple without (resident) children, a single adult with

Table 4.6 Household composition in Harare residential areas in 1991 (per cent)

Household type	High density residential areas		Medium and low density residential areas	
	Owners	Tenants	Owners	Tenants
Nuclear family	56	33	63	61
Nuclear family with relatives	10	7	12	–
Head of household with children	13	5	6	–
Single person	4	36	4	26
Other	17	19	15	13
Total	100	100	100	100

Note: Owners and tenants of main houses combined in medium and low density areas; 'tenants' refers to lodgers in guest cottages and domestic workers' houses.

children and/or relatives, or a single adult. An even higher proportion of medium and high income households, many of which are European with fewer kinship obligations, were nuclear families and far fewer were single person households, but a similar distinction between the owners and tenants of main houses and lodgers was found (Table 4.6). Some of these differences between owners and tenants will be taken up again in Chapter 6.

Compared to some other parts of the world—and compared to African rural areas, where male out-migration has resulted in high rates of de facto female headship—the proportion of female headed households in African urban areas is typically fairly low. This reflects societal marriage norms, women's disadvantaged access to urban economic activities and the relatively young age profile of African cities. Only 7% of low income households in 1991 in Harare were reported to have female heads, half the proportion revealed by the 1982 census for Harare and Chitungwiza as a whole, though whether the difference is real or merely illustrates a definitional problem is impossible to tell. While some had never married, the remainder were separated, divorced or, more commonly, widowed, and almost three-quarters owned their houses. A similarly low proportion of female headed households was found in medium and low income areas. The only exception was the Avenues, where 20% of household heads were women, mostly the tenants of flats. As household heads age, divorce and widowhood are likely to become more common. While these figures do not reveal the full extent of migration by single women, the establishment of independent urban households comprising a single woman still appears to be relatively uncommon. This is due in part to social and parental disapproval of young women migrating, in part to the early age of marriage and in part to the limited range of income earning opportunities (especially respectable ones) open to African women in urban areas, as discussed in Chapter 3. Many of the female headed households which did exist contained children and other relatives.

However, women find it difficult to get access to housing in their own right. They are under-represented on the housing waiting list, to be eligible for which applicants have to be in wage or licensed self-employment and to have children who are dependent on them. Even many of the legal informal economic activities on which women depend require licences, while newly divorced or widowed women are recorded on the date-order waiting list from their date of registration and not their arrival in town, and those supported by their children are not eligible. Married women cannot register without the consent of their husbands, ostensibly to prevent the allocation of two houses to one household, but in practice excluding separated and deserted women. Many households headed by women have no option but to rent, often a single room and often in the lowest rent areas such as Epworth. Those who do manage to gain access to secure accommodation are able to live with their children and add other members such as a mother or sister to increase income earning capacity or security. Investment in an owner-occupied house, if access to one can be obtained and it can be afforded, has high priority as a basis for forming an independent household over the composition of which women can have control, providing a base for income generating activity and ensuring security and a sense of identity. Unlike many male-headed households, none of the women heads in Schlyter's survey wished to return to the rural areas, which is understandable given their lack of entitlement to land (Schlyter 1989).

Urban—rural links

Ties with the rural areas throughout sub-Saharan Africa consist mainly of agricultural rights and kinship obligations. In our 1991 survey, which contained Harare-born and long term as well as recent migrant households, 39% of low income households claimed rights to rural land, a slightly lower proportion than among the recent migrant households surveyed in 1985 and 1988 by Potts and Mutambirwa (1990). Of those that could estimate the area of land that they were entitled to use, a quarter had small plots of less than 0.8 hectare, a third farms of between 0.8 and 1.6 hectares, and the remainder somewhat larger farms. Owners were, in general, more likely to own land and more likely, on average, to be entitled to a larger area, because of the greater age of the house-hold heads and their family responsibilities. Most urban households with access to land cultivated it, with women taking on much of the responsibility and work, though household heads, children, other relatives and wage labour were extensively used also. Production is of subsistence crops, which help to sustain the urban household and, in some cases, of cash crops, adding to household income.

Thirty-five per cent owned cattle, again similar to Potts and Mutambirwa's findings. Of the cattle owners, 62% owned between one and five cows, 23% between six and ten and 15% a substantial herd of eleven or more. Again, older and better off men were more likely to own cattle. Cattle ownership has continued to be important for the reasons noted earlier, though the payment of *roora*, while remaining almost universal, is no longer necessarily made in cattle and has in any case become an increasingly controversial practice (May 1983; Kazembe and Mol 1987). Many women—especially given the control over their labour, household property and children that its payment gives to their husbands or, in the event of death, their husbands' relatives—have come to see it as a capitalist transaction between men in which women are regarded merely as chattels (Kazembe and Mol 1987). Men, however, as illustrated in the government's backtracking over its women members' intention to challenge the system after independence, regard the payment as a token of thanks for bringing up girls, a symbol of a bond between two lineage groups and thus vital to the structure of society, and a substitute for future rights to children of their daughters'/nieces' marriages (Makamure 1970; May 1983; Seidman 1984). The continued health of cattle belonging to urban residents is ensured by communal herding arrangements and supervision by kin. Although land is now allocated by local councils, 'it is men who are allocated land as a right on behalf of the family. In effect it means that men still direct and control women's labour and have first call on the income deriving from agriculture or livestock sales' (Batezat et al 1988: 165; see also Kazembe 1986).

Almost half of the households in the 1991 survey had a rural house, with a slightly lower proportion of tenants than owners. Of those that hadn't (and who expressed an opinion), 62% intended to build in future, especially among tenants, who tend to be at an earlier stage in the life cycle. Building a house at home is thus something that comes with maturity and family obligations—of those with no rural house, the majority also had no land and nearly half of these were single unmarried adults without children. Of those with no house and no intention of building one, a half were aged 60 or more and had been in Harare for over 40 years, a quarter had migrated to Harare from another town, and the remaining quarter were non-Zimbabwean. If all those who intend to build succeed in doing so, eight out of ten urban low income households will have a rural house.

Potts and Mutambirwa were concerned about statements by some policymakers to the effect that urban residents should give up their rights to land, in view of the perceived pressure on land in the over-crowded Communal Areas. They concluded that overall, 85% of the land to which the urban residents in their sample had rights was used productively and could only be reallocated to households permanently resident in the Communal Areas at the cost of adverse effects on the urban households dependent on it for partial subsistence and, in a third of cases, cash income.

A further element in rural ties are the reciprocal economic flows, based on social obligations and cemented by social contacts. The primary economic obligation is of the urban cash earning household to its rural kin: firstly to members of the nuclear family, and secondly to kin of the male head. Three-quarters of low income households in the 1991 survey sent remittances to the rural areas, a quarter regularly and half when needed; only a quarter never did so. The proportion who sent remittances was higher among tenants than owners, not unexpectedly given the fact that more tenant household heads (22%) had a wife living in the rural areas. Typically, just under a fifth of the urban household's income was said to be remitted, though this varied with circumstances. Households with elderly or non-Zimbabwean heads are less likely to send money to rural relatives. In addition, when urban residents visit rural areas, gifts of money or manufactured food and other goods are usually taken. Transfers from rural areas were rarer. Few receive money, occasional gifts of food are more common. Drakakis-Smith and Kivell's (1990) findings from surveys in three suburbs, which suggest that a fifth of households receive gifts of food from the rural areas, bear out this two-way flow.

A third of the migrant household heads in Potts and Mutambirwa's survey, many of whom had no choice as they had no access to rural land, intended to remain in Harare permanently. For the remaining two-thirds, maintenance of rural links continues to be crucial to both short and long term economic security. Urban migrants, Potts and Mutambirwa conclude, juggle the need to increase household security by maintaining two bases for reproduction with their desire to live together as a nuclear family. The dependence on and maintenance of ties with the rural areas by low income urban households has not declined in recent years, and seems set to be an enduring feature of people's social and economic lives and a crucial element in their ability to cope with economic recession and personal misfortune. Maintenance of kinship ties and fulfilment of social and economic obligations to rural kin is not confined to low income urban residents: it is part of the social fabric of Zimbabwean society. A quarter of the households in Drakakis-Smith and Kivell's (1990) survey in middle income Mabelreign cultivated rural land and many middle and higher income households regularly visit rural kin, but they are not so dependent on access to rural areas for supplementing urban incomes and for surviving times of difficulty.

Urban agriculture

Another element in household strategies is urban food production, both on residential plots in low and high income areas (Figure 4.2) and on unused land in and around the urban area. Most houses in high income areas have a vegetable garden and indeed better access to land, labour and finance than low income households. Cultivation of gardens by low and middle income residents was explored in another survey in the late 1980s in the lower income areas of Glen View and Epworth and the middle income area of Mabelreign. The majority of households interviewed produced some crops on their plots: 'In both Glen View and Mabelreign, some four-fifths of those interviewed had gardens in which they grew food crops. In Epworth too, almost all gardens were used for food production, although only two-thirds had any garden space' (Drakakis-Smith and Kivell 1990: 173).

Generally, the emphasis was on vegetable production, though more households in Mabelreign and especially in Epworth produced staple cereals, such as maize and potatoes. Virtually all the production was for the household's own consumption—only in Epworth was a small proportion sold. Keeping chickens was also relatively common. Only about 10% of households admitted to cultivating land elsewhere in the city, although as this use of land is mostly illegal, this is likely to be an underestimate of its full extent. Most of those who did admit to off-plot cultivation lived in Epworth 'where there was more open space and where the influence of the authorities was less marked' (ibid). Of these plots, it was claimed that half were 'owned' by the household and a third by a church. Most were close to where respondents lived, though some were up to thirty minutes walk away (Drakakis-Smith and Kivell 1990).

The cultivation of food in African cities is widespread, and the food produced provides an important nutritional supplement for the poor. The relatively generous size of plots in Harare, even in low income areas (200–300 square metres) and the availability of piped water to every

Figure 4.2 Food production in urban areas. Plot owners here in Warren Park low income housing area have planted a variety of fruit trees, including bananas and pawpaws, and cultivate vegetables on plots (for example in the front garden of the house to the left). Reusable plastic refuse bags line the road ready for collection

plot facilitate on-plot gardening. Those who do not have access to on-plot gardens, however (that is, many tenants of rented rooms or backyard shacks) are forced to cultivate vacant land, of which there is a large amount in the city. Such cultivation of valleys, slopes, undeveloped plots and roadside verges, and even the keeping of livestock, is common in cities such as Nairobi, Dar es Salaam and Kampala, and is increasingly accepted by city councils as a fact of urban life. Harare City Council has traditionally tried to prevent the cultivation of streambank areas, because of the belief that run-off will lead to silting of the watercourses which are important for the city's water supply. Prior to 1985/6 the council tried to educate urban residents on the negative effects of urban cultivation, but when the number of cultivators continued to grow, it began to destroy crops (Mbiba 1994), because urban cultivation contravenes regulations inherited from colonial days or does not fit ideas about the 'modern city' (Drakakis-Smith 1992). In addition, crops on council owned land are slashed when it is needed for development, despite the protests of cultivators, and regulations prohibiting the keeping of livestock are vigorously enforced (Mbiba 1994). Mbiba (1993) is of the opinion that since the severe drought of 1991/2 off-plot cultivation has become more widespread, but that newcomers are finding it increasingly difficult to obtain access to land.

To try to control the activity, the city council allocated periurban areas to cooperatives of cultivators from the urban area (see Chapter 3). Food shortages in 1992 and continued protests when mature crops are slashed may be contributing to a more permissive atmosphere, but the more positive support needed to increase productivity whilst safeguarding against environmental damage has not yet been provided (Mbiba 1994). Given the impoverishment of urban families, the production of staple cereals and vegetables for their own use is for many a vital element in their survival.

Men's and women's lives

For most urban men, life is governed by the routine of the working day, typically starting at 7 or 8 am following a journey to work of between 45 and 60 minutes (often more if going from Chitungwiza to Harare) by bus, on foot or by emergency taxi. Most people are paid monthly so expenditure patterns for household necessities and recreation take on a monthly pattern of variation. The only aspect of men's social lives on which research has been carried out (in the early 1970s) is drinking, which always seems to have been a central social activity. In particular, their social lives revolved around the municipal beerhalls, though some drinking occurred at home and in shebeens (May 1973). Drinking had always been part of rural life, where it fulfilled ritual as well as social and work functions, the latter when beer was brewed as a reward for labour contributions to a work party. For early migrants, the absence of kin group members and the timebound nature of urban employment left leisure hours with little to do except rest and drink. This was recognised, controlled and profited from with the institution of a municipal monopoly on beer sales and the establishment of beerhalls. The social life of men is still centred on drinking with friends. Drinking has always formed a much less significant part of the majority of women's lives, not being considered respectable for married women.

Information on the other important elements in men's social lives, especially the churches, is lacking, while there does not seem to be any other information on women's lives. The only recent follow-up study of the use of leisure time (Child and Heath, 1989) had very limited purposes (to determine actual and potential demand for outdoor recreation facilities used during day, weekend and holiday visits) and a Eurocentric definition of leisure time. Thus it throws little light on everyday use of free time by urban residents, other than to show that in the early 1980s, for a quarter of black households (roughly equivalent to the low income households) the first choice for day visits was city parks, compared to 10% of whites, falling a long way behind dams and lakes as the favoured destination for all races and income groups. For weekend visits, the pattern changes. Over a half of blacks' first choice of destination for a weekend, and over 60% for holidays of a week or more, is the Communal Areas; whereas these, as expected, figure as a preferred destination for only a third of middle and about 7% of high income households.

Church denominations have, as in many African countries, proliferated and church membership is widespread, but no research seems to have been done into its social implications. For some, it results in the forswearing of drinking as a focus of social activity. Many urban residents, especially women, belong to income-sharing groups, in which a small circle of friends and neighbours pool money and take it in turns to receive the pool. As in many other Third World cities, such groups help families to meet occasional expenditure needs. When men do the same, it is generally with workmates. Contributions to burial societies help many to deal with the costs of family funerals, but for everyday borrowing, kinship networks are most crucial.

Urban life provides economic and social opportunities which for many are greater than those in rural areas. This is illustrated by, for example, comparisons between urban and rural incomes (even if the latter include income in kind) and health indicators. In 1980 the income ratio for whites, urban blacks and rural blacks was $39:5:1$. Health indicators also reflected the better access to clean water and sanitation as well as health facilities in urban areas—for example in the incidence of childhood malnutrition, or in infant mortality rates, the ratio for which in 1980 was $1:3.5:10$ per 1000 live births for the white, urban black and rural black populations respectively (Loewenson and Sanders 1988: 134; Davies and Sanders 1988). Everywhere, infant and maternal mortality and child under-nutrition decreased in the years immediately after independence and urban–rural differences probably declined as government spending shifted to the rural areas (Loewenson and Sanders, 1988). However, urban residents have been particularly vulnerable to the effects of structural adjustment programmes, including wage freezes; abolition of subsidies, especially on food; delays in increasing the income ceiling which determines eligibility for free health care; and increases in the cost of infrastructure and services as a result of attempts to improve the financial position of local authorities. All of these are particularly serious for the poor.

In urban areas, men's extra-domestic activity is crucial for family maintenance and social standing, and men are designated heads of household, which conveys various legal rights, despite the legislation ending the minor legal status of women in 1982. However, unlike agricultural activity, wage employment takes place outside the home, thus marginalising the domestic economy, with its productive and reproductive roles (Auret 1990). Wage employment is beyond the wife's ability to influence it, or control its proceeds, thus reducing her informal power as well as reinforcing her economic dependence (May 1979). Crop production in both urban and rural areas is one of the few alternatives open to women in low income households to regain a degree of economic autonomy, given the limited income earning opportunities open to women in town, and the illegal nature of some of these (beer brewing, unlicensed hawking, prostitution) (Seidman 1984). Only a minority of urban black households, even in high income areas, have severed their ties with the rural areas—for the majority these ties fulfil not only social functions but also vital economic functions for both men and women, and there is little sign that they will decline, at least as long as a significant proportion of urban households retain rights to the use of rural land.

5

The land development process

In all cities, the residential property market is dominated by exchanges of the existing housing stock, and construction or purchase of new development forms a relatively small proportion of total transactions. This is true of cities in developing countries and it is, therefore, important to examine the exchange of dwellings. However, the rapid growth experienced by such cities makes the supply of new housing much more important than in the cities of industrialised countries, where demand for new housing often arises out of changes in income levels, household structure and preferences rather than population growth. Land is thus both essential for new building to cope with urban growth and an element in the value of residential (and other) property. Land available for new development is determined by a combination of physical, economic and administrative factors.

It is clear from the discussion in Chapter 1 that physical constraints on Harare's development are insignificant: although there are minor topographical difficulties in some areas, and topography influences the ease with which physical infrastructure is provided, ample land physically suitable for development is available in and around both Harare and Chitungwiza. This chapter will, therefore, focus firstly on the public and private sector actors in the land development process, their aims, motives and behaviour, and secondly on the paths by which land is developed.

Actors in the land development process

Private sector actors

Private sector actors in the land development process in Harare have included the owners of farms initially subdivided and sold by the British

South Africa Company; individual and corporate owners of partly or wholly subdivided land within the city; individual and corporate developers of land for commercial and residential purposes; and intermediaries in the land development process, including estate agents, surveyors and financial institutions. In theory, these actors respond to economic factors of demand and supply. In practice, their motives are mixed, and their actions are influenced not only by market conditions but also by private sector attempts to regulate the land development process and by trends in the country's political economy.

The early development of Salisbury has been described in Chapter 2. While some early owners developed their plots productively for residential, commercial and agricultural use, others were very conscious of the potential value of their land if the township should become established and start to grow. So little investment was tied up in the original land allocation or purchase that landholders could afford to wait. Land was brought forward for development within the town and for subdivision for residential townships outside the original boundary as and when demand increased. The scale of development was small and owners of individual plots or stands generally commissioned one-off buildings. With the exception of the development of flats near the central business district (CBD) (see Chapter 6), most private sector residential development consisted of individual houses. Subdivision of land and development of the housing stock proceeded in fits and starts. Often, subdivision ran ahead of development, but water supply from boreholes and septic tank sanitation made this piecemeal pattern of development feasible. Gradually, as areas within the original and later 1971 boundaries became built up, the infrastructure was upgraded: road surfaces were improved, piped water supply was installed, some areas were connected to waterborne sewage disposal systems, and electricity and telephone connections became universal. Nevertheless, there are still large numbers of stands within Harare's boundary which remain undeveloped today. The ownership of this land and the attitudes and motives of its owners to its development will help to determine the price of land for and the future pattern of urban development.

From the outset, property ownership was every settler's aim. Accurate surveys and clear registration of title were, therefore, essential. The legislation which provided the basis for the system of tenure and title deeds registration and the system established to administer it were modelled on the British system and geared to protect the interests of the settlers. However, they also provided for public access to the Deeds Registry, which is in two parts: a plot by plot record and a personal record showing the extent of ownership for every owner.

From the second half of the 1970s, the increasing success of the liberation struggle was accompanied by economic stagnation and increased white emigration. Investment in residential, industrial and commercial development halted and much property came up for sale. As a result, prices were depressed (see below). Not until the mid-1980s did demand for residential property start to match supply and prices start to rise. By that time a shortage of modestly priced middle income dwellings had emerged. It began to look as if conditions were right for new residential development to start up again, for the first time since the early 1970s. However, very little new land was coming up for sale and few developments were starting. Concern began to be expressed at the amount of undeveloped land available within existing subdivided areas, and speculation was rife about who owned it and why they were holding it vacant.

Studies using the Valuation Roll and Deeds Register tried to throw some light on the issue (Rakodi 1993). There was a considerable amount of vacant land within the overall built-up area of Harare in the mid-1980s. An analysis of the 1985/6 Valuation Roll showed that in the part of the city covered (that is, excluding high density areas), there were 37 922 stands, of which 81% were developed and 7098 undeveloped (Table 5.1). In the so-called built-up area, almost all of the developed residential plots were in private ownership. Most of these contained a single house with domestic workers' quarters. The largest stands were in Borrowdale, followed by Waterfalls, Highlands, Greendale, Mount Pleasant and Marlborough. Five years later, according to a 1990 National Property Association survey, 8545 stands were undeveloped (*Herald*, 17 December 1990). In all these areas, there is arguably scope for more intensive use of the 'developed' land and further subdivision of stands, in addition to bringing forward idle land for development.

The total undeveloped residential area was 6692 hectares, potentially capable of accommodating 16 700 houses if the standard 4000 square metre plot continues to be used and even more if smaller plots were to be permitted. Of this land, a third was in Greendale, followed by Borrowdale with over a fifth, Waterfalls, Harare West and Hatfield. A larger proportion of undeveloped stands than of developed stands were in public sector ownership (28.2% compared to 3.7%), mostly central government. However, these represented only 8% of the total area of undeveloped land. Thus although central government owned over a quarter of undeveloped stands, mostly in Harare South, these were relatively small and accounted for only 4% of the undeveloped area. The city council also owned 4% of the undeveloped area, potentially sufficient for 1300 plots of 2000 square metres. These stands were scattered throughout the city, some inherited from townships absorbed

Table 5.1 Developed and undeveloped residential land in Harare, 1985/6

District	Developed land				Undeveloped land			
	Stands No.	%	Area (ha)	Average size (m²)	Stands No.	%	Area (ha)	Average size (m²)
Borrowdale	2 783	9.0	2 859.5	10 275	1 251	17.6	1 487.9	11 893
Greendale	2 576	8.4	1 404.2	5 451	425	6.0	2 150.1	50 592
Harare C and E	2 324	7.5	394.5	1 697	83	1.2	60.5	7 284
Harare S	3 181	10.3	342.7	1 077	1 611	22.7	66.0	7 414
Harare N	3 120	10.1	897.7	2 877	599	8.4	12.0	3 039
Harare W	3 099	10.0	775.9	2 503	576	8.1	57.5	9 505
Hatfield	2 179	7.1	380.3	1 745	427	6.0	414.1	9 697
Highlands	2 675	8.7	1 643.5	6 144	422	6.0	265.6	6 295
Mabelreign	2 801	9.1	794.0	2 835	158	2.2	301.9	19 109
Marlborough	2 487	8.1	1 002.8	4 032	94	1.3	82.1	8 729
Mount Pleasant	1 903	6.2	919.7	4 833	280	3.9	215.4	7 693
Waterfalls	1 696	5.5	1 042.6	6 147	1 172	16.6	918.4	7 836
Ownership								
City Council	1 047	3.4	301.0	2 875	117	1.6	259.0	22 139
Central government	107	0.3	21.7	2 028	1 887	26.6	269.5	1 428
Private	29 670	96.3	12 134.5	4 090	5 094	71.8	6 163.7	12 100
Total	30 824	100.0	12 457.3	4 041	7 098	100.0	6 692.2	9 428

Source: Valuation Roll.

into the city boundary at the beginning of the 1970s. Some have subsequently been developed by the council for middle income housing. However, over 90% of undeveloped land was in private sector ownership.

Although it is possible to ascertain who owns undeveloped land in Harare, this information is not readily available. The National Property Association survey revealed one owner of 200 residential plots, but confidentiality rules prevented further use of the Valuation Roll to analyse patterns of ownership of undeveloped land in the urban area. From the Deeds Registry it was possible to analyse ownership, not city-wide but for three study areas: Mount Pleasant, one of the oldest privately developed residential areas in northern Harare; Borrowdale, a newer and higher income suburb; and Hatfield, an older area to the south of the city centre. In the Mount Pleasant study area 16 undeveloped stands were identified (with an average size of 5638 square metres), in Borrowdale 19 (again, predominantly in stands of just over 4000 square metres), and in Hatfield 31. In Hatfield, a more varied range of stand sizes was found (mean 1.44 hectares) (Table 5.2).

In all the areas, the stands were predominantly owned by private individuals (83% overall) rather than companies (6%), the city council (9%), or other organisations (2%). However, corporate bodies tended to own larger areas. Of the pieces of undeveloped land, a fifth were one hectare or more in area, with the largest being 15.23 hectares in Hatfield (owned by a private individual since 1969) and 14.53 hectares in Borrowdale (owned by a property company). Of the individuals owning the undeveloped stands studied, 68% did not own another property in Harare, and none more than three. However, of the three private companies, one owned three other properties, one seven and the third twelve. Current owners range from those who have purchased a stand recently to those who bought a stand at the time of original subdivision (mean length of ownership 7 years in Hatfield, 11 years in Mount Pleasant and 12 years in Borrowdale) (see Table 5.2). Although Hatfield was the scene of some of the earliest subdivisions, dating from 1924, its shorter mean length of ownership is due to recent activity in the land market, with a greater proportion of undeveloped stands having been subdivided or sold since 1985. Although there clearly is speculative capitalist investment, especially by larger private corporate landowners, and especially in the more exclusive northern suburbs, many of the stands have been in long term ownership.

Much of the undeveloped land is subdivided, accessible and serviced. The questions then are:

Table 5.2   Undeveloped land in three study areas in Harare, 1991

	Mount Pleasant		Borrowdale		Hatfield	
Stand size, private owners (m^2)						
	No. stands		No. stands		No. stands	
4 000 or less	1		2		7	
4 001–5 000	14		12		5	
5 001–9 999	–		3		7	
10 000–19 999	1		1		6	
20 000 or more	–		1		3	
Total	16		19		28	
Mean	4 638m^2		12 766m^2		14 400m^2	
Owner						
	No. stands	% of area	No. stands	% of area	No. stands	% of area
Private individual	13	83.7	16	37.6	28	85.0
Private company	2	10.9	2	60.7	–	–
Government	–	–	–	–	–	–
Other organisations	1	5.4	1	1.7	–	–
City of Harare	3	n.a.	–	–	3	15.0
Total	19	100.0	19	100.0	31	100.0
Total number of properties owned by private owners in study areas						
	No.	%	No.	%	No.	%
0	7	58.3	8	53.4	19	76.0
1	2	16.7	3	20.0	3	12.0
2	1		2	13.3	3	12.0
3	1	25.0	1	13.3	–	–
7	–		1		–	–
12	1		–		–	–
No record	4	–	4	–	3	–
Total	16	100.0	19	100.0	28	100.0
Length of current ownership						
1 year	2	12.5	3	15.8	8	28.6
2–5 years	2	12.5	4	21.1	5	17.8
6–9 years	5	31.3	2	10.5	8	28.6
10+ years	7	43.7	10	52.6	7	25.0
Not stated	3	–	–	–	3	–
Total	19	100.0	19	100.0	31	100.0

Source: Deeds Registry.

- What is preventing owners developing the land?
- What measures can government or the council take to ensure that land ripe for development is brought forward for development or sale?

Some possible answers to the first question will be explored here and the second taken up again in Chapter 7. The cost of constructing new housing has, since independence, been above the cost of secondhand properties (see below), deterring new investment and encouraging owners to retain land in their ownership on the assumption that demand will increase in the future. Although conditions are more favourable today, the cost of credit for construction has increased and building materials are in short supply. Owners include emigrants who were unable to sell land on their departure and with some of whom their agents have lost contact. Some owners have held their land for a long time, and their motive may not be short term profit; some, especially the elderly, may be unaware of the value of their land. In addition, if the capital is not needed in the short term, the uncertainties over whether a seller of land will benefit from the proceeds may have deterred many from selling. Thus many underdeveloped stands in the CBD belong to emigrants, who are prohibited from exporting most of the proceeds of sale and instead have to invest much of the sale price received in government bonds. They prefer, therefore, to continue to receive rents, even though these are less than the land could yield if redeveloped.

Public sector actors

The public sector actors that intervene directly in the land development process are the local authorities, through their acceptance of responsibility for providing land for low income housing and industrial development. However, they also have indirect roles in planning and regulating land use, and in raising property taxes—as does central government through policy formulation and legislation, administration of the tenure system, and its financial and other powers over local government.

In Chapter 1 I described the settlers' need for urban centres to provide services to mining and agricultural enterprises and a base for the development of manufacturing, and I analysed the policies that were adopted to ensure an adequate but controlled supply of unskilled and semi-skilled black labour. The adoption of a strongly interventionist role in economic policy, especially the development of industry, and in labour supply led logically to particular urban policies, notably the allocation of land for future urban uses and the provision of rented housing and associated social services for the 'temporarily' resident migrant labour supply. The evolution of a locally financed system of urban government designed to achieve a high quality environment for the urban white population and what were considered appropriate (but lower) environmental standards for the urban black population has been described in Chapter 1. The land administration, planning, property taxation and local government systems were inherited largely intact from the settler government. Post-independence changes in central–local relations, local government structures and the management of urban development were also sketched in Chapter 1, and aspects of the administration and development of Harare itself were described in Chapter 2. To flesh out the picture so far presented, the remainder of this chapter will analyse the land development process in more detail, and the subsequent chapter will concentrate on housing.

The paths by which land is developed

Patterns of interaction between economic and non-economic factors determine the paths by which land is developed and the capacity of land supply mechanisms to meet urban demand. Land supply for urban development in Harare is dualistic. The supply of land for formerly European housing (broadly, upper and middle income group housing) has been expected to be provided by the market, while almost all property transactions in this sector are private. In non-settler colonial cities in migrant labour systems, where the expatriate administrators were also regarded as temporary residents, the public sector took responsibility for providing them with rented housing and thus much land was retained in public ownership. In the settler societies, reliance on the market was greater. The supply of land for housing 'low income' groups (formerly Africans), however, has always been regarded as a public sector responsibility. Rights in land have both economic and social dimensions—they are viewed as a commodity and a factor in production, but also represent social relations and cultural assumptions. Typically, in the cities of developing countries, systems of overlapping tenure arrangements exist, including a formal official statutory system, an informal system, and indigenous or customary tenure. People may own and deal with land in more than one legal system, while land itself may be affected by more than one system, giving rise to conflicting rights and duties and considerable confusion (Farvacque and McAuslan 1991). In Zimbabwe, an imported tenure system was introduced into the large areas of the country appropriated by the colonial settlers, while communal tenure, which is not registered through the formal system of title deeds, persisted in the areas allocated to the African population (Chapter 1).

Private sector residential and commercial development

The market in undeveloped land and supply responses to changing demand can be assessed by the examination of prices and exploration of the reasons why so much land in the city remains undeveloped even though physical infrastructure is available. The second issue has already been discussed above, so this section will concentrate on the first. However, in any city and especially in Harare, land markets are affected strongly by policies and procedures, including tenure and title deeds registration, land use regulation and land taxation, and these also need to be incorporated in the analysis.

In studying land markets, it is desirable to examine and explain both long term trends in land prices, which affect patterns of urban development, and short term trends, which illustrate the relationship between demand and supply. Land price information in Harare is not published, but the use of the Deeds Registry information collected for the three study areas referred to above together with advertised sale prices for land enable a picture of the market in undeveloped land to be built up (Rakodi 1993). The price of each transaction in the pieces of undeveloped land identified in Mount Pleasant, Borrowdale and Hatfield was recorded in the Deeds Registry. The samples were too small to provide wholly reliable data on price trends. Also, they indicated wide variations in prices paid, both between the areas and for different stands within the areas. Strictly, account should be taken of possible influences on price, including zoning, size of stand, location within an area, topography and service provision. It has not been possible to do this, so prices for transactions in a single year have been averaged. Wide variations in prices within the areas conceal inter-area differences but, generally, land has changed hands at higher prices in Mount Pleasant and Borrowdale than in Hatfield, which might be expected from their relative locations. Overall average prices for all the areas, subject to some adjustment and interpretation, have been plotted in Figure 5.1. Because of the lack of appropriate indicators for the long time period covered, they have not been corrected for inflation. The graph indicates rising prices in the late 1940s as in-migration and postwar economic recovery generated demand for land and housing. Prices also rose in the second half of the 1950s, during federation. A fall

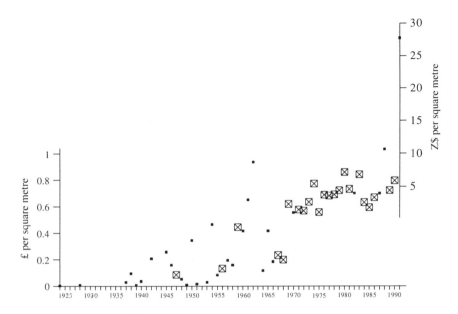

Figure 5.1 Long term trends in land prices (three study areas). ■ average for year; ⊠ average based on more than 4 transactions

in the mid-1960s illustrated the impact of wider economic problems, but was followed by a recovery and gentler increase through the 1970s, while confidence remained high. Falling prices at the end of the 1970s and in the first half of the 1980s showed the effect of political uncertainty and European emigration. They were succeeded by increases in the second half of the 1980s, but to little more than the 1980 level, even in cash terms.

In order to ascertain geographical patterns in the price of undeveloped land and to analyse recent trends in more detail, data on the asking price of land offered for sale were collected for June–August 1990, January–August 1991, and August 1993. As far as possible, land advertised more than once was eliminated, and land zoned for the development of flats or for industrial or commercial purposes is not included. A total of 452 stands were offered for sale during the study period, two-thirds of them (64%) in the northern and northeastern suburbs, 18% in the southern suburbs including Hatfield and Waterfalls, and the remainder in west or east Harare. Of the plots offered for sale, 39% were of 2500 square metres or less in area, a proportion heavily influenced by the coming on to the market of a single subdivision of 144 serviced stands of 2000 square metres each in Marlborough in February

1991; and 31% were between 2501 and 5000 square metres in size, predominantly the standard one acre (4000 square metres) stands. The remaining 30% of stands were larger than 5000 square metres, some (7%) of two hectares or more. These were predominantly concentrated in the northeastern suburbs.

The price of land varied with stand size and location. The price per square metre was highest for land zoned for the development of flats and town houses, and the few sites available for sale were mostly located in Avondale. However, the price per square metre for 4000 square metre plots was also slightly higher than that for larger stands, especially those which would need subdivision and the provision of infrastructure. Prices and price trends also varied geographically. The highest prices (per square metre) were in the most prestigious north-eastern suburbs, though the northern, western and eastern suburbs did not lag far behind (Figure 5.2). Over a study period from June 1990 to August 1991, the price trends in these areas were generally upward, with some variation around the trend. Prices in the southern suburbs were lower, reflecting their less desirable location, and the upward trend in prices was less marked. A small number of landholdings without significant agricultural or building development were advertised for sale in the urban fringe (up to about 50 kilometres from the city) at prices about a quarter of those within the city boundaries, but ten times or more those of agricultural land.

The overall average price of land increased from about Z$14 per square metre in mid-1990 to well over Z$30 per square metre in mid-1992. Allowance for inflation can be made by plotting this increase against the Consumer Price Index for high income urban households (Figure 5.3). The increase in land prices was, until mid-1991, markedly higher than the inflation rate, but then fell back in nominal terms to a level similar to that at the end of 1990, while inflation continued. Around the turn of the decade, price trends would have led us to expect an increase in the supply of land, subdivided stands, and new speculative housing coming on to the market. The data on vacant land do not, however, indicate any consistent recent upward trend in the amount of land offered for sale. Land is physically available, as we have already noted, but the presence of undeveloped land cannot be equated with a ready supply of building land. Other significant influences on the rate of new construction include constraints on construction itself, and policies and procedures related to tenure, land use planning and land taxation.

As the urban centres were built on 'European' land, it was not until the later 1970s that Africans could do more than rent houses owned by employers or municipalities in them. Formal freehold and leasehold

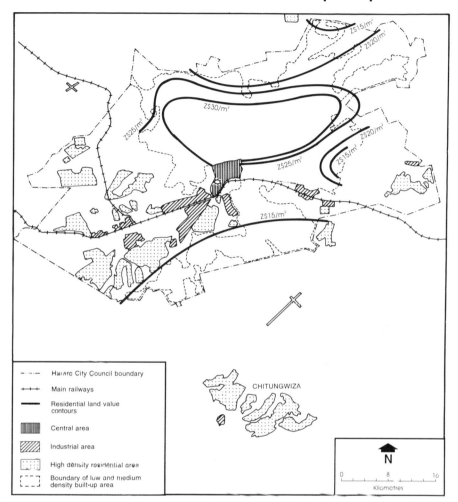

Figure 5.2 Residential land values (early 1991)

tenure was thus introduced by the settlers, but it was adopted and reinforced by the post-independence government. Perhaps because of the earlier exclusion of urban Africans from secure tenure and property as a source of accumulation, house ownership is a high priority for all income groups and was politically endorsed from the outset by the new government. The government's aim, therefore, has been, firstly, to transfer the areas of previously municipally owned rental housing to tenants by means of an Agreement of Sale under which freehold ownership is transferred on completion of the necessary payments (see

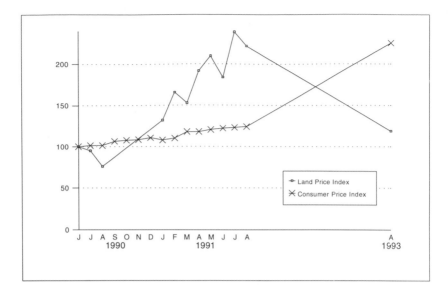

Figure 5.3   Land price trends in Harare, June 1990 to August 1991. Sources: CSO 1991, 1992; Monthly Digest of Statistics 1993. (CPI recalculated from 1990, no longer distinguishing between higher and lower income groups)

Chapter 6) and, secondly, to base new urban development on the existing formal system of land tenure. Informality has not been tolerated (see Chapter 2). Unlike other cities in Africa, therefore, informal and customary systems of tenure do not, at present, coexist and overlap with the formal system in urban areas.

Private developers may acquire land on the open market, subdivide it and service it for development, or they may be sold land by a local authority. If the land is outside the urban area, the Ministry of Lands, Agriculture and Rural Resettlement must certify that the government has no interest in acquiring it. Transactions are normally handled on behalf of the buyer and seller by estate agents and conveyancers. Title must then be registered (Figure 5.4). Subdivision permission is sought from the relevant local authority and when it is obtained, a cadastral survey is carried out, an activity which need only take a few weeks, but, in practice, because of the shortage of surveyors, may take months. The survey has to be approved by the Surveyor General, whose department is itself short of staff. If the developer services the land, the process may be completed in 12–18 months (Butcher 1989). A crucial set of actors is omitted from the diagram—namely landowners—as are later stages in the process of development, including procedures for

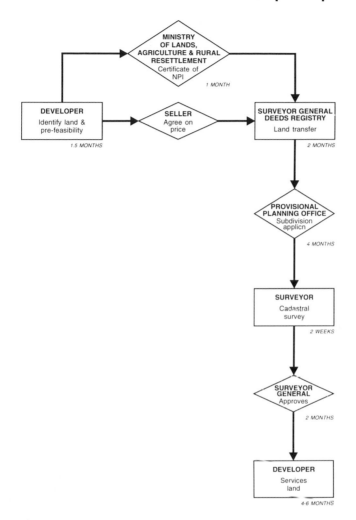

Figure 5.4 Land delivery procedures followed by private developers (average lead time 1–1.5 years). Source: Butcher 1989 (with permission)

obtaining development permission; mechanisms for securing finance by developers, contractors and purchasers alike; and the process of construction, which is subject to delays and constraints (see Chapter 6).

The system of registration is painstakingly administered. However, there are only two Deeds Registries (in Harare and Bulawayo) to cover the whole country, the system is entirely manual, and procedures are complex and slow (Mutizwa-Mangiza 1991b). Delays may occur less in the title registration process than in the requirements for individual boundary surveys of each plot, given the shortage of registered surveyors. Although well organised, the capacity of the system to keep pace with urban growth and its suitability for low income owner-occupiers is less clear.

Land use planning and regulation has been discussed in Chapter 1 and its application in Harare in Chapter 2. Although ostensibly modelled on the British system, the Southern Rhodesian system of planning was more of a zoning system within the areas covered by Town Planning Schemes, complemented by controls over subdivision. The standards adopted in Town Planning Schemes were high, influenced by attitudes to land and space, the cultural divide between the dominant European group and the subordinate African majority, and engineers' ideas about appropriate standards for road construction and sanitation in an African context. Minimum plot sizes were reinforced by minimum building clauses designed to ensure a minimum quality of construction. The existing Outline Plan and Town Planning Schemes, with their rigid land use zoning, which provided the basis for development control until 1976, in practice continued to do so for many years, though they have gradually been replaced by a Master Plan and Local Plans, as described in Chapter 2.

Permission for development must be sought under Part IV of the 1976 Regional, Town and Country Planning Act, which requires the local authority to carry out appropriate consultations and may require the applicant to notify neighbours to the proposed development and invite objections and representations. Applicants may appeal to the Administrative Court against refusal of permission or the conditions imposed, and to the Supreme Court on points of law. Provision is made for controls over subdivision, including the reservation of land for public uses, and for enforcement. The main way in which flexibility in the face of changing circumstances is allowed for is by a provision for 'special consent' to be given where the development would benefit the public and/or would not adversely affect the character or amenity of the neighbourhood. A review of the development control system concluded that it was basically efficient and was only responsible for delays in determining the outcome of applications in a limited number of cases (Manyere 1989). However, only 38% of applications in 1988 were determined within three months, and there was evidence of increasing pressure on the system: an increase in special consent applications, a decrease in the proportion of decisions reached in under three months, an increase in the number of appeals and enforcement notices, and an increase in illegal development (together with an increasingly sympathetic attitude to it by the Administrative Court). If many delays are due to applicants incorrectly completing applications, this may illustrate difficulty in understanding complex requirements.

Because in so many African cities development control systems are ineffective and unauthorised development is widespread, it is important to understand how and why Harare is different. The development control system in Harare appears to be successful in the sense that the administrative procedures work well if bureaucratically, little illegal development has occurred, there is a general culture in which the right of the city council to take action against unauthorised development is accepted, and the system creates a climate of certainty with respect to development. However, plan preparation is non-participatory, the approach to planning and development control is inflexible and reactive, and the standards imposed are unnecessarily high. The climate of certainty provided by a relatively rigid planning system benefits property capital, especially large scale commercial investors and high income residents, who maintained political dominance until 1980. Although it penalises the lower income residents, who suffer from planning standards supposedly imposed in the public interest, rigid density controls and the periodic demolition of illegal structures, the majority appear to have accepted the city council's right to enforce the system. Residents of low income areas were excluded from the direct implementation of control over private development for many years, though not excluded from its influence. Its gradual extension into the parts of the city where they live is likely to give rise to increasing problems.

In addition to tenure and land use planning, the third set of policies and procedures which influence patterns of new construction are those related to land taxation. Revenue for local government operations and services in the former European areas was generated by user charges for services such as electricity, water, sewerage and refuse removal, licences for vehicles, shops and bars, and rates on land and property. Services such as water and electricity (responsibility for which was transferred to the Zimbabwe Electricity Supply Authority in 1986/7) are expected to recover their costs. Rates are levied on residential, commercial and industrial property and based on capital value. They are set annually, subject to central government approval, and revaluation is supposed to take place every seven years. The system of collection, notification of arrears and enforcement is backed up by an acceptance among urban residents and councillors that the rates must be paid and that annual increases are necessary (Pasteur 1992). Until recently, arrears were not a serious problem, though it is said that this is changing as a result of the adverse impacts of the intensified structural adjustment programme on urban residents. In 1984/5, rates contributed 18.6% of Harare City Council's total revenue, despite being based on a 1975 assessment

(Wekwete 1989c). Quite a large proportion of property is exempt from rates, mainly central government property, public sector uses and charitable and educational institutions. The Tax Commission's recommendation that central government buildings should pay 50% of their rate liability (Zimbabwe 1986a) was rejected by government. The main purpose of property taxation is to raise revenue. Although the rates on land and buildings are differentiated, the relatively small differential (1.399 c/Z$ and 0.982 c/Z$ respectively) has not helped to solve the problem of unutilised land discussed above. Former African residential areas have, to date, been subject to a different system of taxation, which will be discussed below.

For capital expenditure, councils are dependent largely on borrowing from central government. Although Harare City Council is allowed to borrow from private sector institutions, this right has been severely curtailed since independence. The funds for infrastructure investment made available by central government have been less than needed. So far, however, Harare's ability to invest in general infrastructure provision has been greater than that of many other urban centres. This can be explained by its political importance, relatively healthy financial state, ability to cope with the infrastructure needs arising from population growth by incremental investment, and plentiful undeveloped land in areas already provided with infrastructure.

Low income residents and the supply of housing land

The government's commitment to improving living conditions for its low income urban population since independence has been expressed in increases in minimum wages (see Chapter 3), improvements in health and education, and housing policies and programmes. These last have focused on the 'right-to-buy' previously municipal rented housing (see Chapter 6), and the continued provision of serviced plots for house construction. The provision of serviced plots depends, among other inputs, on a publicly administered land supply programme.

Land in public sector ownership from the outset, or purchased from farmers who are willing to sell, has been used for public housing schemes and allocated to households on the local authority's waiting lists according to criteria applicable at the time. In the years leading up to independence, emphasis in public housing policy shifted from the provision of municipal housing for rent to serviced plot programmes for home ownership. The focus on home ownership in sites and services schemes has been maintained since independence. Individual property ownership has been regarded as compatible with socialism, explicitly 'to provide security of tenure and expand credit facilities [that is, building society finance] for the beneficiaries of housing schemes funded by the Public Sector' (Zimbabwe ndb: 4). Implicitly, the ideological importance of access to land and ownership of property, and the use value of owner-occupied housing, have underpinned the emphasis on home ownership. However, the supply of new housing has failed to keep pace with the need arising from population growth. There are a variety of reasons for this failure, some of which will be discussed in Chapter 6. Here, the question of the extent to which land supply is a constraining factor will be addressed.

Until the mid-1970s, rates of urban growth were relatively slow, and Harare inherited large areas of publicly owned land from the British South Africa Company and surrounding township councils. More recently, it has been necessary to purchase land for low income housing development. On paper, this presents few problems, since local authorities have the legal powers to do so by agreement or compulsory purchase. In practice, administrative and financial constraints have caused delays and prevented the city council from developing a medium term land purchase programme (Butcher 1989).

In theory, urban local authorities sell serviced plots to low income beneficiaries at current market values, the proceeds being made available for future land purchases. The cost of infrastructure provision, operation and maintenance is fully recovered from allottees. In practice, while supplementary and other charges have traditionally been set at levels sufficient to cover costs, land is sold at its so-called intrinsic land value (ILV), which is set by the council itself. In sites and services projects in the 1980s, the price charged for land constituted only between 6.5% and 8.4% of total serviced plot costs. By the end of the decade, the council was using an ILV which was nearer to the market value of land, but still accounted for only 11% of serviced plot costs and 3% of the costs of a core house (Butcher 1989). The proceeds of land sales are insufficient to finance new land acquisition, partly because prices for the sale of serviced plots are less than the market price for new land being acquired, and partly because the number of plots being serviced and sold is far below the incremental need for new development. When Harare City Council has needed to purchase land, willing sellers have come forward, encouraged by the hindrance to farm operations posed by wood cutting, stock thefts, fires, etc. (Butcher 1989).

City councils are permitted to borrow from the building societies for the purchase and servicing of land, but Harare has only done so to a limited extent, partly because the interest rate charged is higher than that on funds borrowed from central government. For example, Harare borrowed from the Central Africa Building Society (CABS) to finance the servicing of two recent sites and services areas, because it was anticipated that sale of the plots using building society mortgages would enable rapid repayment (see Chapter 6). In addition, such borrowing has to be approved by the Ministry of Local Government and Rural and Urban Development (MLGRUD), which has tended to regard it as a last resort and so has been reluctant to approve it. Most land purchases which cannot be undertaken using the local authority's own reserve funds are, therefore, financed by borrowing from central government. Loans from the General Loan Fund (administered by the MLGRUD) are available for land purchase and off-site infrastructure and from the National Housing Fund (administered by the Ministry of Public Construction and National Housing) for on-site infrastructure (Figure 5.5). Loans are made at an annual interest rate which had increased to 10.5% in the early 1990s, repayable over 25 years. Both ministries have to submit annual budget estimates and proposed lending to the Ministry of Finance, Economic Planning and Development (MFEPD) for approval. This ministry does not seem to approve of land banking and will not allocate funds until the need is critical, preventing councils, even if their own planning is sufficiently well advanced, from developing medium term land purchase programmes which would enable them to ensure a continuous supply of land for subdivision (Butcher 1989). Allocation of funds for land purchase would, of course, need to be accompanied by loans for infrastructure provision, which are in equally short supply.

Although low income residential areas are not covered by the main land use planning and development control system, the prevailing standards adopted in European areas influenced expectations and the standards adopted, making it difficult to reduce minimum standards even when financing and affordability problems emerged. Since plots in these areas have been sold, development control is being exercised within the framework of 'local plans' which are merely the original layout plans. The new Harare Combination Master Plan now provides a policy framework for development decisions, though it remains to be seen whether its proposals for westward and southward extension can be translated into implementable programmes. Gradually, the old layouts will be replaced by Local Plans as has occurred for Highfield, new housing areas will be developed in accordance with local plans, and these areas will be incorporated in the development control system. As yet, consideration does not appear to have been given to the implications of incorporating high density residential areas into a 'one city' system, in terms of simplifying procedures, modifying planning standards and publicising the requirements among residents and small builders.

Revenue in Local Government Areas came from rents, supplementary

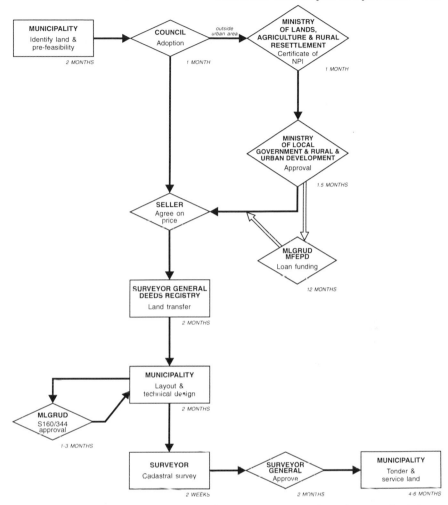

Figure 5.5 Land delivery procedures followed by municipalities (average lead time 1.5–2 years). Source: Butcher 1989 (with permission)

charges and beer profits. After independence a policy decision to match the changes in local government administration by a 'one city' policy which would merge these separate financial systems was taken, but progress in Harare has, for practical rather than political reasons, been slow. Water, sewerage and waste management accounts have been merged. Separate housing accounts are used for revenue from rents and supplementary charges, which finance expenditure on a similar range of services to the rates. Before independence, they were set at levels which ensured cost recovery for expenditure on roads, street lighting, cleansing and administration, while beer profits were used to provide welfare facilities and services. Since independence, these profits have been eroded by government control of prices and increased excise duties and sales taxes (Jordan 1984; Zimbabwe 1986a). The increasing involvement of external agencies in funding particular housing schemes has reduced the scope for adjusting charges between areas to allow for varying historical costs.

Valuation of high density residential areas took place simultaneously with the revaluation of low and medium density residential areas in 1990, both in Harare and Chitungwiza. The intention is to substitute rates for supplementary charges, based on the capital value of property rather than its area. It is hoped that residents will, on average, pay much the same as before and that yields will not decrease. Higher rates on commercial property and the capacity of the new system to take the quality of construction into account will, it is hoped, increase equity.

The ability of the councils to increase the supply of serviced plots to keep pace with demand is limited by resource shortages and administrative processes. Although the system of charging for services enables the cost of infrastructure and services to be recovered, the councils are dependent on borrowing, mainly from central government, to meet initial land purchase and development costs (Mutizwa-Mangiza 1991c). What funds are made available do not go as far as they should because of the relatively high standards for plot size and infrastructure adopted (see Chapter 6), while the practice of charging below market rates for land represents an implicit subsidy which will become harder to sustain as the supply of land for low income housing already in local authority ownership runs out. The process of land delivery for low income housing is estimated by Butcher (1989) to take between one and a half and two years, though lengthy delays may be incurred in obtaining the necessary funding, central government approvals and surveys. Central government procedures, legal requirements and some local authority administrative processes need to be simplified and streamlined in order to increase the supply of land for housing.

Although land made available for purchase by low income households is relatively cheap, the associated costs of servicing and house construction are very considerable and supply has been limited. As might be expected in this situation, squatting has occurred. However, as discussed in Chapter 2, the government before and since independence has opposed illegal land occupation and eradicated squatter areas as they occurred. Small settlements continue to form today, but they are only tolerated briefly, do not generate widespread working class support, and are frequently demolished at the cost of considerable hardship to their residents. Only in Epworth, which was not strictly a squatter settlement, has regularisation and improvement been grudgingly accepted (Chapter 2). Squatting tends to occur when the supply of affordable new plots and houses fails to keep up with urban population growth and when the ability of public and private landowners to enforce evictions is eroded, in the case of the former by political considerations and in the case of the latter generally by absence. Sometimes, however, private owners may allow illegal settlement on their land in return for the payment of rent, subsequently being unable to control the squatting. Recent migrants from the rural areas perceive undeveloped land as unused and thus, under customary tenure, available to those who can make constructive use of it, or, in urban areas, house construction. These processes and attitudes can all be seen at work in other African cities, for example Lusaka. Elsewhere, for example in Ghana, land under communal tenure abutted cities and could be allocated by traditional leaders to those entitled to use it by virtue of kin relationships. The more extensive and longer duration of the control exercised by Southern Rhodesia's settlers has reinforced the ability of property owners to resist encroachment, while Zimbabwean Africans are, because of the history of land tenure in the country, very aware of the nature of property rights based on European law.

Typically, squatting is an early response to the limited supply of land for low and even middle income housing. Later, as the land market has become more commercialised, the nature of both these processes has changed. Allocation of land under customary tenure has tended to become commercialised, as the token gift which was previously expected has been monetised and even, in some places, has begun to operate as a 'price' for the land. Elsewhere, illegal subdivision and sale of privately owned land has become more important. These processes have not occurred in Zimbabwe, with one recent exception. Just outside Harare's southwestern boundary, a farm belonging to a black opposition leader was, much to the annoyance of the local planning authorities, illegally subdivided and let for house construction by urban residents. Court action against the landowner was used and the occupants forced to vacate their plots. Unless the supply of affordable serviced plots is increased, however, it may only be a matter of time before the limit of tolerable overcrowding in existing housing areas is reached and residents take the matter of access to land into their own hands on a much larger scale than hitherto.

6

Housing

The housing which accommodates the population of the city and which, second to work, has the greatest influence on its quality of life, is produced, consumed and exchanged through a series of processes that essentially involve the private sector. However, the degree to which these processes are marketised varies between cities in different countries, within cities and over time. The institution of private property, the basis of the capitalist system, provides opportunities for accumulation and profit in its production and exchange. It is an important element in the wealth of landlords and owner-occupiers, to whom it is an asset which they hope will continually appreciate, but to its consumers it also has use value. Invariably, public bodies intervene in the processes of house production and exchange in order to achieve development goals, compensate for perceived market failure and regulate the process of urban development. For the private construction sector to take advantage of demand for housing, an adequate supply of the necessary components (land, services, materials, labour and capital) must be available, in addition to effective demand for the dwellings they can offer (incomes which enable households to afford to buy or rent, together with a system of long term credit). As the population and wealth of a city grows and the financial sector becomes more developed, private construction firms expand, and the potential for producing housing on a speculative basis increases. Although this does occur in African cities, in many it is still relatively limited and on a small scale. More commonly, housing is produced for a corporate or individual client. Where employers or high income households commission housing, the construction firms operate within the formal sector, generally but not always complying with land tenure, planning and building regulations.

The majority of urban households are, however, not high income and in many cities they either cannot get legal access to land or cannot afford to comply with planning and building regulations. They organise the construction of a house for their own use, using a combination of household labour and the services of artisanal builders. Such housing also has potential market value, which may be realised by renting it out or by sale.

In any city, the production of housing will be organised in a variety of ways, reflecting both the nature of producers and their access to resources and the demands of consumers. The relative importance of different modes and forms of production varies between cities and over time, depending on local economic circumstances, the nature of the urban land system, the institutional framework, and the speed and pattern of urban development. In many African cities, rapid population growth, limited administrative capacity, underdeveloped large scale construction and housing finance sectors, and widespread poverty have limited the large scale production of formal private or public sector housing. While the formal private sector produces housing for high income households and employers, the public sector generally succeeds in producing housing for only a minority of low and middle income households, many of whom may be its own employees. The scarcity of such housing and its subsidised nature make it a scarce prize, and therefore corruption and favouritism in house allocation and leakage of dwellings intended for low income households to those higher up the income distribution are common. In most cities, therefore, the majority of dwellings have been produced by individuals, either for their own use in areas of semi-authorised or unauthorised development or as petty landlords for rent.

In this chapter, I analyse the processes of housing production, consumption and exchange in Harare and the effect on these of policy interventions to date. In the first part of the chapter, I describe the components of the housing stock, seeking an explanation of their production in the organisation and financing of the construction process. Factors which influence housing supply are then examined, and the extent to which they constrain production is assessed. The consumption of housing is determined by the ability of urban residents to afford the dwellings on offer, and this in turn is influenced by whether credit is available. Although production and consumption of new housing are important for a rapidly growing city, most transactions are in second-hand housing. The implications of housing exchange will also be examined.

Components of the housing stock

The production of different types of housing over time, by production processes organised in different ways, cumulatively makes up a city's

Table 6.1   Population living in main dwellings and outbuildings in Harare, 1987

	1982 population	1987 population			Total	% Increase, 1982–7
		Nos. in main dwelling	In outbuildings No.	%		
Harare						
LDRAs	218 604	225 719	65 869	23	291 588	33
MDRAs	11 542	13 359	2 222	40	15 581	35
HDRAs	412 045	540 023	94 021	15	634 044	54
Other areas	16 173	20 258	–	–	20 258	25
Chitungwiza						
HDRAs	172 456	216 601	46 789	18	263 390	53
Epworth	18 000	18 705	13 545	42	32 250	79
Total	848 820	1 034 665	222 446	18	1 257 111	48

Source: HCMPPA 1988c: 40.

LDRAs Low density residential areas.
MDRAs Medium density residential areas.
HDRAs High density residential areas.

housing stock. Four are significant in Harare: the private production of housing for high and middle income groups, private sector rental housing, public sector house production, and unauthorised house production (Rakodi 1990; Rakodi and Mutizwa-Mangiza 1990). Independence was marked by continuity rather than change, though housing policies have continued to evolve and minor innovations to occur.

The only overall figures for Harare's housing stock were produced in 1987 during the preparation of the master plan. Because these data are the only suitable ones available, they are shown in Table 6.1, despite their shortcomings. Just over a third of the households in the conurbation in 1982 and about a quarter of the population in 1987 were accommodated in legally produced private sector housing for main plot occupants and 'servants' quarters' for their employees in low and medium density areas. All except about 2% of the remainder lived in residential areas developed under public sector auspices, but including local authority houses, self-built houses, rented rooms and illegal backyard shacks. The 2% in the regularised squatter area of Epworth is thus an underestimate of the proportion in illegal or semi-legal dwellings.

The private production of high and middle income housing

The 'low density' areas, which in 1987 accommodated 23% of the city's population, occupied 76% of the total residential area and included both relatively high density apartment areas immediately north of the city centre and low density areas, mostly with very large plots occupied by the bourgeoisie, but including some areas of somewhat smaller plots developed either for the black middle class or for the white proletariat. The apartment blocks, which were speculative or employer developments requiring relatively large amounts of capital, will be discussed under the heading of rental housing. Most of the other housing was constructed by the buyers of subdivided plots. The early development of the township and the process of subdivision in the townlands, within the original municipal boundary and beyond, have been discussed in Chapter 2. Farms subdivided in this way included Avondale, Mount Pleasant and Borrowdale, the last two outside the municipal boundary until 1971 (Figure 6.1). Minimum plot sizes and building clauses helped to maintain white exclusivity and property values, even though exclusivity was already protected by tenure legislation, which precluded Africans from owning or occupying houses in the European parts of urban areas, with the exception of domestic workers.

Not all housing for whites was in low density areas, nor was it all produced by the private sector: the main exception was Mabelreign, the earliest part of which was a housing scheme initially developed by the central government for in-migrant artisans after the Second World War (see Chapter 2). In addition, to accommodate and foster the growing black middle class, a limited home ownership scheme was introduced in the 1960s, making plots available, mainly on long leases, in Marimba Park (Ashton 1969; Teedon and Drakakis-Smith 1986: 321). The classification of areas into low and medium density varies: in some accounts Mabelreign, containing a mixture of 2000 square metres, 4000 square metres and smaller plots, is classified as medium rather than low density, while in 1987 a more restrictive definition of medium density areas was adopted. They are shown by the figures given in Table 6.1 as containing about 2% of the stands in the conurbation and 1.2% of its population.

Separate figures produced by Harare City Council for the number of 'housing units' show 37 358 in 1986 and a 5% increase to 39 409 in 1991. These appear to exclude some of the housing units included in the 1987 figures. As they do not distinguish between main houses, domestic workers' houses, guest cottages and apartments or row houses, it is not possible to arrive at a total for the number of dwelling units. Nevertheless, it is clear from these figures that there have been few additions to the high and medium cost stock in recent years.

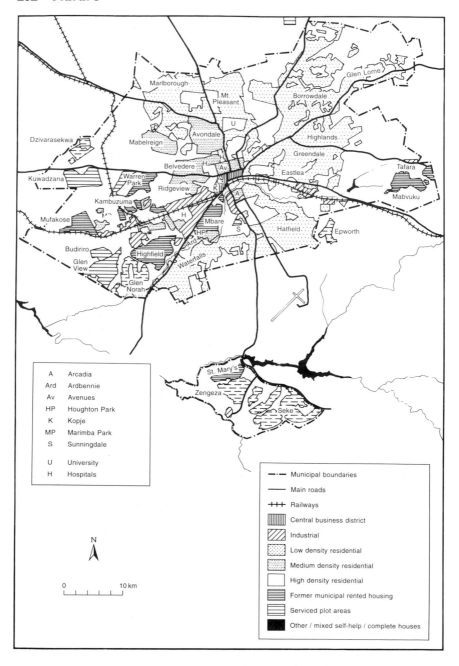

Figure 6.1 Components of Harare's housing stock in 1991

In east and central African colonial societies, the temporary nature of expatriate administrators necessitated the provision of rental housing for them. This was usually heavily subsidised. When, on independence, the civil service and other public sector bodies were indigenised, the new employees expected to inherit the same salaries and conditions of service enjoyed by the colonial administrators. Subsidised tied housing in cities where private formal sector capacity to produce housing was limited was a major entitlement to which, once established, civil servants and others were reluctant to give up their rights. Efforts to reform the system by increasing rents to market levels or encouraging public sector employees to build their own houses had to be implemented by the very people whose interests were threatened. Reforms generally came to nothing, for example in Zambia, and the burden of housing an enlarged civil service continued to be a drain on government revenue, while the availability of this housing to a major group of employees hindered the development of construction sector capacity to supply adequate numbers, especially of modestly priced houses.

In the settler state of Southern Rhodesia, in contrast, even civil servants were generally permanent residents and were expected to own their houses. As a result, not only did newly employed African civil servants not expect to be provided with subsidised rental housing in the city, but also the substantial private sector housing market which existed was associated with considerable capacity in the construction sector and a more developed housing finance system than in most other African countries with the exception of South Africa. The housing sector producing for high income households in Zimbabwe can, therefore, be analysed as a private market-based sector, though subject to extensive government regulation.

Sources of information other than those used above, such as building plan approvals, property sales and house prices, throw further light on trends in the high income residential property market. On average, 2289 high cost dwellings were approved each year between 1970 and 1973. This then fell off dramatically, rising only to 149 in 1979 (Figure 6.2). Private sector high cost dwellings fell from 26% of the total in 1970 to 3% in 1979. The construction of new houses for the European population was directly affected by the increasing success of the liberation struggle during the later 1970s and the emigration of whites. After 1980, there was a marked increase in the value of building plans approved (Figure 6.3), but very few of these were for high cost dwellings. Instead, construction was of industrial and commercial as well as government buildings. Only 28% of the value of this construction was residential nationwide, compared to 53% in 1979, though the bulk of new construction in Harare continued to be comprised of public low cost

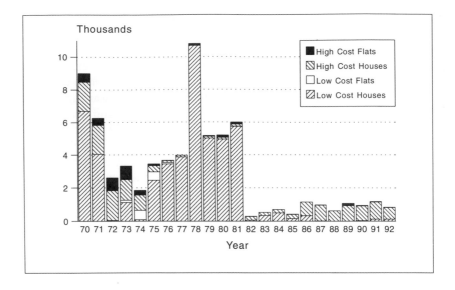

Figure 6.2 Building plans approved in Harare, by dwelling type. Source: CSO Quarterly Digest of Statistics December 1990, pp. 56–7

housing programmes (Figure 6.2). The value of new construction increased in the immediate post-independence economic boom, then fell off during the years of economic difficulty and drought (see Chapter 1), only picking up again from 1985 onwards. For the country as a whole, under a third of new construction was residential until the mid-1980s.

Although the value of new construction increased between 1980 and 1982, this did not represent an increase in real terms. The fall off in new construction in cash terms during the mid-1980s is shown by Figure 6.3 to have been even more marked in real terms. By the mid-1980s the downward trend in the real value of building plans approved was reversed, but the increase in cash value of new construction in the later 1980s did not represent an increase in real value, as the costs of new construction (represented by the Building Materials Price Index) escalated. From an average of 231 high cost dwellings each year between 1980 and 1985, a faster but still relatively insignificant rate of new construction commenced: 824 in 1986, increasing to a peak of 1050 in 1991 but then, affected by declining property prices (see below), falling off again (Figure 6.2).

Between three-quarters and four-fifths of houses in low density areas are owner-occupied. An examination of trends in sales and prices helps to explain why so little new house construction occurred for owner-occupation until the late 1980s. The number of property sales was

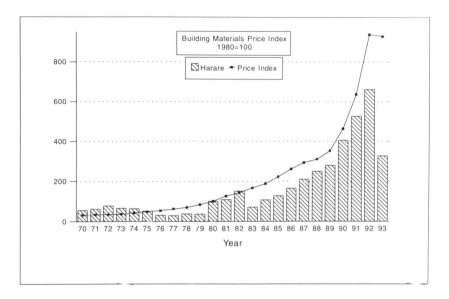

Figure 6.3 Index of value of building plans approved (all types). Building Materials Price Index—materials for a typical 3-bedroom house (materials weighted 1968). 1993 figures are for January to June, BMPI for June. Sources: CSO Quarterly Digest of Statistics December 1990, December 1991, December 1993

relatively high in the early 1970s, fell off between 1975 and 1978, and increased again as independence approached. Although sales in all urban areas increased by nearly 30% in 1979 over 1978, the average value of urban property sold decreased by 6%. This reflected both the purchase of houses in medium density areas by black Zimbabweans (see below) and depressed prices due to excess of supply over demand, as large numbers of emigrants placed their houses (often unsuccessfully) on the market. One estimate for Harare was that only a fifth of properties offered for sale actually changed hands, mostly at the upper end of the market, to accommodate the increase in embassy staff which accompanied independence (RAL September 1980).

The trends in property sales noted at the end of the 1970s also characterised the early 1980s. While the total value of sales and the average value of property sold increased, this represented a continued decline in real terms until 1984. Not until 1986 did the increase in average property sale prices start to keep pace with inflation, following increased sales in the previous three years. Depressed property prices made it possible for black Zimbabweans to buy into the low and medium density areas, though this opportunity was somewhat constrained by the shortage of mortgage finance. This process of exchange was most active in, though not confined to, areas near the main commercial and industrial employment centres and near the existing high density areas, especially those containing smaller and older houses and plots (Harvey 1987) (see Chapter 4). Houghton Park, a medium density area of 800 square metre plots, was 80% black by 1979. In Mabelreign, in-movement in the early 1980s was accompanied by a steady increase in the value of properties, as the supply released by owners moving out to low density suburbs roughly matched demand from potential buyers. The proportion of houses occupied by blacks within the suburb was positively associated with lower property prices. By the mid-1980s over half the occupiers in four of the six sub-areas were black (Cumming 1990).

In 1984 the property sector was noting an increase in supply of houses for sale once again, as emigrants attempted to take advantage of the limited time provided for them to invest the proceeds in external bonds (RAL September 1984). By 1985 those who had not yet bought began to realise that the market was tightening up, as price levels started to increase, though they were still only 60% of the cost of new construction (Zimbabwe 1985b: 10). The National Property Association estimated that house prices in the low density areas increased on average by 26% in 1985, 53% in 1986 and 28% in 1987, well above the rate of inflation, while the increase for small dwellings and flats was faster (RAL December 1987; Cumming 1990). Even more rapid increases occurred between 1987 and 1991. However, since then prices have fallen, by an average for residential, commercial and industrial property of 35% between mid-1991 and the end of 1992 (RAL December 1992).

Again, a range of explanatory factors is involved. Bond (1991, 1993c) considers the price increases to have been driven solely by a dramatic and sudden increase in lending by commercial banks and building societies after the mid-1980s and attributes this to a crisis of accumulation in the primary circuit of capital, especially in manufacturing. Surplus capital accumulation since the mid-1970s by the banks, which by the mid-1980s accounted for about half of all assets/liabilities held by the financial sector, was sunk into a large number of mainly commercial mortgage bonds in 1984. This led to a flurry of speculative activity by institutional investors in the central business district (CBD) property market (see Chapter 2). The following year, the building societies increased their mortgage lending, mostly to middle and upper income housing for which prices soared. Other reasons for the price increases included a reduced supply of secondhand housing for sale as a result of reduced out-migration in the second half of the 1980s; a shortage of smaller houses and flats for high income elderly households, reducing the supply of larger family houses for sale; and continued high demand from embassies and companies for luxury houses (RAL, various dates). At the peak in 1991, senior private sector managers were still able to purchase houses, but even houses in medium density areas were moving beyond the reach of middle range private and upper range public sector employees. Financial liberalisation and the collapse of share prices on the Zimbabwe stock exchange heralded the end of the speculative boom. Falling commercial property rents and prices did not initially halt large scale bank lending (Bond 1993b). However, changes to interest rates as part of the economic structural adjustment programme and declining real wages led to reduced flows of deposits into the building societies and a reduction in the number of new mortgages issued (CSO 1993). By mid-1993, prices of houses in medium density areas had almost returned to their 1990 level.

In the later 1980s, the surplus of supply over demand for secondhand houses had disappeared and the value of these houses was approaching their replacement cost. However, the figures quoted at the beginning of this section show that there was no immediate response from the private construction sector. Gradually, small developments of luxury town houses, single houses for corporate clients and houses commissioned by owner-occupiers began construction during the later 1980s. Demand for top-of-the-range houses continued to offer sufficient opportunities for development and construction firms, for the most part, to remain uninterested in building medium price housing. The shortage of modestly priced housing has led to the letting out of 'guest cottages' and domestic workers' houses in low density residential areas, as described in Chapter 4.

Surveys in some typical high and middle income residential areas in 1991 have already been drawn on in the analysis of economic and social characteristics of households in Chapters 3 and 4, and bear out aspects of the general analysis above. Of the main houses in all the areas, 80% or more were occupied by their owners, and the remainder by tenants either of private landlords or employers; practically none was occupied by more than one household. Most had bought their current house in the years since independence (64% in Mount Pleasant, 87% in Hatfield and 93% in Mabelreign). Over half of all households had bought their houses during the 1980 to 1984 period, when house prices were most depressed. Households of both European and African racial origin had benefited, with equal proportions of black and white households acquiring property in Mount Pleasant and mostly black households elsewhere at this time. Today, two-thirds of the households in the previously white area of Mount Pleasant are white and a third black. The sample in Houghton Park was selected from a part of the area developed with speculatively built housing in 1986 (Figure 6.4). At that

Figure 6.4   Houses in a medium income area: Houghton Park

time, the selling price was Z$45 000 for the land and a three bedroom house, equivalent to a building cost of Z$120 000 in 1991. However, advertised resale prices in mid-1991 averaged Z$193 000, the large profit to be made illustrating the severe shortage of medium cost houses.

The small proportion of households in these areas with incomes below Z$1000 per month (Table 3.9) were mostly elderly, supported by pensions and/or help from their children. The lower modal income in Mount Pleasant is explained by the presence of a larger proportion of elderly households in this area, but its higher average income (Z$3312 compared to about Z$2500 in the other areas) is accounted for by the presence of a larger proportion of very high income households. Household incomes ranged widely in all the areas, including households at the lower end of the income range who bought houses (especially in Mount Pleasant, but also in Hatfield) early in the area's development, when their incomes were higher, or during the years of depressed prices, as well as households at the upper end of the income distribution. While the high proportion of high income households in Mount Pleasant is unsurprising, because of its large plots and substantial houses, it is unexpected in the medium density areas. Here it presumably arises from the mismatch between household incomes and property prices in the later 1980s, which has led high income households who might previously have aspired to residence in areas such as Mount Pleasant to settle instead for a smaller house on a smaller plot. Unlike low income households in high density areas, the great majority of which are dependent on a single wage income, most of the owner households in these higher income areas contain two or more income earners, particularly in the areas other than Mount Pleasant (51%, compared to 83% in Hatfield, 81% in Mabelreign and 70% in Houghton Park; see Chapter 3).

Housing costs comprise both mortgage payments and other charges (rates and utilities). The proportion of household incomes paid out in housing-related costs varied both within and between areas. The range overall was from about 5% to over 45%. In Mount Pleasant, Hatfield and Mabelreign, many of the owner households took out their mortgages some time ago when house prices were depressed, though for some, housing-related costs absorb more than the 27.5% of income ceiling used by government to guide policy. In the more recently developed area of Houghton Park, however, only for 28% of households did total housing related costs consume less than a quarter of their incomes. For the one in two households who were paying over 30% (and in particular for the 23% paying over 40%), obtaining access to housing has imposed a considerable strain on household resources. Areas such as Houghton Park provide one of the few sources of new housing for owner-occupation, other than serviced plots in the high density areas (see below), for which many middle income households are not eligible. Purchasers are clearly willing to make considerable sacrifices in order to gain access to a house in such an area. Whether they will be able to maintain payments through the 1990s, as interest rates increase and real wages fall, remains to be seen. However, because of the shortage of this type of house, prices are high and resale is more likely than default, except for the households who bought at the peak of the property boom and now have negative equity in their houses.

Some middle income households are reported to be experiencing difficulties with meeting the costs (of housing and transport) associated with living in low density areas. However, these are a minority. The survey showed that subletting of parts of the main house to tenants has not yet occurred. An alternative is to let the guest cottage or domestic workers' houses. This has not occurred in Mount Pleasant, but over a quarter of owners in Mabelreign and Hatfield obtained rent from this source (see Chapter 4). An unexpected finding was the high proportion of domestic workers' houses which were deliberately being kept unoccupied (27% in Mount Pleasant, 32% in Hatfield and 39% in Mabelreign). In Chapter 3 I noted the decline in domestic employment. Not all households in medium and high income areas employ domestic workers today, while, although a large minority of owners in Mabelreign and Hatfield have decided to let this accommodation, for many neither financial difficulties nor housing market pressures have been sufficient to tempt them to risk 'quiet enjoyment' of their property in order to raise income from rents.

Private rental housing

There are a number of different submarkets for rental dwellings under the general heading of private rental housing. About a fifth of the main houses on low and medium density stands are rented either from private landlords, some of them resident in South Africa or overseas, or from employers. In addition, rented flats form a significant element in the housing market, especially in the Avenues and Avondale areas north of the city centre (Figure 6.1). Despite the policy emphasis on owner-occupation in new housing areas for low income households, some plot owners let out the main house. However, more significant in terms of quantity are privately let dwellings occupied by 'lodgers', mainly one or two room units in wholly or partly let houses in high density areas and in illegal structures within these plots. This last category of housing bridges the divide between legality and illegality—registered lodgers have been legal since family housing was first built for Africans in the 1940s; theoretically, letting to unregistered lodgers is not permitted, while the construction of side-structures is certainly illegal. The scale and dynamics of each of these rental submarkets will be analysed in turn.

After independence, the demand for houses for rent grew in response to the influx of short term personnel in the public and diplomatic sectors. Owners who had been unable to pass on rising costs in the depressed demand conditions of the late 1970s increased rents (RAL September 1981). Once this demand was satisfied, periodic oversupply of houses was reported until the mid-1980s. Since then, houses for rent at higher rent levels have been in short supply, as have cheaper houses and flats.

To rent control, which had been introduced in 1982, have been added periodic rent freezes imposed as part of national anti-inflation policy. While initial rents are fixed at close to the market level, increases have failed to keep pace with inflation, or, from the point of view of the landlord, to provide an adequate return on investment. The result has been to encourage the sale of rented property and to deter new construction for rent (NCSI 1985). While benefiting some, notably long-standing tenants, such provisions discriminate against new tenants or those unable to buy their flats when disposed of by the landlord. By 1987, the Rent Board became more aware of the need to increase rentals

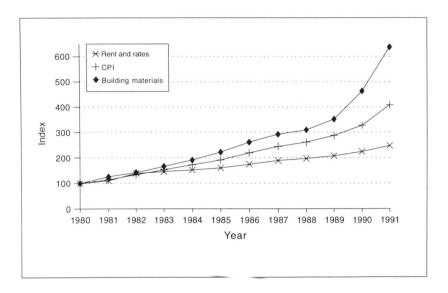

Figure 6.5 Rent levels in urban Zimbabwe. CPI = Consumer Price Index for high income urban families. Sources: CSO Quarterly Digest of Statistics December 1990, December 1991

in order to provide realistic returns, but rental increases remained below the consumer price index and well below the cost of new construction (RAL March 1988) (Figure 6.5). Average rents in Mount Pleasant in 1991 were almost double those in Hatfield and Mabelreign, though they varied widely around the average. Rents in Houghton Park were, as expected, even lower. Generally, the socio-economic characteristics of tenant households in low and medium density areas and their housing conditions were similar to those of owners, except that tenant households generally appeared to be at an earlier stage in their life cycles, and many may seek to purchase houses in future.

There were estimated to be 810 blocks containing 11 864 flats (apartments and row houses) in Harare in 1989 (Pritchard 1989). Over 40% of the blocks, representing over 60% of all dwellings, were in the Avenues area, where blocks of up to eight storeys are allowed and perhaps half the flats are small bachelor and one bedroom flats. The second most important area was Avondale, where construction is generally limited to two storeys. It contains over a quarter of the blocks but only a fifth of the dwellings, and a larger proportion of two and three bedroom flats. Apartments (flats) were advertised for rent in the range Z$350–800 in July 1986 and Z$550–1000 in July 1989. Increases in the lowest rents at which flats were available were less than 15% per annum in 1986/7 and 1987/8, but more than 20% in 1988/9. Between June–August 1990 and March–May 1991, rents, on average, increased by about 25%, 4% above the consumer price index for high income households (CSO, 18 August 1991) and considerably more than the increase in average earnings. Pritchard (1989) noted a considerable difference in the rents set by the Rent Board, rents charged by employers to their employees and rents for privately leased flats. He suggested that the rents for the last were typically more than three times the first and that the Rent Board only controlled the rents of about two-thirds of rented dwellings. After 1991, unlike sale prices, rents continued to rise, as liberalisation made it easier for landlords to set rents which ensured them market rates of return.

A sample of 51 tenant households in the Avenues in 1991 showed that half had two members in employment. While 43% of the households were nuclear households, a third were single people, many of them living with unmarried relatives (usually brothers and sisters). An unusually high proportion of household heads had never married (29%). As a result, the average household size (3.1) was relatively small. This submarket within the private rental sector clearly meets the needs both of young households comprised of one or more adult wage earners and young nuclear families. The latter were most dissatisfied with their current accommodation, but were finding it increasingly hard to move into the owner-occupied sector.

Despite the more recent increases in rents noted above, the impact of rent control has been to encourage landlords to sell blocks of flats, to employers or for non-residential uses, or to dispose of individual flats. Pritchard's inspection of the Valuation Roll showed that in 1980 blocks of flats owned by investors accounted for 85% of the dwellings. The owners included pension funds, insurance companies, building contractors and individuals, especially continental Europeans. Between 1980 and 1986, an average of 18.4 blocks per annum were sold to employers and companies. The number of sales of individual flats increased once legal tenure issues were clarified, and by 1988 rented flats accounted for only 40% of the total (Pritchard 1989). Many of the individually owned flats are themselves rented out, and turnover tends to be greater than in blocks owned by companies.

Prices of flats have increased rapidly, as increased prices for detached houses have forced potential buyers to purchase smaller units. Between 1986 and 1989, the prices of the smallest flats nearly doubled, and those of larger flats increased by two-thirds. The rate of increase in sale prices then accelerated and in *each* of the subsequent two years (1989/90 and 1990/91) the average price of bachelor flats doubled and the price of medium sized flats increased by 50% (Table 6.2). The increase in sale

Table 6.2   Mean advertised sale prices of flats in Harare, 1990–1991

Type of flat	Avenues		Other areas		Total		% increase 1990/1
	1990	1991	1990	1991	1990	1991	
'Bachelor'	43 480	75 500	–	60 000	43 480	75 081	72.7
1 bedroom	86 783	120 105	81 000	130 286	85 957	120 871	40.6
2 bedrooms	138 773	236 276	167 724	254 040	155 235	246 212	58.6
3 bedrooms	80 000	250 000	212 539	318 333	203 072	315 425	55.3

Source: *Herald*, June–August 1990 and March–May 1991.

prices was more than twice the rate of inflation and twice that for rents, illustrating the dampening effect of rent control. After 1991, prices of flats decreased, though by less than those of houses (10% by mid-1993 for small one and two room flats). Despite the increase in demand, little new construction has taken place. Between 1970 and 1981, a total of 3326 high cost flats were built, accounting for 28% of all building plans approved (Figure 6.2). From 1982 to 1992, plans for a total of 211 flats were approved, including both private and city council developments, accounting for 3% of a much reduced total volume of building plans approved.

As is often the case, the intentions of rent control were good—to protect tenants against racist or rapacious landlords and excessive rent increases. However, it is a difficult policy to get right and Zimbabwe has been no exception in this respect. Pritchard (1989) estimates that in the 1980s profits of 20–30% were to be made from construction for sale, compared with a return of 5–10% over 10–15 years if building for rent. Although the Rent Board has responded to landlord pressure by setting rents nearer market levels in recent years, in general rents have been about two-thirds of this level. In addition, the administrative delays in settling appeals, together with government rent freezes, have made it difficult for landlords to ensure regular and appropriate rent increases. The ease with which individual flat owners can flout the legislation further deters corporate investment, while even the threat of enforcement has been sufficient to encourage landlords to sell or convert flats to other uses and to discourage new construction. The result has been a decreased stock of flats for rent in the face of increased demand. The results of rent control policy have not matched up to its aims and it is overdue for a review. The reasons why the private sector has not responded to price increases by constructing new flats for sale are similar to those inhibiting the production of houses in low and middle density areas and will be examined later in this chapter.

Since the 1960s, subletting of municipal rented housing has been tolerated. However, the desire to maintain control over influx and urban residents, as well as to ensure payment for services, led to an insistence that subtenants be registered. Thus in 1974 nearly 8000 registered lodgers were recorded in Salisbury's high density housing areas (13% of all households). Even at this date, however, it was acknowledged that lodging was more extensive than shown by the official figures (Cubitt and Riddell 1974: 42). Just over a fifth of Harare's public sector low income housing stock (21% including hostel accommodation) is rented today. Most of the remaining hostels have been renovated but quality is still poor, overcrowding typical and illegal subletting common, despite the council's attempts to prevent it and to improve maintenance (Harare City Council, Department of Housing and Community Services 1987, 1988).

Rental rooms in high density areas are produced in large numbers. Rationalised first in terms of the temporary nature of African rural–urban migration, once stabilisation became the official policy (see Chapter 1) the arguments in favour of lodging shifted to those of assisting married couples in achieving home ownership (Mafico 1991). Policy emphasis since the later 1970s has been on achieving home ownership for all (see below). With varying degrees of explicitness, it has been acknowledged that a significant low cost rented housing sector exists and will be necessary in future, both to provide for low income households and to enable allottees of serviced plots to afford their repayments. While national housing policy has been silent on the issue, the World Bank has actively supported the production of rental dwellings by participants in the serviced plot schemes it has been assisting (World Bank 1984). Because of the official insistence that lodgers be registered and that unregistered lodgers were illegal, it was in the past difficult to obtain accurate city-wide estimates of the extent of rental house production. A survey of recent migrant households in a limited number of areas at the end of 1985 found that just over a third were lodgers (Potts with Mutambirwa 1991), and another estimate at about the same time suggested that 40% of all low income households were lodgers (Butcher 1986: 10). Better figures were available for Chitungwiza, where waiting list priority is given to registered lodgers and thus there is more incentive for them to be registered. In 1985 53% of the registered adult population were lodgers (Schlyter 1989: 137). Even in 1982, 95% of Kambuzuma and 65% of Glen View houses had been extended to accommodate lodgers (Figure 6.1). The proportion of absentee landlords was 13% in the new area of Glen View and 21% in the older areas of Glen Norah, Highfield and Kambuzuma (Hoek-Smit 1982).

By the middle of the 1980s, warnings were being given that the housing stock was near saturation point (Patel 1984; World Bank 1985). More recent information does not enable us to gauge whether 'saturation point' has been reached, but does illustrate how varied the behaviour of owners with respect to the production of rental housing continues to be, and the continued differences in the characteristics of owner and tenant households. The areas included in our 1991 survey did not include the most crowded inner city areas and so do not constitute a city-wide random sample, but they do permit analysis of the characteristics of lodger households and comparisons with owner households in the same areas (Rakodi with Withers 1993).

Lodging was most extensive in the older serviced plot area of Warren Park D (Figure 6.1), where 68% of all plots contained lodgers and over half of all households were renting, resulting in an average of 2.1 households per plot. Close behind were the owners of ceded plots in Kuwadzana, of whom half were landlords. Renting is less common in the areas with smaller houses (average 3–4 rooms), including the old municipal housing area of Mabvuku, where small plots limit the scope for house extensions, and the newly developed serviced plot area of Budiriro, where lodgers were renting temporary shacks pending completion of the main house where more lodging may be expected in future. In Mabvuku, nevertheless, the proportion of households who were renting out rooms had approximately doubled since 1982. Absentee landlordism was most extensive (17% of stands) in the samples of ceded plots in Kuwadzana and Mabvuku, where the possibility of buying houses had provided an investment opportunity for people who would otherwise not be eligible for council housing. In other areas, absentee landlordism was less common. Self-help home ownership areas, therefore, give the most opportunities to owners to build additional rooms. Lodging in such areas starts early in their development and becomes more extensive as they mature. The scope for accommodating lodgers is less where houses are ready-built, especially where these are small and on small plots, but even in these areas lodging has become more extensive. Although the growth of absentee landlordism may be a pointer to the future, most of the rental accommodation in low income areas in Harare, as in similar areas in the urban centres of Malawi or Zambia, is provided by petty landlords on a small scale and generally as a supplement to other sources of income.

There are a number of socio-economic characteristics with respect to which owner (or municipal tenant) and non-owner households are different, in addition to their housing conditions: age of the household head, household size, and household income. Owner household heads were, on average, ten years older than non-owners, the majority of whom (63%) were between the ages of 25 and 34 (Table 6.3). This difference is closely related to the eligibility criteria for public sector housing, which has, since family accommodation first began to be built, depended on the head having dependants to support. As households who have been longest on the waiting lists are allocated housing first, length of residence in the city has also been important. Thus 38% of owners were 45 years old or more, while a larger proportion of non-owners were young (16% under 25) or elderly. The most marked difference between owner and non-owner households with respect to marital status was the higher proportion of never married household heads among the latter (27% compared to 3%) (see also Chapter 4). As a result, average household sizes were less than for owner households (2.7 compared to 5.4) and many lodgers lived in one or two person households (Table 6.3). The findings of other surveys have been similar. Although a larger proportion of non-owner households than of owners had relatively low incomes, this is also, to some extent, a life cycle effect and the class characteristics of landlords and tenants are similar.

Households living in rented dwellings generally had a long experience of similar accommodation: on arrival in the city, most stay with relatives, from where they move to what is generally one of a long succession of rented rooms. One in five were able to rent from relatives, benefiting from lower room rents than would have been charged by an unrelated landlord (Z$42 compared to Z$50 on average). Renting from a relative also seems to provide a certain amount of security, with a fifth of households renting from a relative having lived in the same place for ten or more years, compared to 3% renting from ordinary landlords. Non-owner households had dwellings on average less than half the size of the dwellings occupied by owners, and almost three-quarters lived in one room (Table 6.3). Although the small families were not over-crowded, more than double the proportion of renters than owners lived at an occupancy rate of three people per room. Nearly a quarter of one room rented dwellings were occupied by households with four or more members.

A ceiling room rental was set in 1980, but this proved impossible to enforce for registered let alone unregistered lodgers. The average rent paid for one room in the sample areas was Z$50 in 1991, though some households paid as much as Z$100. In addition to rent, most lodger households are required to make a contribution to monthly water and electricity bills. Total monthly housing costs for one room ranged from Z$20 to Z$103 (average Z$56), accounting for between 5% and 63% of household income (average 16%). Between 1982 and 1991, rents increased at 17% above the rate of inflation and 125% faster than minimum industrial wage increases. Although the supply of rooms for

Table 6.3 Characteristics of households in low income areas by tenure

	Owners	Non-owners
Age of household head (years)	42	32
Average household size (persons)	5.4	2.7
1 person	4%	36%
5+ people	65%	18%
Household income (Z$)	%	%
1–200	3	7
201–400	20	35
401–600	28	28
601–800	19	16
801–1000	14	9
1001+	16	5
Total	100	100
Dwelling size		
Average no. rooms	3.4	1.4
1 room	6%	73%
5+ rooms	18%	2%
Room occupancy (persons/room)	%	%
1 or less	24	43
>1–2	48	21
>2–3	21	18
>3	7	18

Source: Rakodi with Withers 1993: 172.

rent had not, therefore, fully kept pace with demand, it had not fallen so far behind that rent increases were sufficient to drive the majority of households to run the risk of squatting. Hardly any non-owner households spent less than the 27.5% ceiling recommended by government, suggesting that income is not the only barrier to obtaining better housing for many non-owner households.

The majority of tenant households interviewed in 1993 were dissatisfied with their housing conditions, mainly because of the lack of space, and would, given the opportunity, move to better accommodation. The vast majority would not choose to rent again. The lodger households headed by women whom Schlyter interviewed (1989) regarded lodging negatively because of conflicts with landlords, lack of privacy, and insecurity. They preferred absentee landlords. It tends to be assumed, especially by the aid agencies, that the economic benefits of renting out rooms outweigh any disadvantages for landlords, though

the reasons why some poor households choose, given equal opportunities, to sublet and others do not are unknown. Even if the supply of
houses or plots for sale is increased, and despite its unpopularity as a
tenure, renting has always been and will continue to be a significant
component of total housing production and will be the tenure of choice
for some households. Given this, more needs to be known about the
motives and experience of landlords and tenants, and greater policy
attention needs to be paid to the sector, with a view to reforming rent
control, increasing supply and overcoming the main disadvantages of
the tenure, mainly from the point of view of tenants, but also from that
of landlords.

Public sector housing production

The policies of the settler government towards African urban labour and
the local administrative and housing policies to which these gave rise
have been analysed in Chapter 1. Early housing provisions for urban
labour were based on three premises: that African migrants were
temporary and so should be provided with rental housing; that they
were predominantly men and so should be accommodated in single-sex
hostels; and that they should not be a drain on the purse of white urban
residents, so should live in dwellings built to minimum standards and
separately financed and administered. Although following the policy of
stabilisation, construction of family housing overtook hostel accommodation in importance, even by the end of the 1970s a third of the
dwelling units in the city were hostel beds (Table 6.4). The early
residential areas (Mbare, Highfield, St Mary's, Dzivarasekwa, Tafara)
comprised small houses to rent and hostel accommodation, the latter
mostly in Mbare (see Figure 6.1). As early as 1963, however, the national
government started to develop owner-occupied core houses in
Kambuzuma, despite opposition from Salisbury's right wing white
councillors who feared the increasing numerical domination of the city
by blacks. By 1978/9 15% of family units in Harare, concentrated mainly
in Kambuzuma, Mufakose and Highfield, were owner-occupied,
compared to 2% in 1974 (Whitsun Foundation 1980: 101).

Construction of rental and core houses in Zengeza paved the way for
the development of Chitungwiza in the later 1970s (see Chapter 2).
House ownership was more extensive in the new settlement—27% in
1978/9 (Whitsun Foundation 1980: 101). Because of the urgent perceived
need to resettle war refugees from squatter areas, and the influence of
international donor agencies, especially the Red Cross, ultra-low-cost
two room core houses were built in Zengeza at less than two-thirds the

Table 6.4 Municipal housing stock types at independence

	Detached (including serviced plots)	Semi-detached houses	Terraced houses	Flats	Total	Single berths
Harare	10 591	29 688	2 824	1 198	44 301	28 086
Chitungwiza	6 770	5 435	1 100	–	13 305	120
Total	17 361	35 123	3 924	1 189	57 606	28 206

Source: Whitsun Foundation 1980: 100.

cost of a conventional two room core house (Mills 1979; Underwood 1987). The government originally hoped that this house type would constitute nearly two-thirds of the post-independence large scale low income housing programme (Teedon 1990). This realistic way of reducing the cost of owner-occupied housing was, however, abandoned in 1982 in response to widespread criticism of the low standard it was felt to represent (Simon 1986; Zimbabwe 1987a).

By the end of the 1970s, recognition of the desirability, for political reasons, of increasing home ownership, added to resource constraints; and growing concern over the ability of urban Africans to pay for municipal housing had led to a major shift in emphasis towards home ownership, and also to reliance on serviced plot provision for new housing supply. Also, by the end of the 1970s a decision had already been taken to sell the existing rental housing stock to sitting tenants. However, two categories of rental housing were considered unsuitable for sale to their occupants: berths in hostels, and houses with shared bathroom and toilet facilities. Although some hostels have been demolished, many blocks have been refurbished and converted into family units. They provide small, cheap, low quality dwellings in environmentally poor surroundings, but are popular because of their location in Mbare close to the city centre. Many are sublet, much to the city council's annoyance. They pose ongoing management and maintenance problems. Gradually, the houses—many of which are semi-detached (Table 6.4)—have had their sanitary facilities improved where these are considered to be substandard (for example in Tafara, Dzivarasekwa and Highfield), though lack of available funds has limited progress. Once provided with self-contained facilities, the houses are considered suitable for sale to their occupants.

Local authorities were required to sell rental units to the households which were, at that time, the main tenants, at a discount reflecting the length of their tenancies. In Harare nearly two-thirds of the total stock was sold in the first stage, which began in 1981 but was not completed until 1985/6. The sale price was determined by capitalising the current rent paid over 25 years and the discount meant that tenants of more than thirty years' standing became outright owners. A number of cases were found where the tenant was not resident, or where the tenancy had been illegally transferred to another household. In the former case, the absentee tenants forfeited their rights of purchase, while in the latter, sympathetic consideration was given to regularising long-standing arrangements, particularly those involving inheritance. The city council was reluctant to sell its entire stock, because of the continued need for rental housing, but, following pressure from government, it embarked on a second programme of sales in 1986. Sales started in 1988, following a wrangle between the city council and central government over how to calculate prices, and by the end of 1990 37% of the 6980 houses available had been sold. At the end of March 1979, 22% of family housing units were individually owned (Patel and Adams 1981: 12). By the end of the second phase of sales, 82% of the former rental housing stock will have been sold into individual ownership (Harare City Council, Department of Housing and Community Services, various dates).

The beneficiaries of the sale of municipal housing have included original tenants, well established lodgers with absentee landlords, and the children of original tenants. In Mabvuku, half had previously been sitting tenants and the remainder had inherited the house or been granted the right to buy as a subtenant of a long-absent main tenant. The original tenants were overwhelmingly nuclear families with male heads in formal sector employment and thus did not include the poorest. These characteristics are still displayed by the current owners of previously rented housing, though in the older areas they have been complicated by life cycle factors. In Mabvuku, for example, 28% of the owners had lived there since the 1950s, and the average age of the household heads was 54 in 1991. Some households' incomes have declined with the retirement of the wage earner; others have increased as a result of long service or the employment of adult sons and daughters. A quarter of the households contained three or four generations of the same family and half had two or three working members, though a third of the household heads had retired. Average household incomes were Z$579 but they varied widely round the average because of the variations in household situation. Because of the relatively low quality of the houses, a relatively small proportion of incomes on average (13%) was spent on housing and related costs. The children of the original municipal tenants are privileged with respect to urban housing because of their right to inherit, a privilege which gives them an advantage over other young heads of household. Nevertheless, those who have benefited from the rent-to-buy programme mostly experience relatively modest housing conditions because of the age and size of the houses they have bought. They are certainly not in the same income group as many of the owners of plots in serviced plot schemes, so they are not the 'elite' of the urban poor.

Harare has never pursued a policy of building complete new 'low cost' houses for sale, and since the late 1970s most of the public sector low income housing programme has concentrated on the provision of serviced plots, with or without some form of wet core (tap, toilet, maybe a sink and/or shower) or core house with one or two rooms. Such a model had been promoted by the World Bank and pursued by many developing countries since earlier in the decade. The early post-independence achievements represent the coming to fruition of pre-independence programmes, and many of the initiatives implemented in the early 1980s had been decided before independence.

In Glen View, over 7000 plots of 200 square metres had been allocated by 1980 (Figure 6.1). Allottees were expected to complete one room in three years and an entire house (36 square metres) within ten years, the freehold of the plot to be transferred when the house was complete (Teedon 1990). In the initial absence of construction loans and technical assistance, progress was slow (Patel and Adams 1981; Mutizwa-Mangiza 1985a). Later, some loans were made available, but progress varied markedly: by 1984, over half the plots contained houses with seven or more rooms and only 13% had less than four rooms, though some occupants had not yet managed to start building and were still living in temporary shelters (Teedon 1990).

Despite the apparent success of Glen View, policy differences between central government and Harare City Council resulted in delays to planned housing development. The standard pre-independence plot size of 200 square metres was considered too small to accommodate a complete house and provide sufficient space for vegetable gardening (Underwood 1987), despite the fact that the larger plots would be 20% more expensive to service (Whitsun Foundation 1980: 105) and the evidence, recognised by the government itself, that many of those on the waiting list earned very low incomes (Rhodesia 1979). Administrative and policy confusion at the centre lessened with the publication of the three year Transitional National Development Plan (TNDP) in November 1982, which set out national housing policy as follows (Zimbabwe 1982: 15):

• A focus on the provision of serviced plots on an aided self-help basis (that is, 'self-help' construction with financial and technical assistance).

- The establishment of building brigades for construction and the production of building materials, in order to bring down costs.
- strict enforcement of standards, which were set at a minimum plot size of 300 square metres (normally 12.5 x 25 = 312.5 square metres) and a core house of four rooms (50 square metres) extendable to seven rooms, with a separate kitchen and bathroom/toilet.

Progress began to be made with serviced plot schemes in both Chitungwiza and Harare, adjusted to the policy principles set out in the TNDP. Target income groups varied slightly, but the schemes were generally aimed at those with incomes around Z$150—compared to the estimated median monthly income in the city of Z$175 in 1982 (Hoek-Smit 1982). Cash loans were made available, and on 10% of the plots, houses for rent were constructed to meet central government concerns, inter alia, for housing their own employees (Taylor 1985). Allottees had to build a four room core house within 18 months (with an additional six months' negotiable grace period). Increased reliance on self-help aimed at reducing costs through inputs of residents' own labour, overcoming the housing backlog and giving residents flexibility to produce at their own pace.

In the early 1980s, 6594 plots were made available in four areas in Harare: Kuwadzana, Warren Park D, Dzivarasekwa and Hatcliffe (Figure 6.1). Kuwadzana was the largest and lowest income of the four. It was partly funded by USAID, which insisted that the plots be allocated to families from the housing waiting list with a maximum income of Z$175 (Schlyter 1985; Mutizwa-Mangiza 1985a; Mafico 1991). A relatively small average plot size was allowed in this area, planning for which had already been underway when the government policy changes noted above occurred, so that 60% of the plots were less than 300 square metres in area. Within a few months of the start of construction, 2200 artisanal builders had registered on the site (Gore et al 1985). Most participants used this private sector hired labour for construction. Allottees were eligible for a building materials loan, the size of which was related to their incomes. Although by mid-1985 a fifth of the houses had been completed to a habitable stage, many households had underestimated the costs of building and had started four rooms, exhausting their loans before completing a single room. All except 4% of allottees were formal sector employees, and nearly three-quarters had no savings from which to finance construction once the loan was exhausted (Patel 1985). Nevertheless, 82% of those surveyed in 1985 had invested additional funds from their own resources (Holin 1985). Although some households with incomes above the ceiling had been allocated plots,

Figure 6.6   Kuwadzana serviced plot scheme, developed with USAID assistance in the mid-1980s. Many households had completed seven room houses, but others had been unable to extend the original core house, as seen in the background

these were relatively few—the project had been successful in reaching its initial target population. This, however, is not the whole story—many residents were lodgers, and the impact of plot sales must be taken into account (see below).

Plotholders were permitted and even encouraged to build additional rooms for rent (Holin 1985). For USAID, the scheme was seen as a success and the development of rental housing was explicit and welcome; the city council's view of the scheme was also positive—for the council, building for lodgers was inevitable, though not an explicit part of the current policy. It was left to Schlyter (1990) to point out that while the median household income for the whole city was Z$175 in 1982, a third of the population had incomes of less than Z$70. These poorer households could not afford to participate in a self-help housing scheme, even an aided one.

In Phase 2, 502 plots were sold to employers (Potts with Mutambirwa 1991: 9), from whom demand greatly exceeded supply. By 1989, 6702 stands had been allocated in this area alone, on two-thirds of which at least one room had been completed. Construction was still proceeding at the beginning of the 1990s, though at a less dramatic pace (Figure 6.6), and security street lighting and many facilities had been provided, overcoming some of the deficiencies faced by residents in the early years. However, shortage of foreign exchange had prevented the installation of domestic electricity.

Despite the difficulty experienced by many allottees in Kuwadzana in building a four room core within 18 months, this unnecessary requirement and the new minimum plot size of 300 square metres were generalised to all other new schemes (and to all urban areas) (Zimbabwe 1986b). The city council wanted to develop the first stage of Warren Park D in a similar way to the successful Glen View scheme, with one and two room core houses and freehold title to be issued on the completion of the house. Eventually, the 1325 mostly 200 square metre plots serviced in Phase I were provided with a mixture of one and two room core and complete houses, while 366 larger (400 square metre) plots were laid out between the area and the Bulawayo Road, concealing the lower income houses from the view of passing motorists. In response to central government's concern with the appearance of Glen View, however, allottees were required to build four rooms within 18 months. Instead of allowing temporary dwellings, the council decided that plots could not be occupied until a permanent room had been built, meaning that the resources of the lowest income households were unnecessarily strained by having to buy building materials and pay a builder at the same time as paying rent elsewhere (Figure 6.7). When the plots were advertised, over 20 000 applications were received. A minimum income of Z$130 per month was required for a one room core house, while the ceiling was set at Z$325. Allocations started in mid-1981 and were completed a year later, to households in the target income group. Again, most occupants used the model house plans provided by the council, and hired builders. As in Glen View, a relatively large proportion had extended their core houses by the mid-1980s (Teedon 1990), but for those without extra resources, the threat of eviction if they did not fulfil the scheme requirements, even if rarely enforced, increased their sense of insecurity and vulnerability.

Our sample survey in 1991 (Rakodi with Withers 1993) found that a third of the plots were occupied by the owner alone, 60% by the owner and one or more lodgers, and 8% by the tenants of absentee landlords. On average there were 2.1 households per plot. Most owners occupied four or five rooms, while the great majority of lodgers rented one room. The owner household heads, most of whom (70%) had been allocated their plots in 1984/5, were long term urban residents (average 21 years) with steady employment and average household incomes of Z$892 (compared to Z$555 for lodgers), significantly supplemented by rents. Although slightly more than 43% of owners in 1991 fell within the officially defined 'low income' group (less than Z$650), the majority, including original allottees whose incomes had increased and purchasers

Figure 6.7 An incomplete house in the Warren Park D sites and services scheme. Some owners started to build large houses and ran out of money before any rooms were complete, but scheme rules forbade them to live on the plot in a temporary shelter. This house is still unoccupied five or six years after the plot was allocated

of partly developed plots, were no longer low income. Original allottees paying Harare City Council loan instalments were not paying a lot more per month than lodgers (Z\$67 compared to Z\$60), but this constituted a relatively small proportion of their incomes (average 14%) and provided them with a substantial dwelling of 3.7 rooms and a separate kitchen while Z\$60 was the typical rent for one room. Over half the owners had managed to complete a habitable structure within a year of allocation, and most had subsequently embarked on a more or less continuous process of extension and improvement, mostly financed from their own savings. A quarter had completed seven rooms but over half had fewer than this (Figure 6.8). A second phase in Warren Park and smaller schemes in Dzivarasekwa and Hatcliffe completed the first post-independence programmes (HCMPPA 1988c; Mafico 1991).

In the public sector, therefore, more than one form of house production is operating. The industrialised production of physical infrastructure and core houses signifies the presence of large scale contractors able to make a profit because of the size of public sector contracts and the standardised nature of the components. That the units, especially complete houses, are then not affordable by the majority of the population is as much a function of the standards and speed of

Figure 6.8 Completed houses in the Warren Park D sites and services area. Few women can get wage jobs, so most are at home during the day. Social contacts between neighbours are important

construction insisted upon by the public authorities as the profits expected by private contractors. Also operating, especially in Harare, are small scale labour-only building contractors, used by owner-occupiers for house construction or extension. Hired labour of this type is more important in the construction process than domestic labour inputs from the household itself. Teedon (1990) in Warren Park and Glen View found that only householders who were themselves engaged in construction trades tended to build with their own hands. The government in 1982 intended to reduce the supply costs of housing by the establishment of building brigades. They were to be established by local authorities and were ultimately expected to replace private contractors in low income house construction, but proved expensive and unpopular (Mutizwa-Mangiza 1985b; Mutizwa-Mangiza and Marciano 1987).

Cooperatives, in general and in the housing sector (Zimbabwe 1987a), have been encouraged, at least in theory, as representing a move towards the socialisation of production. However, they have not proved attractive to participants in urban serviced plot schemes. The few cooperatives which have been established in Harare and Chitungwiza have run into difficulties in obtaining access to land and housing finance: allocation policy allows plots to be allotted only to individuals, and access to building society loans is impeded because cooperatives are not covered by the government housing and loan guarantee scheme (Butcher 1990; Zimbabwe 1991b).

The next phase of low income housing programmes started in 1984, with the approval of Glen Norah C, which, along with Sunningdale and Budiriro, was developed with the assistance of World Bank financing under the first Urban Development Project (World Bank 1984). The plots were allocated to households with an income ceiling of Z$400, and it was expected that 70% would be allocated to families with incomes below Z$200, in accordance with the income profile of the waiting list (World Bank 1984: 69). In practice, a minimum income of Z$190 was necessary to afford a plot. Rising costs led to an increase in income ceilings in 1988 and 1989 (Harare City Council, Department of Housing and Community Services 1989). The standards and regulations to be adopted were those standard at the time. The main departure was in the arrangements for housing finance (see below). Building society loans have been made available to cover the capital costs of the plot and house construction, at building society interest rates (12.5% at that time), repayable over 25 years. Initially, there were delays as the societies developed appropriate procedures, but by 1988 the backlog of loan applications had been cleared. Repayments, after a five month grace period, were not supposed to account for more than 25% of the allottees' incomes, but it was expected that other resources would be available to builders, especially income from lodgers. Indeed, the World Bank anticipated that there would be three or four households on each plot (World Bank 1984). Title to plots was issued to applicants and bonded to the building society, enabling the local authority to recover the plot development costs much more promptly than in previous projects. By 1989 a total of nearly 5000 plots had been allocated (Harare City Council, Department of Housing and Community Services 1987, 1989). They went to those in the target income groups, but households' ability to afford repayments restricted the size of loan for which they were eligible to less than half the cost of a plot and complete four room house (Potts with Mutambirwa 1991).

Budiriro was located on three farms, to the southwest of the city, in an area ultimately capable of accommodating at least 7000 plots (Figure 6.1). In Phase I, 1197 plots were allocated in the normal manner to people on the waiting list, and 1200 were allocated to employers for their employees. The latter allocation was something of an experiment, and so it was evaluated in some detail in 1991/2 (Withers and Rakodi 1993). Further phases are under development.

Allocation in Budiriro Phase I was delayed from early 1987 because of the need to persuade and prepare building societies for their new role. However, by June 1989, of the 1200 employer assisted plots, 694 allottees had title, 124 had started construction and 59 had completed at least a four room house (Figures 6.9 and 6.10). Construction had been slowed down by shortages of cement (see below). On the plots in the sample surveyed in 1991, an average of 3.3 rooms had been built, though only 43% of beneficiaries had been able to fulfil scheme requirements and build a four room house within 18 months of allocation. While the majority of companies involved provided credit to employees on a concessionary basis, in general, employer assistance in the form of paying the plot purchase price up front benefited the city council most, in that they were able to recoup plot servicing costs relatively quickly. Some employers, however, also gave top-up loans for house construction and financing, while the additional assistance they gave with the construction process was generally welcome, if not vital to allottees. Employers' assistance is also of interest to building societies, in that company-guaranteed mortgages are cheaper to process than individual mortgages requiring government guarantees. To companies, aware of the adverse impact of living in distant and overcrowded rental rooms on worker productivity, the benefits seem sufficient to encourage a continued positive response to offers of serviced plots for their employees. For employees successful in obtaining company nominations, the main benefits are the reductions in waiting period for some and in costs for others. Although those who were allocated plots in Budiriro I were from the low income group, including a third with incomes under Z$400, high costs seem likely to pose repayment problems. However, disadvantaged groups were excluded from the scheme: women heads of household, a smaller proportion of whom can get access to formal sector wage jobs, and those in informal sector employment. Employer aided self-help programmes are unlikely, therefore, to change the bias of established plot allocation processes and will instead reinforce the privileged position of those in stable wage employment.

We are now in a position to summarise total public sector house production over time. Between 1971/2 and 1979/80, 23 378 units were produced in Harare (an average of 2598 per annum). This was reduced to an average of 2434 per annum between 1980/1 and 1984/5 and fell even further, to 2180 per annum, between 1985/6 and 1988/9). By mid-1990, the waiting list stood at 60 000, and was growing at 900 a month, while the council was only able to service about 1500 stands a year (Harare City Council, Department of Housing and Community Services 1990).

At independence, there were about 13 500 municipally owned houses in Chitungwiza, in addition to 7300 houses on serviced plots (Patel and Adams 1981: 12). Squatter resettlement continued after 1980 in ultra-low-cost houses in Seke, and continued house construction meant that

Figure 6.9   Building under way in Budiriro Phase I

Figure 6.10   Budiriro sites and services area. New and more sensible rules permitted allottees to live in temporary shelters on their plots while building. Thriving businesses have developed for the production of wooden panels for use both in sites and services areas and to build illegal backyard shacks

end of 1988 the housing stock had grown by over 40% to 29 500 houses. Despite the rapid rate of house construction, the council has been unable to keep pace with demand, as illustrated by the waiting list, which had reached 30 000 households in mid-1991 (*Herald*, 23 August 1991), and the growth of backyard shacks for renting.

The majority of governments which have attempted to meet low income housing needs by relying on the provision of serviced plots have encountered similar problems of keeping pace with growing numbers of households and affordability. In part, as in Harare, this can be attributed to problems with the standards adopted and the design of programmes (van der Linden 1986). In some countries the shortfall is exacerbated by their lack of technical, administrative and financial capacity, especially at the local level, but this is less of a constraint in Zimbabwe. In addition, problems have arisen because serviced plot programmes, especially those financed by external agencies on a project by project basis, have not alleviated wider sectoral supply constraints (Rakodi 1991b). This last factor will be considered more systematically below.

Unauthorised dwellings

The attitudes of both pre- and post-independence governments to the unauthorised production of housing have been discussed in Chapters 1 and 2. The first government of independent Zimbabwe inherited a number of squatter areas near Mbare and between Harare and Chitungwiza and continued with the earlier policies of demolition, combining the temporary movement of families into hostels no longer used for single male migrants with relocation to serviced plot schemes of various sorts, and pressure to return to the rural areas. Thus in 1981 Mbare Musika squatter area and Chirambahuyo transitional squatter resettlement area in Chitungwiza (30 000 people) were demolished, despite Patel and Adams' (1981) attempt to argue for upgrading. The following year, demolitions continued (Butcher 1986) and 'Operation Clean-Up' was initiated by the central committee of ZANU-PF, taking the form of a purge of squatters, along with people labelled as 'prostitutes' and 'vagrants'. Squatter homes were burned or bulldozed throughout the city, and their residents were arrested but released on condition that they returned to the rural areas, if they had access to land, and did not squat again. Similar measures, which have also periodically been used in other African countries, have continued to be taken since.

Patel attributed the government's approach to urban squatters to 'a mixture of national pride and concern over health hazards, visible productive activities, and reducing criminal elements' (1988: 212).

Squatter settlements are seen as eyesores, and a first step on the slide to the urban characteristics and problems which politicians and officials alike abhor in other African cities. Although there is now widespread recognition of the need to encourage informal sector activities to fill the growing gap between the labour force and available formal sector wage employment (see Chapter 3), this is combined with a (probably incompatible) desire to regulate and license this sector—more difficult if activities are located in areas which are themselves unregulated. Finally, Patel regards the belief that squatter areas harbour criminal elements as a myth, underlain by criminalisation of some informal sector activities, ranging from unlicensed vegetable selling to beer brewing or prostitution. The vulnerability of squatters to government action has led all who can to settle in legal housing areas, so that the desperate families who opt for squatting or sleeping rough are the poorest and most marginal. Although demolition threats generate a measure of support from concerned high income individuals and bodies such as the churches, widespread working class support is not forthcoming.

The only exceptions to the demolition policy are Epworth and illegal backyard shacks. In Epworth, which has been described in Chapter 2, halting progress has been made with infrastructure improvement and regularisation since 1983 (Patel 1984, 1988; Butcher 1986). In recent years, housing shortages have also led to the construction of wooden backyard shacks or side-structures adjacent to houses to which extensions are not officially allowed. In 1987 it was estimated that 15% of the population of Harare's high density residential areas and 18% of Chitungwiza's population lived in outbuildings (HCMPPA 1988c). Periodic attempts to demolish these shacks have been much less effective than the raids on squatter settlements, partly for physical reasons (they are in the yards of permanent legal houses, many built by the councils themselves) and partly because they have been constructed by voters on privately owned land. Present signs are that increasing housing shortfalls will be met by a proliferation of backyard shacks rather than squatting on vacant land. Indeed, businesses have been established in those areas where demand is greatest to supply prefabricated wooden wall and roof panels for the easy construction of such dwellings. An added advantage over squatting is the access they provide to piped water and other services, though of course the house is not free.

Factors influencing housing supply

Potentially, since 1980, the housing provided by each of the forms of production discussed above could have accommodated population growth, depending on its capacity to expand production, on its compatibility with the development policies of the new government, and on particular constraints on supply. The factors which influence and potentially constrain the supply of housing include land and tenure (see Chapter 5); the availability of infrastructure; the capacity of the construction sector; the supply of building materials and construction skills; and certain legislation, especially planning and building regulations (see Chapters 1, 2 and 5) and rent control (see above). The extent to which these constrain the production of housing in Harare will now be assessed. Several are expected to be addressed in a new USAID funded programme announced in 1992 (USAID 1992).

Land constraints

Our consideration of land supply in Chapter 5 concluded that physical availability of land was not a constraint on the future development of the city, though there are bottlenecks affecting the supply of land for development and sale on the private market. Much of the undeveloped land which is suitable for development is within the existing municipal boundary and the first priority must be to find means of deterring the hoarding of this land, in addition to modifying and streamlining policies and procedures to ensure that private owners respond to increased demand for land for new housing development.

Land has been made available for public sector low income housing development on an ad hoc basis. In Harare, this pragmatic approach has resulted in the continuation of pre-independence patterns of:

1   confining the low income population largely to the southwest and south of the city by expanding areas such as Warren Park, Dzivarasekwa and Chitungwiza; and
2   using peripheral locations for large scale development, again in Chitungwiza, but also in Kuwadzana and Budiriro, the locations of which appear to have been determined by the chance availability of land for sale.

Although some land is available in council ownership, and planning is underway for the servicing of additional plots, the numbers are well below those needed to keep pace with growth in population and the waiting list, and plans are afoot to acquire more land. This approach to land supply for housing reflects the short term project orientation of the housing department in the council, the lack of strategic guidance in face of the long delays in master plan preparation, and the reluctance of government to approve funds for advance land purchase.

Financial constraints affecting the purchase and servicing of land have resulted in an insufficient number of plots being made available, but the supply problem is exacerbated by the generous plot sizes for houses and social facilities. Large plot sizes have been entrenched in policy and regulations, both for low income development and high income housing. Official policy has been to close the gap between low and high density areas of the cities by requiring quality construction for low income residents, regardless of its feasibility. The outcome is that public sector programmes satisfy the housing demands of the growing middle income group while the poorest are increasingly marginalised. Until recently, pressure to reconsider these standards was resisted, but the conditions attached to new USAID funding (USAID 1992) produced a reduction in the minimum plot size to 200 square metres for high density areas, and some consideration is being given to the possibilities for higher density infilling and the subdivision of large undeveloped plots in the northern suburbs.

Infrastructure constraints

Harare has a high standard of utility provision: 90% of low income plots have individual water connections, though these are often shared by two or more families occupying the plot. Current sources of supply are thought to be sufficient to meet the needs of the city for the remainder of the twentieth century (see Chapter 2). A similar proportion of low income areas has waterborne sewage disposal. Many of the low density areas, however, rely on septic tank sanitation which may be a constraint to locating higher density development in the northern suburbs. While only half the low income plots have electricity connections, all official areas have street or tower lighting. In the past, all low income plots have also been provided with road access, despite low rates of vehicle ownership. The high standards of physical infrastructure continued (Zimbabwe 1986b), despite the demands placed on public capital for development and the cost to individual plot buyers. Harare City Council appears to have the technical and administrative capacity to implement large scale infrastructure programmes, but since 1983, the availability of public sector finance has been a major constraint on the supply of serviced plots (Zimbabwe 1986b: 7).

Allocations at both national and city levels have fallen short of both need and targets in each year since 1980 (Zimbabwe 1986b, 1991b; Mafico 1991; Mutizwa-Mangiza 1991c). The shortfall has been exacerbated by the high space and infrastructure standards that have been adopted, which result in roads and surface water drainage typically accounting for over half the cost of a serviced plot (Atkins 1983; Musandu-Nyamayaro 1993). The high standards of water supply and sanitation increase water consumption, capital costs (though not as much as the extravagant access standards) and recurrent charges. Plot occupancy rates in many of the low cost areas are high (8.3 on average) (Zimbabwe 1991b: 31) and may increase as residents build more rooms and backyard shacks for rent. There are, therefore, some grounds for retaining these standards for water and sanitation, though alternative sanitation technology is available. Even if individual piped water supply and waterborne sanitation are retained, a recent study by Musandu-Nyamayaro (1993) shows that dramatic cost reductions could be achieved by reducing the size and frontage of plots and modifying road access.

Construction sector constraints

The capacity of the construction industry is influenced by its organis-ation, the availability of capital and other necessary inputs, including equipment and sufficient suitable labour, technology choice, and the supply of building materials. Materials are discussed separately below.

Residential construction is divided between the public sector, which has, in recent years, initiated most new development, and the private sector. Little had been published about the private construction sector until 1991, other than references to its declining contribution to GDP and considerable underutilised capacity, despite a post-1980 loss of skilled manpower and increasingly obsolete equipment (Colquhoun et al 1985; Zimbabwe 1986b). It is dominated by large contractors, who are awarded most of the large public sector contracts. In October 1990, there were 875 registered construction contractors in Harare. Three had over a thousand employees, but the great majority were very small (Giersing Rose 1991).

The largest and some smaller firms are members of the Construction Industry Federation of Zimbabwe (CIFOZ), the body traditionally representing the construction industry in negotiations with government. It has used its standard-maintaining powers, the technical superiority of its members, and strict (and expensive) membership rules to further the interests of a small number of white owned companies and to exclude newcomers. As a result, it has had little influence on govern-ment since 1980, making it more difficult for the sector as a whole to obtain access to the resources it needs (Giersing Rose 1991). As a reaction to the racist and exclusionary attitudes of CIFOZ, black contractors formed a rival organisation, the Zimbabwe Building

Contractors' Association, in 1985, to better represent their interests. Indigenous contractors have experienced a range of problems, some arising from various discriminatory practices by CIFOZ and its members, and some typical of a newly developing industry. Giersing Rose identified lack of management skills and experience, difficulties in obtaining access to foreign exchange for the import of equipment and vehicles, and difficulty in obtaining access to contracts. The contract access problem is attributed partly to CIFOZ practices, partly to the large size of government projects, and partly to the lack of affirmative action in the award of public sector contracts.

To operate, contractors producing housing for public or private clients or developers need capital, equipment and skills. Access to formal sector capital is easier for large well established firms, and government efforts to make credit available to small enterprises have met with only limited success. In a survey of CIFOZ members it was found that a third of plant and vehicles were over 15 years old, a third were obsolete, unusable or in very poor condition, and 15% of usable equipment was immobilised awaiting spares. Difficulties of getting access to foreign exchange prevented replacement of this equipment (Giersing Rose 1991). The loss of professionally qualified whites, both by emigration and from the depressed construction industry to other sectors, and a lack of local replacement staff have given rise to shortages of professional, technical and supervisory staff, which affect the large scale sector more seriously. Trade skills are more widespread, as is demonstrated by the ability of artisanal builders to meet the house construction needs of individual plot holders in sites and services schemes.

While demand for large commercial and office buildings has been buoyant in Harare, investment in speculative private sector house construction has been limited, and the response to growing unsatisfied middle income residential demand has been slow. The reasons for this are complex. They include price differences between the price of secondhand and new houses; the rigidity of standards incorporated in development plans, which increase costs; difficulties in purchasing, replacing or repairing equipment; the escalating cost of building materials; the plentiful availability of work, especially from the public sector, obviating the need to undertake risky speculative development; the difficulty many small and medium contractors experience in obtaining access to bank or supplier credit even if they decide to build speculative houses; and the higher costs faced by middle income families if they individually commission a builder. At the other end of the market, the demand for 'low cost' houses has been dampened by the shortfall of serviced plots and by the mismatch between building

costs implied by minimum standards and the incomes of many poor
urban households, even though very small scale contractors can build
large numbers of low cost houses on the basis of labour-only
contracts. As a result of the constraints on their operations, eight out
of ten of the contractors who responded to Giersing Rose's survey in
1991 were unable at the time to take on more work. That the capacity
of the construction industry is limited, despite its potential, reflects
both the defensive conservatism of firms which existed at independence, and the failure of government to recognise the importance
of a healthy construction sector to its economic development aims,
which has led to policy neglect. Trade liberalisation has enabled
construction firms to import needed equipment, but the extent to
which this benefits those firms producing low cost housing rather
than those producing commercial buildings and luxury accommodation needs to be monitored.

Building materials

As a result of government support and years of sanctions before
independence, Zimbabwe has a building materials supply industry
which is well developed compared to many African countries. It was
estimated that only 7.6%, by value, of the materials necessary for a four
room low cost house had to be imported in the mid-1980s (Martin et al
1985: 8). Basic cement, iron and steel industries were developed in the
1960s and 1970s (see Chapter 1). A wide range of materials is manufactured locally by formal sector enterprises, many of which are
monopolies or near monopolies (Colquhoun et al 1985). Before
independence formal sector enterprises were encouraged by the absence
of competition and after independence by strict exchange control
regulations and control over new investment. Until the mid-1980s,
demand was so depressed that there was spare capacity in many of the
industries, despite the age of the equipment being used (Colombard-
Prout et al 1986). An increase in demand from 1986 onwards resulted in
sudden and growing shortages even of locally produced materials,
especially cement and bricks.

Cement shortages resulted from a combination of factors, including
breakdown of obsolete machinery, difficulty of obtaining foreign
exchange, and price control (Colombard-Prout et al 1986; Giersing Rose
1991). By 1990, black market prices of at least twice the controlled price
were being paid, especially by households and black contractors
(*Financial Herald*, 11 May 1990; *Business Herald*, 16 May 1991). The
shortage of cement had ripple effects throughout the construction

sector—there was a severe drop in the supply of cement based products such as roofing tiles, asbestos roof sheets and building blocks. In August 1991 price control was abolished overnight and import controls lifted (*Herald*, 9 August 1991). This has enabled local producers to re-equip and increase supplies, while increased imports have helped meet demand in the interim.

Two basic types of bricks have traditionally been produced in Zimbabwe: farm bricks, which are produced by their users, mainly in the commercial farming areas, and cannot be sold on the open market; and burnt bricks, for which there are several production units in Harare. Between 1970 and 1985, 71% of the municipal houses in Harare were built of brick (Colombard-Prout et al 1986). However, by 1989/90 brick production was sufficient to satisfy only two-thirds of total demand. Despite the advantages of bricks (the raw materials are widely available, the capital cost of a new brickfield is relatively modest, and some machinery for small scale production can be produced in Zimbabwe), investment in their production is not given priority over concrete block manufacture. However, new investment in brick production near Harare was occurring by the beginning of the 1990s (*Herald*, 22 March 1991).

A further problem has been the rapid rise in costs, on average by 16% per annum between 1979 and 1989, despite the dampening effect of price controls. Price rises of 31% in 1990, 37% in 1991 and 47% in 1992—greater even than the rapidly increasing rate of inflation—reflected the removal of price controls, increased demand and the initial impact of the structural adjustment programme. The 1980s price increases have been explained by the increase in labour costs resulting from minimum wage legislation (HCMPPA 1988c; CSO 1988: 55, December 1991: 36). However, the monopoly production of certain materials, the increase in demand following a period of depression and the downtime of obsolete equipment are more important factors in recent years. The system discourages innovation in building materials: the state uses tenders with materials already specified, architects and contractors are conservative, there is little local research into alternative materials, there is a lack of competition, and the by-laws are restrictive. Eventually, the national guidelines for by-laws were changed in December 1992, allowing the use of farm bricks, soil cement bricks and prefabricated panels in house construction in urban areas (*Herald*, 22 February 1993), and the rate of price increases, especially of imported materials, fell dramatically in 1993. However, as imported materials are hardly needed in the construction of low cost houses, this decrease in prices may benefit commercial and high income clients rather than low income households.

The consumption of housing

Housing needs are usually defined in relation to normative standards of acceptable accommodation. While this is necessary, it does not take into account resource availability at both national and household levels. The result is that at national and city levels, the supply of acceptable units can never be sufficient in volume to satisfy total estimated need, while at the individual level, many urban households cannot afford to pay for the housing units produced. Recognition of these problems has led to increasing emphasis on the analysis of effective demand, and on an insistence, especially in internationally funded housing programmes, that the units supplied be affordable. The resources available to individual households determine their consumption of housing, but may be influenced by government, especially in the arrangements made for housing finance.

Housing needs, effective demand and affordability

Two indicators of housing need have been used in Zimbabwe: the official housing waiting lists, and estimates of need based on population projections. However, the latter type of estimate, which takes into account population growth, household characteristics and ideas about minimum standards, does not appear to have been made for Harare since 1979. The housing waiting list in Harare (then Salisbury) was added to on a chronological basis. By 1977 it had reached 20 000 (Smout 1977d: 50) and by 1984 36 000 (Taylor 1985) or 63 000 including Chitungwiza (Mutizwa-Mangiza 1985b: 85). Although this was used as a guide to housing need, it was recognised to be out of date. Many households did not bother to apply, as the chance of being allocated a house or plot was so remote. In 1984 the list was reformed, in two stages. First, all those who wished to be placed on it had to reapply and a system of annual updating was adopted. In 1985 it had dropped to 23 000 because of non-renewal of applications, but since then it has increased on average by over 20% each year to 90 000 in 1993. The Chitungwiza waiting list included 30 000 applicants in mid-1991 (*Herald*, 23 August 1991).

The second reform of the list saw a scoring system introduced to replace the simple queuing system that had previously operated, taking into account mainly the applicant's length of urban residence but also household size, income etc. In order to be eligible for registration, a household head must be in wage employment or acceptable and licensed self-employment, must be married or have parental responsibilities, may not own or rent a house elsewhere in the city, and must have an income below a ceiling which in 1985 was increased from Z$450 to Z$600 per month and was later abolished. The reliability of the waiting list as an indicator of need has been questioned. Some people are unaware of the need to register; others are discouraged by the size of the list; households currently in employers' accommodation only apply as a safeguard against unemployment or retirement; information on the list is outdated; and many are ineligible. Although the situation has improved since the reform of the waiting list, certain categories of household are ineligible, especially those with household heads who are not working in wage or registered self-employment. These include many households headed by women—but not those headed by widows, who are permitted to stay in houses already allocated to their husbands. Despite improvements in women's property rights since independence, female heads of household are discriminated against in a variety of ways—for example a mother or sisters who undertake domestic tasks to enable a household head to work are not counted, unlike the wife of a male head (Schlyter 1989).

In addition, plots and houses are allocated to people who are not waiting list priorities. In some cases, this is because public sector bodies make a special case for their employees; in others it has been because the plots advertised are too expensive for those at the top of the waiting list. However, in yet others there is evidence of malpractice, allegations of which have surfaced periodically during the years since 1980. An internal city council investigation which reported in March 1992 found 'massive' irregularities, including allocations to city council employees and their friends and relatives; allocation to those earning more than Z$650 per month, the income ceiling for eligibility for housing in high density areas; and allocation to applicants who had falsified information, especially that relating to their length of employment in the city (*Herald*, 17 March 1992).

Estimates of housing need, whether based on self-registration or more systematic analysis, can rarely be translated into effective demand, because of a mismatch between the cost of housing and residents' ability to afford it. Analyses of affordability in Harare show that this city is no exception. Estimates of the ability of each group in the income distribution to consume housing require accurate information on household income, together with the proportion of that income available for expenditure on housing and utilities, and on the ability of households to mobilise resources from other sources, including the household itself, the extended family and credit.

References to problems of affordability occurred in Rhodesia as far back as the 1950s (Ashton 1969). The Whitsun Foundation, based on the wage distribution of black employees in 1977, estimated that only 20%

could afford standard low cost housing and 27% could afford core housing (Whitsun Foundation 1980: 107–8). Mutizwa-Mangiza (1985b) made a similar calculation using the income figures available from Hoek-Smit's 1982 survey updated to 1985. Using the rule of thumb of the Ministry of Public Construction and National Housing (MPCNH), that households should not spend more than 27.5% of their incomes on housing, only 16% of low income households could have afforded the official four room core house (Mutizwa-Mangiza 1985b).

At the same time, the World Bank (1985: 64) concluded that four room houses were affordable (at 25% of income spent on housing) only by the top 25% of all urban households, using an income distribution based on the updated figures from the 1976/7 Expenditure Survey. In the first World Bank projects it was intended that 70% of dwelling units provided would be affordable (allowing for rental income from lodgers) to those with incomes less than Z$70, supposedly following the income profile of the waiting lists (World Bank 1984). Room rental was calculated to be affordable down to the thirteenth percentile—that is, below the poverty line. However, to pay for a four room house would have required an income more than that earned by three-quarters of the households on Harare's waiting list. It was, therefore, assumed that every owner household would rent out three rooms, bringing in an income sufficient to cover nearly three-quarters of the monthly costs, and making house ownership affordable to those on the poverty line. The practical impossibility of this was not acknowledged. The household income that was counted for the assessment of eligibility for loans by public sector institutions in Zimbabwe did not include potential rental income, so there was no way in which households with incomes below that sufficient to repay a loan for the cost of a four room house could have qualified for such a loan in the first place.

That this was indeed a problem is demonstrated by the gap between mortgages granted to allottees in recent serviced plot schemes and the cost of completing a four room house, as specified in the conditions for participation. However, that it is not a long term problem for all allottees is shown by the progress with construction made over a number of years, generally using households' own savings, in older serviced plot schemes such as Glen Norah (Potts with Mutambirwa 1991) or Warren Park (Withers and Rakodi 1993).

The official calculations were updated in 1991. Surveys for the housing indicators' report showed that the average income in urban high density areas was Z$400 (Zimbabwe 1991c). Only those earning over Z$900 per month, it was estimated, could have afforded a standard four room core costing between Z$18 000 and Z$20 000. Those earning under Z$200 could only have afforded the rent for a single room or backyard shack (Z$50), often at the cost of other essential expenditure. Of the households on the city's waiting list in 1988/9, 9% earned less than Z$200 and 54% less than Z$400. Only 12% earned more than Z$800. Although there are a number of problems with these simple 'rule of thumb' estimates of affordability, they do illustrate the mismatch in housing policy in Zimbabwe between the normative standards embodied in the conditions imposed on allottees in 'low cost' housing schemes and the resources available to poor households.

The households most in housing need in Harare are those renting rooms and backyard shacks. Using our 1991 costs and survey results (Rakodi with Withers 1993), it was estimated that even a one room house would have been unaffordable by 61% of non-owner households. This was not only due to poverty (only about one in five of these households were estimated to be below an updated poverty line), but also to the high costs implied by large plot sizes, high infrastructure standards and good quality construction. Not all tenants aspired to home ownership, but 58% expressed a desire to move, given the opportunity. They wanted, on average, four room dwellings, and were prepared to pay roughly the proportion of their incomes assumed by the MPCNH (27.5%), but few would be able to afford even a one room core house in a typical present day sites and services scheme such as Budiriro. As has already been noted, although low income households have been allocated plots in Budiriro, there is cause for concern with respect to their ability to build four roomed houses and to sustain housing related costs which often absorb a third or more of their incomes. The prospect for the great majority of lodger households being able to satisfy their need for more space and security by owning their own homes seems remote, unless the rules which govern sites and services schemes are significantly changed.

Housing finance

The amount families can afford to pay for housing is not, in the case of home ownership, solely determined by their monthly incomes. The availability of savings and importance of inter-household transfers varies from place to place, and the latter especially is an important source of finance for households in some cities. However, the cost of housing in relation to household income makes the availability of credit crucial. Zimbabwe has a well established housing finance system, which has recently been harnessed to provide loans for low income house builders in serviced plot schemes.

The system relies primarily on the building societies, of which there are three. Traditionally, these have been the main source of funds for high income households' house construction or purchase. They operate within the 1965 Building Societies Act, which aims, by requiring relatively high reserve and liquidity ratios, to ensure that they are run on prudent, conservative lines with little risk to investors (Building Societies' Role 1987). The availability of credit depends on the ability of the societies to attract savings, while its suitability for low income borrowers depends on the design of lending instruments and procedures. Savings are affected by wider fiscal policies, including taxation rates, interest rate regulation and the government's need for finance. Building societies in Zimbabwe lost out in the early 1980s from changes in tax and interest rates and in 1984 from the loss to the Reserve Bank of many millions of dollars' worth of blocked funds belonging to emigrants. Although the government requires a certain proportion of building society funds to be invested in government bonds, it relies primarily on the Post Office Savings Bank (POSB). When budget deficits increase, interest rates paid by the latter are increased over those which building societies are allowed to pay. As a result between 1980 and 1984, while POSB deposits increased by 90%, building society deposits increased by only 7% (NCSI 1985); and while the POSB increased its share of total savings with financial institutions by over 60% between 1982 and 1986, the share of building societies declined by almost as much (commercial banks maintained a relatively steady share of about 37%) (Building Societies' Role 1987: 20).

By 1985 the building societies had financed 30 000 houses since their establishment (World Bank 1985). This finance had all been for higher cost dwellings and took the form of level repayment mortgages (Zimbabwe 1991b: 42). The societies had not participated in lending for low income housing for a mixture of more or less valid reasons: security of tenure was lacking (many local authority housing areas were unsurveyed and even owners could not obtain title deeds), while local authorities imposed restrictions on resale; lower building standards were used in high density areas than those acceptable to building societies; the high cost of administering a large number of small loans; lack of resources and experience; and fear of a high default rate (Beresford 1990a). Central government, urged on by the international agencies, was anxious to replace the direct role of local authorities, in on-lending government funds for house construction and purchase, by the use of private sector institutions (NCSI 1985; Zimbabwe 1985b, 1986b; MPCNH 1986). By the 1980s, the World Bank and USAID had identified the limited volume of mortgage funds which the public sector was able to make available as one of the main constraints on the larger scale provision of serviced plots. A desire to tap into private sector funds for low income housing, an ideological belief that private sector institutions would be more efficient in disbursing and recovering loans than public sector institutions, and an underlying desire to extend the reach of international and domestic large scale capital, led to a major focus on housing finance. Attempts were made in a variety of countries to create self-supporting financial intermediaries capable of making loans to low and moderate income households and to reduce and restructure housing subsidies (especially to eliminate subsidised interest rates) (World Bank 1993). In sub-Saharan Africa, Zimbabwe appeared to offer good prospects for a successful experiment. Since the mid-1980s, the development of housing finance has illustrated government's attempts to balance its need to maintain revenue with its desire to rely on the private sector for credit for both low and high income housing.

In 1986, building societies were given permission to issue 9% tax-free PUPS (permanent paid up shares—that is, for two years). These, it was hoped, would enable building societies to attract additional investment funds, on condition that 25% of the funds so mobilised would be available for lending for high density housing. Of the latter, 25% was to be lent to the NHF (National Housing Fund) for on-lending to local authorities and the remaining 75% was to be for individual mortgages. Although the advantage of the POSB has not been removed, the flow of savings into building societies was healthier between 1986/7 and 1991 and mortgage finance was, as a result, sufficient to meet demand (Beresford 1990a: 4; Building Societies' Role 1987).

Beverley Building Society, the second largest and most innovative of the three societies, was the first to become involved, followed by the Central Africa Building Society (CABS), the largest. Founders Building Society, the smallest and most conservative, was reluctant to participate, though its issue of tax-free PUPS ensured that it had to contribute to the NHF and become involved in individual lending to a limited extent. The lending instrument changed little when the societies extended their activities to low income housing—level repayment mortgages were offered over 25 years at 12.5% for residential loans of less than Z$12 000 in 1989. By late 1991, the threshold for a 'low cost' house had been raised to Z$35 000 to reflect increased building costs, and interest rates for owner-occupied housing had been raised to 15% below this ceiling and 17% above it.

Building societies lend an amount for which repayments do not exceed 27.5% of single or joint cash income (Founders), 25% of gross single or joint income (Beverley), or 30% of single or joint income (plus an additional Z$50 per month from anticipated 'lodger' income) (CABS). All will lend more in employer assisted schemes (see below). CABS will also lend to self-employed applicants and is currently negotiating the grant of mortgages to a group of Korsten basket makers for whom Chitungwiza municipality is servicing plots. These limits, it should be noted, exclude the housing-related costs which are included when the MPCNH uses its 27.5% rule of thumb. Early problems with lending to low income households led to adjustments in the details of procedures and practice, but to few real innovations. Building societies had to adjust their building standards requirements downwards; have lengthened the repayment period from 25 to 30 years; allow a longer grace period for self-help houses; and issue a 25% advance to enable construction to start, rather than require progress to foundation level before issuing a loan as is their practice in low density areas (Beresford 1990b).

Beverley is the only building society to have introduced a low start mortgage (the Red Door bond), in which repayments are set at between 60% and 80% of the flat rate, increasing by 15% per annum approximately until the sixth year. If it were to be made available to lower income households, Musandu-Nyamayaro (1993) estimated that even households with incomes of Z$150 would be able to afford small core houses on small plots with pedestrian and service vehicle access. Although Beresford's (1990a) caution—that building societies cannot extend loans to the 60% of households on the Harare waiting list with incomes of below Z$480, or for loans of less than Z$6000—should be taken as typical building society prudence, the societies' inherent conservatism may inhibit further measures to make formal sector housing finance available to very low income households. In practice, the fear expressed by the building societies of a high default rate among low income borrowers has proved unfounded. Defaults are rare, partly because low income borrowers in difficulties can resell at a profit in order to pay off the mortgage.

The programme has, in practice, been fairly small scale in relation to the funds available and the scale of the problem. In the first three years of implementation, nearly 14 000 mortgages for low cost houses were made available countrywide, fewer than for high cost houses (Table 6.5). While the building societies emphasised that nearly half of all loans advanced between 1987 and 1989 were loans for houses in high density areas, they made less of the fact that these accounted for under 20% of funds lent. The main limitation on progress was said to be the lag of local authority serviced plot supply behind targets, need and demand, exacerbated by building materials shortages (Beresford 1990b).

For low income house buyers, even a downpayment of 10% may cause problems. At least one of the building societies is sympathetic to this problem and will assume that self-help labour contributions by the builder represent 10% of total house value, effectively entitling the borrower to a 100% loan. However, their preference is for employer

Table 6.5 Building society lending for home ownership, 1985–1989

	Low density areas		High density areas		Lending in high density areas as a % of total	
	No.	Average	No.	Average	No.	Average
1985	4 166	14 886	–	–	–	–
1986	4 811	16 504	–	–	–	–
1987	4 754	23 494	3 641	6 372	63.4	17.2
1988	4 765	31 024	4 600	7 591	49.1	19.1
1989	6 263	41 445	5 351	9 550	46.1	16.5
Total	24 759		13 592			

Source: Based on MPCNH 1991: 44.

assisted schemes. Many companies have an employee housing policy. In the past, employers have constructed housing for rent or have leased local authority houses for subletting to their employees. Employers have also purchased serviced plots for sale to their employees. Employers recover the cost of the plot and loan repayments to building societies at source, approve and even supervise building contractors, and give top-up soft loans for legal costs, the down payment and furnishing. Such arrangements appear to be acceptable to employees, though many older or casual employees do not qualify, and employees of small firms are less likely to benefit. They are also favoured by employers, local authorities (who get quick returns, making it possible to service residential areas using private sector loans or to recycle funds), and building societies (who regard employer involvement as reducing the risks of lending to low income borrowers, at no cost to themselves).

While the measures discussed above have succeeded in making formal sector housing finance available to lower income people, if not in sufficient volume to meet all the needs, the lowest income people are excluded by a variety of factors, such as the refusal of building societies to make loans of less than Z$6000 on grounds of administrative costs, standards which result in unaffordable construction costs, and insecurity of employment or income. The MPCNH has at times acknowledged a need for shelter assistance programmes for workers with below the minimum wage, 'informal sector employees', and the unemployed (Zimbabwe 1985b: 37, 45). However, the ministry has not developed such programmes and has, instead, perhaps under pressure from the international agencies, emphasised its objectives of minimising subsidies and providing affordable shelter. Although much has been achieved with respect to provision of serviced plots and loans for house construction, and recent adjustments in standards may help make sites and services schemes more affordable, the quantity is insufficient to meet needs, and the poorest are excluded.

In addition, declining real wages and massive interest rate changes associated with structural adjustment policies since 1991 led to a fall in building society deposits, a reduction in the number of new mortgages issued and increased defaults (CSO 1993). The mortgage programme for low income households effectively came to a halt, revealing the vulnerability of reliance on private sector housing finance to meet the needs of the urban poor. Implicitly acknowledging the contradictions in their own programmes, USAID announced a new housing package which is to include funds for the building societies (part loan, part grant) which, on condition they borrow matching funds locally, will enable them to lend to low income households at a subsidised interest rate (USAID 1992). The sticking plaster approach adopted by USAID does not, however, deal with the basic contradictions in the policies advocated by these agencies. It is seen as a transitional measure to maintain the flow of mortgage lending during the high interest rates associated with the early years of structural adjustment, with a view to enabling building societies at a later date to borrow sufficient funds at reasonable interest rates to continue lending for low cost house building without outside assistance. There would, in practice, seem to be little certainty that interest rates will come down as anticipated. The financial instability produced by rapid structural adjustment policies, as advocated by these agencies, has called into question the basis of their own lending to the housing sector.

The exchange of housing: who benefits?

People exchange dwellings to meet changing family needs, following a change of job or economic circumstances, as a hedge against inflation or simply for personal preference. Systems of exchange may be either formal or informal and may be subject to a greater or lesser degree of government regulation. The process of exchange increases in importance as the housing stock ages, and its smooth functioning is essential for market mechanisms to produce smooth adjustments to housing demand or supply (Rakodi 1992). It has been suggested that a downward filtering process typically operates in Western cities, by which older and less well maintained dwellings, often in inner city areas, become cheaper and more affordable to low income urban dwellers, while higher income buyers trade up and purchase new and more costly houses. Few studies of residential mobility and filtering or of the process of exchange exist for Third World cities, but it is known that upward filtering may occur when unauthorised housing is regularised and upgraded, or the supply of subsidised public sector housing units falls short of demand. First, the system by which the sale of property in Zimbabwe is handled will be briefly described. Of particular concern, because little is known about it, and because of its implications for housing policy, is the process of exchange that is occurring in the housing which has resulted from public sector initiatives and which is intended for low income households. The remainder of the chapter will be devoted to an examination of this process.

The system of exchange

Exchange is usually organised through a system of intermediaries, the nature of which may be important in determining which groups consume particular types of housing. All of the actors involved are likely to be pursuing their own interests, which may have an impact on the supply of housing, on whose interests are advanced during the process of exchange, and on who will benefit from the profits and fees generated (Rakodi 1992).

The exchange of industrial, commercial and high income residential property in the former European areas of Zimbabwe's cities is handled by a well organised system of estate agents and conveyancers, almost all of whom are registered. In response to pressure from within and outside the profession, in 1970, under the Estate Agents Act, a council was established to regulate the sector. Its members comprise six estate agents and three government appointees, and its purposes are to protect the public from loss by the creation of a compensation fund and to raise standards of practice, for example by regulating the commission charged. Small claims against malpractice by agents are generally handled outside the grievances procedure, the mere existence of which serves to ensure honest practice, while a serious claim only arises every two or three years. Other criteria by which the practices of estate agents may be judged include efficiency and the effect of their attitudes on house exchange. The regulatory mechanism in Zimbabwe is not designed to ensure efficiency. For example, it has been suggested that setting minimum and maximum rates of commission discourages competition and thus reduces efficiency. Estate agents have been accused of holding racist attitudes, which have served to slow the penetration of black Zimbabweans into the highest income white areas and to discriminate in favour of white buyers or tenants. Pressure has been brought to bear, not least by means of a TV 'soap opera', to change such attitudes, but that they persist, modified to some extent by class attitudes, among some practitioners, was clear to the author during interviews. Information on property for sale is mostly disseminated via the daily paper. The process of securing a mortgage and transferring property with formal title seems to operate reasonably efficiently. The main government role is in the registration of deeds, which can cause delays in property transfers (see Chapter 5), but safeguards the interests of buyers and sellers.

Commodification of public sector housing

Generally, the intention of public sector housing programmes is that the beneficiaries come from a population group which is considered to be in housing need and that even when the initial occupant of a house moves on, that house is available for those in social need in perpetuity. When public sector housing was almost all rented, this was relatively easy to achieve. The shift in policy towards owner-occupation has, however, given rise to concerns about the ultimate beneficiaries of public investment. In Harare, in theory, as soon as an Agreement of Sale is signed between low income purchasers of municipal rented houses and an urban council, the owners can sell their properties. In practice, the deeds to the property cannot be registered even when the purchaser has fully paid for the house because the vast majority of plots in ex-rented housing areas have not been individually surveyed. Although the councils have been intending to survey the ex-rental housing areas, they have had neither the financial nor the qualified manpower resources to do so, and owners wishing to register the deeds to their properties have had to pay for individual plot surveys. Because of the shortage of surveyors, this causes delays as well as being expensive. As a result, relatively few legal private sales in these areas can occur independently of the city council.

In the interim before receiving freehold, the householder in the process of renting-to-buy or having completed payment of instalments can apply to the local authority for permission to cede. Soon after independence, the MPCNH had proposed a 30 year ban on cessions, but Harare City Council felt that if residents couldn't sell it would discourage investment in self-help construction and prevent those with a legitimate reason for selling from doing so. Early on, it had been decided that cession of an undeveloped stand or one with only foundations would not be allowed and that such stands would be reallocated by the council to people on the waiting list. The council also tries to insist that those to whom the plots are ceded are eligible for the waiting list, and operates a policy of one person, one house, at least within the high density areas for which it has a record of ownership. By 1983 it had introduced a ban on cessions for the first three years of new schemes and required the permission of the spouse of the head (Teedon 1990), as Agreements of Sale are normally, if unjustifiably, in the name of the male head. However, the council does not try to regulate the financial transactions between buyers and sellers, and since the income ceiling for the waiting list was removed the only grounds for ineligibility are ownership of another property, lack of wage or legitimate self-employment, or lack of dependants.

In all areas of Harare, over 1000 cessions were recorded between 1985 and 1989. Most occurred in Mufakose, where a large number of the sellers were non-Zimbabweans intending to return to their countries of origin, followed by the older mixed and self-help housing areas of Warren Park and Glen View respectively. Cessions also appear to be used to handle inheritance before outright ownership is achieved. In Mabvuku, of a sample of 42 ceded houses, 17% had been inherited rather than bought, reflecting the older average age of Mabvuku's long-standing tenant population. There was a greater incidence of absentee landlordism amongst the ceded houses (17%) than among the houses bought by their original tenants (5%). This indicates that increased commodification of housing is occurring, even in an area of such modest opportunities as Mabvuku, and that investors are purchasing houses as part of accumulation strategies rather than for their use value.

The characteristics of households who owned houses in Mabvuku obtained under the cessions procedure were in many ways different to those purchasing houses under the rent-to-buy programme. Households owning ceded houses were on average smaller than those renting-to-buy (5.3 compared to 5.9); fewer of them were three generation households (5% compared to 25%); their heads were younger (41 compared to 54); more had been born in Harare (21% compared to 12%), and of the remainder, more had come to the city since 1980 (a quarter compared to 12%) and they had lived in Harare for a shorter time (21 years compared to 32). A slightly higher proportion of households acquiring by cession had female heads (14% compared to 10%). Their economic circumstances were also different. Households in ceded houses had average incomes of Z$699, compared to Z$579 for the owners of former rented houses. However, despite the difference in averages, the income ranges for the two samples of owner households were not dissimilar. The existence of relatively high income households in the ceded houses was due to a larger number of higher wage employees, while in the rent-to-buy houses, it was because of the greater incidence of households containing more than one wage earner (51% compared to 26%). However, fewer households who had bought houses had low incomes. Most of those who had bought by the cessions procedure had had to pay cash and only 7% had had access to loans from their employers to purchase the houses.

The cessions procedure is complex. Because of delays in obtaining city council approval to a cession, many people sell privately without the services of estate agents and lawyers, giving opportunities for owners to sell to households who are ineligible for the waiting list, investors interested in absentee landlordism, and to more than one buyer. Such transactions are, strictly, illegal, and sometimes give rise to disagreements, as the new 'owners' later try to formalise their ownership. The purchaser may end up without clear entitlement to the property as a result (*Financial Gazette*, 16 November 1990). Another practice is for the seller and buyer to agree a price, for the seller to use part of this to pay off the remaining amount owed to the council, and for the house subsequently to be transferred, with or without title deeds, to the buyer without the need for council approval (Rakodi and Mutizwa-Mangiza 1990). However, sales of former municipal houses have been constrained because of the lack of freehold tenure and thus of title deeds; the limited control still exerted by the Harare council, though its ability to enforce its one person, one house and waiting list criteria is diminishing as people become more aware of these and thus more able to evade them; and the general reluctance, given the limited supply of new housing, to sell. Even if owners of formerly rented houses retire to the rural areas, they keep ownership of their urban houses for the sake of their children. Nevertheless, the volume of sales of houses which have been rented-to-buy has been growing.

In the serviced plot areas developed in the 1970s, plots were sold and loans issued under an agreement with the city council, and freehold is not transferred until repayments are complete. In those areas where individual plot surveys are not available, difficulties similar to those in the rent-to-buy areas occur. Undeveloped plots (or those with only limited development) are, eventually, reallocated by the council to other eligible households. Influence may be brought to bear on the council during the reallocation process, resulting in allocation to households outside the initial target income group.

In the areas developed since independence, individual plot surveys are available. In those areas where housing loans were issued by the city council, it attempts to regulate private sales by approving cessions. In the more recently developed areas for which building society loans are available, freehold is transferred at the outset and, although the World Bank preference was for sales not to be allowed (Potts with Mutambirwa 1991), in practice it is hard to prevent them and easy for all sales to be

Table 6.6 Average advertised prices (Z$) for houses in high density areas

Area	1986	1987	1988	1989	1990	1991
Tafara/Mabvuku	17 188	–	–	25 500	28 000	39 952
Mbare	–	–	–	–	46 500	63 769
Mufakose	23 500	–	23 107	–	43 182	44 615
Dzivarasekwa	24 053	19 750	34 143	26 333	48 000	71 667
Glen Norah	23 879	25 000	18 292	25 300	44 833	94 961
Glen View	22 028	21 000	28 141	29 000	68 539	100 473
Highfield	24 067	19 000	30 125	40 000	66 666	175 228
Kambuzuma	22 417	32 833	26 154	33 143	75 000	131 667
Kuwadzana	20 350	12 500	23 596	27 615	62 143	104 167
Warren Park	25 000	20 600	23 450	37 500	89 000	117 083
Budiriro	–	17 000	40 000	–	50 333	105 909
Total	22 583	23 841	25 724	30 068	61 133	99 789

Source: *Herald*, various dates.

registered. Because of the total absence of small plots or speculative housing for sale outside the local authority schemes, and the great shortage of houses for sale in the high density areas, such houses command relatively high prices. In March/April 1991, advertised prices ranged from Z$30 000 to Z$175 000 in Harare (Table 6.6), with a mean of Z$90 000, compared to the cost of a serviced plot and four room house of about Z$18 000 at the same date.

Using press advertisements, average prices per house and per room in high density areas in Harare were calculated for 1986–1993 and are given by area in Table 6.6. The average price of houses for sale increased in line with inflation between 1986 and 1989, then more rapidly, by 103% and 63% respectively in 1990 and 1991. The same pattern is evident in the price per room (Figure 6.11). By 1993, however, prices had levelled off and had begun to fall, by 11% since 1991. The average house price tends to be lowest in Mabvuku and Tafara, which are characterised by small houses on small plots. The figures are averages and conceal a very wide range of prices asked for houses of the same size in the same area. This is partly accounted for by differences of plot size, location and quality of construction, but also by the different ideas of owners about the selling price of houses in a situation where relatively few are on the market. Prices in Harare in 1990 were, as expected, 25% above those in Chitungwiza, because of the latter's distant location and lower level of facilities and services, as well as the presence of small core houses.

Already in 1986, the average cost of a house for sale in Harare's high density areas was more than one and a half times that of the cost of

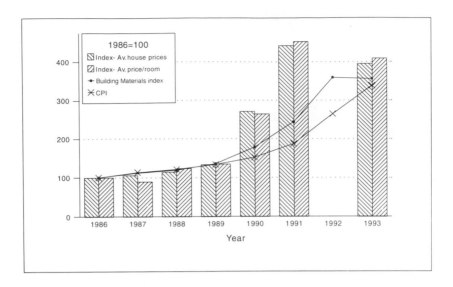

Figure 6.11 Index of average advertised sale prices of houses in high density areas of Harare. Sources: CSO Quarterly Digest of Statistics December 1990; The *Herald* various dates. 1992 sale price data not available

purchasing a newly serviced plot and building a four room house. By 1990 the margin had widened to four and a half times. High and rising prices essentially reflect a shortfall in supply because of the shortage of new housing and the relatively small number of houses for sale. The price spiral, fuelled by fear on the part of non-owners that unless they bought quickly, prices would increase beyond their reach, further reinforced rising prices, while sellers inflated prices in response to the increased demand. Underlying this were other factors, including the investment opportunity offered by renting, unsatisfied demand for middle income housing, and the availability of housing finance. The high prices placed houses beyond the reach of typical low income households (Rakodi with Withers, forthcoming).

A survey in Glen View, an early serviced plot area for which housing loans were not available, found that 14% of the plots had been ceded between 1979 and April 1984. Two reasons for ceding were identified: financial difficulties, or as part of a strategy of investment and accumulation; and those ceding for the former reason had, on average, lower incomes than those ceding for the latter reason. The incomes of purchasers were, on average, considerably higher than those of cedents, and the differential was greater as the size of the house purchased increased. In Seke in Chitungwiza, likewise, in the early 1980s, incomes of cedents were less than those of households to whom houses were ceded (Teedon 1990).

In Kuwadzana, applications for cessions were dealt with strictly to ensure cessionaries met income and other criteria. The practical difficulties in such vetting have led to its gradual relaxation, and now the only requirement is that the purchaser be on the waiting list. The majority in a sample of cessionaries in Kuwadzana surveyed in 1991 had purchased their houses since 1988. Their characteristics were compared with those of original allottees surveyed in 1985 (Holin 1985). In 1991, 17% of the plots had absentee owners. The resident owners of ceded plots were, on average, younger (37) than owner household heads in Warren Park D (42), a scheme that was implemented at the same time as Kuwadzana. Thus cessions give access to households with younger heads, because of the importance of length of time on the waiting list to priority for allocation of serviced plots (25% of cessionary household heads were under 30, compared to only 14% of the original allottees), though these are by no means recent urban residents—15% of the heads of owner households on ceded stands had been born in Harare and a further two-thirds had lived in Harare since before independence. The proportion of households headed by women, though still very small (9%), was three times higher among ceded stands than among original allottees (3%), suggesting that the market is less discriminatory than formal public sector allocation procedures against single, separated, divorced or widowed women with incomes adequate for home ownership. The mean income of households who had bought houses was Z$723, double that (updated in line with average earnings) of the original allottees. Only 14% had incomes of Z$400 or less, and those with incomes of over Z$1000 had all moved into the area between 1988 and 1990—that is, following the relaxation of cessions procedures and eligibility checks. The differences between original owners and pur-chasers in this sites and services scheme were quite similar to those in the ex-rental housing area of Mabvuku, suggesting that city-wide, where commodification of public sector housing is occurring, the outcome may be expected to be similar.

Controls over the right to dispose of property at open market prices have been limited to attempts to prohibit disposal of newly built houses for a certain number of years after allocation of serviced plots. They have proved difficult to implement. Other controls, such as a local authority option to buy publicly provided housing at cost with a reasonable profit, or retain part of the equity in order to ensure future buyers come from the eligible group, have not been attempted, so that rights of ownership in theory result in houses entering directly into the private market. In practice, the absence of freehold tenure and residual controls exercised by local authorities to which residents are paying purchase instalments or loan repayments have placed a brake on such free market transactions to date. The shortage of new serviced plots for those able to contemplate owner-occupation means that there is intense competition for houses which come up for sale, resulting in market prices many times in excess of replacement costs. Given the lack of alternatives, relatively few owner-occupiers wish to sell (despite the temptation to realise the very considerable value of their assets), further fuelling the price spiral. Although prices fell following the collapse of the property boom in 1991, the rate at which they decreased was less than in the high income housing sector. In such a market, buyers are not from the lowest income group, and the evidence from available data is that the incomes of owners of ceded or purchased houses are higher than those of original owners in the same area. This is unsurprising, given the shortage of dwellings suitable for middle income owner-occupation, and the income to be realised from renting out rooms. The emergence of absentee landlordism is symptomatic. Although the councils are attempting to prevent multiple house ownership and the growth of large scale landlordism, their control over the housing stock is diminishing.

7

Issues in planning and managing Harare's future development

Harare's first decade as the capital of independent Zimbabwe was, as has been repeatedly stressed in this account, marked by continuity rather than change (see also Davies 1992). It is unsurprising that the recent settler legacy, at its strongest in the urban settlements, which were created to serve settler interests, is persistent, not just in the city's built form but also in the way it is planned and managed. What is more surprising is that many aspects of the settler-created city have been accepted and perpetuated since independence. Nevertheless, there have been changes: some deliberate, obvious and symbolic, such as the enfranchisement of the urban population and the changing of street names; some slower and less obvious but more important, such as the implementation of the one-city concept in administration; and some apparently unexpected and unintended, such as the emergence of a housing market in the high density residential areas or the outcome of rent control policy.

In this final chapter, I discuss some questions that arise in trying to assess the city's capacity to cope with future growth and development and with problems arising out of the disjuncture between an inherited urban form which embodies the ideology, politics and social structure of an earlier era and the principles upon which Zimbabwe is trying to develop its economy and society as the millennium approaches. Issues of the future role of the city, appropriate management for the city region, the administrative and political implications of implementing the one-city concept, housing supply, the capacity of the development and planning system, and the future urban form are discussed in turn.

Harare's future role

Harare was established to facilitate accumulation by capital and control over the surrounding territory. An environment conducive to capital, much of which was in foreign hands, and the maintenance of lifestyles for European residents, was achieved by infrastructure provision, land use planning and the implementation of measures necessary to ensure a low cost pliable workforce. One of the manifestations of the internationalisation of capital, which started with colonialism and has gathered pace in recent decades, has been the emergence of a hierarchy of cities with particular roles in the world capitalist system. Not unexpectedly, given Africa's marginality to the world economic system, none of the 'world cities' which occupy positions at the apex of the urban hierarchy are located in Africa. Although some African cities, such as Nairobi, play an international role, this is political rather than economic, so even the second tier of cities in the world hierarchy is not fully represented in the continent. It seems to be generally agreed that in the third level in the hierarchy can be placed national cities that are foci for national accumulation but that also provide a location for transnational corporation offices and operations, banks and corporate services, and that are thus linked into the world economic system, albeit not on their own terms (Simon 1992; Sit 1993). Harare performs this role for Zimbabwe, especially since sanctions were ended with majority rule in 1980.

Despite the relatively large volume of domestic demand which is a legacy of its settler past, its ability (in normal years) to feed itself and its diversified resource base, Zimbabwe still has a relatively open economy. Open economies, such as the Asian NICs (Newly Industrialising Countries), which have been able to find markets for manufactured exports have made remarkable progress since the Second World War. Open economies which depend on exports of primary products to earn foreign exchange for importing fuels and manufactured goods, however, have suffered from global price instability and the long term decline in the terms of trade for primary commodities. Zimbabwe is, like most African countries, heavily dependent on primary exports, of both minerals and agricultural products. For some, notably tobacco and asbestos, prices have been buoyant; for others, less so. Some diversification has been possible, for example into cut flowers and vegetables for the European market, but finding export markets for manufactured goods has been more difficult—though Zimbabwe exports more manufactures than many African countries, and exports increased in response to a package of incentives and supports implemented in the mid-1980s. The manufacturing-based economy of Harare, therefore, produces largely for the domestic market. It relies partly on imported and partly on domestically produced materials and components and is more diversified than that of most African cities, but ultimately its expansion is limited by the continued poverty of the majority of Zimbabweans, both urban and rural.

The stabilisation policies adopted in the 1980s and, even more so, the structural adjustment policies implemented since 1991, far from spreading the benefits of economic growth more widely, seem certain to exacerbate inequality overall. Clearly, Zimbabwe inherited an economy with a number of structural weaknesses, as did all ex-colonies. However, because of the country's particular history, its economy in 1980 also had a number of strengths. Certainly, some of the policies adopted in the 1980s were poorly designed, and the escalating budget deficit was unsustainable. But into this particular economy was imported a standard set of structural adjustment policies. Although it must be said that industrial capital, backed up by agricultural, mining and commercial capital, supported trade liberalisation (Skalnes 1993), as did some political and technocratic interests, the abdication of any independence of thought in designing a programme has made the country vulnerable to World Bank influence. In part, of course, this is involuntary: it arises from the country's aid dependency, which has increased dramatically since independence and is now on a par with that of many other African countries. Some components of the standard package of policies that has been adopted have met with approval from fractions of capital which have benefited from trade liberalisation and other changes. However, yet other changes threaten these and other capitalist interests and have given rise to widespread criticism (Riddell 1992).

Crucial to the structural adjustment programme is the reduction of the budget deficit. There is widespread agreement that to achieve this, the loss making parastatals must be reformed. However, privatisation is resisted because of the government's determination to wrest control of major economic sectors from foreign and white capital, and reform, implying job losses, is politically difficult. Similarly, the intended reduction in size of the civil service is problematic, not least 'because of the need to balance "rewards" among different ideological and ethnic subgroups' (Herbst 1989: 81). As a result, public expenditure cuts have fallen disproportionately on the education and health sectors, with adverse effects on the poor, especially in urban areas. The urban poor have also suffered from declining real wages, increases in food prices as subsidies are abolished, and increases in the cost of basic services as service providers' costs increase and they are simultaneously pushed to ensure cost recovery.

Harare will, of course, continue to function as a national city, but given the constraints on its future economic development and the achievement of majority rule in South Africa, it seems unlikely that it will be able to compete with Johannesburg to emerge as a regional or continental city in years to come. While mutually beneficial economic interaction in southern Africa may develop, Zimbabwe has grounds for concern about the impact on its economy of South African competition. Prospects for increased trade with other African countries or even with northern countries seem poor without significant reforms to global trading arrangements very different from those currently proposed. Without a change in the marginalised position of Africa in the world economy, and independence from the political conditionality that accompanies the resulting aid dependency, prospects for future economic development, even in a relatively diversified, stable and prosperous country such as Zimbabwe, seem poor.

For Harare, in this situation, to retain its economic base, capable administration and ordered physical development will be difficult. In one scenario, those with political and administrative responsibility for the future development of the city will adopt a more flexible and developmental approach, accommodating and supporting small scale enterprises and residents' own solutions to the housing shortage. The city will become more like other African cities, but what is lost in physical order will be compensated for by greater diversity of economic activity and a more vibrant urban environment. In another scenario, the privileged will defend their quality of life and levels of consumption, informal activities will continue to be penalised, inequalities of income and service provision will widen, and there will be widespread impoverishment. Eventually, however, the poor will find a political voice and protests will escalate, threatening the legitimacy of the local authorities and reducing their ability to provide services and regulate urban activity. Urban conditions will deteriorate, except for the elite, who will retreat even further behind fortresses of security fences, electric gates and guards.

To avoid the nightmare scenario of a polarised, disorderly, unhealthy city, the contradictions and inconsistencies in the policies advocated and supported by the international agencies at both national and urban levels need to be challenged and the policy initiative regained. Inevitably, this involves a political struggle, internationally, nationally and at city level. The content of this struggle, which has both political and practical elements, is the concern of the remainder of this final chapter.

Issues at the regional level

The future growth of Harare and Chitungwiza depends on regional resources, especially water. Investment in expansion of storage and treatment capacity has ensured that water supply to date has been sufficient to cope with urban population growth. Although conservation measures implemented during periodic droughts and many dry seasons ensure that Harare's water supply is not unsustainably depleted, water use is extravagant. Some of the water used most extravagantly, to water parks and sports facilities, comes from boreholes, and does not directly compete with domestic supplies for the majority of urban residents. However, the impact of abstraction from a large number of private boreholes on the water table needs to be monitored. Continued urban growth will create demand which will, it is anticipated by Harare City Council, exceed the supply capacity of the current sources by later in the 1990s. At that stage, the council expects that a new source of supply will need to be found and major investment in a dam to the northeast of the city may be required. The development of such a new source will affect existing users of water from that river catchment. Attention should be given to the needs of these users, especially if they include Communal Area farmers, as well as to the cost.

Water engineers worldwide tend to make more or less straight line projections of water demand related to industrial needs and population growth, and then to design engineering solutions which will increase supply to meet that demand. Rarely is the scope for conservation or reconsideration of water supply and treatment standards built in to the planning process. Conservation may be achieved by, for example, legal restrictions on particular activities (such as filling swimming pools), as already used by Harare City Council, improved maintenance to reduce wastage and leakage, and pricing structures. The last approach may also be used to provide a cross-subsidy from high to low income users, to ensure that the latter have sufficient water for everyday needs. As has been noted in Chapter 2, Harare City Council, which also supplies treated water to Chitungwiza, has been able to ensure the continuation of relatively high standards of treatment and supply, in part because of a pricing system which is sound if not progressive.

However, the disposal of sewage is more problematic. It presents engineering difficulties because of the city's location on a series of watersheds, and it poses problems for water supply, in that treated sewage is discharged into watercourses in the water catchment area and waterborne sanitation itself requires large volumes of water to function. Both investment in treatment facilities and efficient ongoing operation and maintenance are crucial to enable the system to cope with a growing population. Because of its limited revenue base, Chitungwiza's problems are worse than those of Harare: they include inadequate treatment capacity and pollution. In addition, although low income residents benefit from the high quality of environmental sanitation achieved, the high capital and operating costs of the system increase their financial burden. The sustainability of a city-wide sanitation system which uses large amounts of water, either in a waterborne system or septic tanks, does not appear to have been questioned. It is assumed that widespread waterborne sanitation is desirable and achievable. The use of alternative technologies which might conserve water and reduce costs, while still providing adequate levels of environmental sanitation, is dismissed out of hand at present. However, serious consideration needs to be given to water conservation measures appropriate to areas where houses have multiple taps, large gardens, swimming pools and waterborne sanitation, as well as to the use of cheaper technologies in pilot projects as part of a process of innovation in housing development for the poor.

Water supply and sewage disposal are merely the most obvious regional issues that arise from the development of Harare and Chitung-wiza. In Harare, the practice of drawing the municipal boundary tightly around the urban area gave rise to the piecemeal pattern of planning and development which was inherited in 1971 by the enlarged city. Subsequent developments, such as Kuwadzana, immediately outside the boundary to the west, have been incorporated by a process of ad hoc extension. Similarly, sufficient land for the first phases of development in Chitungwiza was carved out from the surrounding Tribal Trust Land. The disadvantages of such tightly drawn administrative boundaries for strategic planning purposes became clear when the preparation of a revised plan for the city was embarked upon. In the absence of an appropriate administrative unit which approximated to the city region, a somewhat arbitrary boundary was drawn for a study area which incorporated part, but not all, of the surrounding administrative areas. The technical team that undertook the planning exercise was dominated by Harare and the central government, and not until much later was a planning authority established, on which all relevant local authorities were represented, to reach decisions about appropriate policies and directions for future growth.

There is no discussion of implementation in the plan, but it would appear to depend on a set of disparate local authorities agreeing to coordinate their investment and development control policies. A number of factors make this far from straightforward: the rural councils are currently undergoing reform, as rural and district councils are merged into rural district councils; they have few resources and fewer staff. Chitungwiza, as was noted in Chapter 2, despite being economically part of Harare and deprived of revenue because of its limited economic base, is anxious to maintain its independence. Presumably, the intention is that once further investigations have been undertaken in the areas identified in the master plan for future urban expansion, boundary extensions will be made to incorporate appropriate areas into both Harare and Chitungwiza. It is clear that cooperation cannot automatically be assumed from the surrounding local authorities, who were not full partners in the plan preparation process from its beginnings many years ago.

At present, Harare and Chitungwiza's boundaries are drawn too tightly for forward planning, but the Combination Master Plan study area is too widely drawn. In addition, responsibilities for implementation, monitoring and revision of the strategic policies and land allocations included in the master plan are not clearly defined and allocated. This position is unsatisfactory. While there would be considerable logic from a physical and financial planning point of view in extending Harare's boundaries to include Chitungwiza, as well as sufficient land for urban expansion and associated uses for the next twenty or thirty years, the political resistance to this, especially by Chitungwiza, must be taken seriously. A more appropriate solution may be to establish a metropolitan authority with appropriate powers to undertake policy formulation, strategic plan preparation and major infrastructure investment for the city as a whole. Such a structure would provide a forum within which the councils could negotiate priorities, and a means for more equitable sharing of revenue. It could leave the urban councils with significant functions related to the development and operation of local services, housing programmes, regulation of development and so on. Whether it makes more sense to include some of the surrounding councils in their entirety or to incorporate relevant parts of their areas within the boundaries of the two urban councils would have to be subject to detailed investigation.

Implementing the one-city concept

Progress towards a unified city administration within Harare, in which equity of access to facilities and fairness in contributions to revenue generation are achieved, has been patchy. The new government had no plans to reorganise local government. Instead, the aim was to de-racialise the representative bodies, in stages. De-racialisation of the democratic system occurred immediately, though the franchise, which was radically extended at independence, is not universal. The transfer to a more representative council appears to have been fairly smooth in Harare, and its political life since independence has avoided major scandals of the sort which have affected some other urban local authorities. However, as the city has grown, decision making by the council has become more and more remote from ordinary residents. Although there is a certain amount of administrative decentralisation, there has been little progress in developing a political structure at local level and there are few community organisations. As a result, low income residents have little say in city government and it is by no means clear that there is much understanding of or sympathy for their problems and needs among councillors and officials. This is demonstrated particularly by the repressive attitude adopted by the council towards informal sector economic and housing activity (see below).

Local authorities continue to operate similar committee and departmental systems to those existing in the 1970s, and administrative change in Harare has focused largely on integrating the previously separate administrative areas and financial systems. Change has progressed steadily, if slowly. The result is that the city council has maintained political stability, considerable administrative capacity and an adequate local financial resource base, especially if compared to local authorities elsewhere in Africa. The council's finances are in a relatively healthy state, especially in revenue terms. The heavy reliance on full cost recovery by means of user charges where possible has reduced the burden on other taxes, especially those on property, as did the pre-independence insistence on the former African housing areas being self-sufficient in revenue terms. Despite delays in revaluation, revenue from rates has kept pace with inflation, and although there are fairly extensive exemptions, the system is relatively efficiently administered. Progress towards a unified property tax system is slow, but is being made, and it appears that the system will be relatively equitable. In addition, the city council had large reserves on which it has been able to draw since independence when revenue has lagged behind costs.

As is by no means unusual in developing countries, major difficulties appear to be caused for the city by its relationship with central government. Government has not always allowed realistic increases in rates and charges; it has passed responsibility for the provision of certain services to the local authority without adequate financial backing; and it has allocated inadequate loan funds to finance capital investment, leading to lags in expanding service capacity and especially a shortfall in the supply of serviced plots for low cost housing development (Mutizwa-Mangiza 1991c). The second World Bank funded urban project is an attempt to overcome this problem and is being used as a vehicle to further improve the city's financial management. However, evidence is already emerging that under pressure from the economic structural adjustment programme reforms and the World Bank, and in the absence of a strong political voice for the poor, the solutions to problems faced by the city will be 'efficiency' and market orientated, and will fail to meet the needs of the increasingly pressured poor majority. The impoverishment which is resulting from structural adjustment, at least in the short term, itself may threaten the goal of good governance, if lower real wages and increased unemployment result in higher defaults in payments.

Chitungwiza's finances are much more precarious—although economically part of Harare, it derives no revenue benefits from the private sector development of industry, commerce and housing in the latter. As a result, and despite the revenue it raises from its low income population through supplementary charges, it has continued to depend more heavily on central government than any other urban council in the country. The worst fears of the new town's planners have been realised: a low density, monotonous and undistinguished residential environment has been created, with large areas of unused space; the majority of workers still have to commute daily by inadequate public transport services to Harare; and the physical and social infrastructure and services that Chitungwiza provides to its residents are of poorer quality than those in Harare. New-found political and commercial confidence is giving rise to a determination to find solutions to the town's problems, though this quest is inhibited by conflicts between different interests and by shortage of resources.

The style and structure of management in urban local authorities is traditional, bureaucratic and sectoral. The administrative system is based on using correct procedures and avoiding mistakes (Jordan 1984), so the emphasis of local authority policy is cautious and regulatory. Ongoing tasks (service provision, operation and maintenance, regulation) are performed reasonably efficiently. However, underlying assumptions about the nature and future suitability of traditional provisions and ways of doing things are rarely questioned, and there appears to be little in the way of corporate policymaking and management. While there are virtues to system maintenance, especially if compared to the breakdown of service delivery so common in other African cities, it tends to reinforce the position of those who already benefit from the system: high and middle income residents continue to occupy a privileged position. Although councillors are elected and have real power to make decisions, residents have little direct say in urban administration. This is partly due to the traditional preoccupation of councils with delivering services and regulating development, matters in which the scope for resident participation is limited, and partly to the irrelevance of local government to the overriding problems of employment and inadequate incomes faced by most urban residents, as well as the decreasing ability of the councils to solve housing shortages and public transport problems. The challenge is for the city council to become more innovative and proactive in solving urban problems, while maintaining its traditionally strong administrative and financial base, and for Chitungwiza council to increase its attractiveness to commercial and industrial investors at the same time as improving services to its predominantly low income residents. Unless the city administrations become more responsive and flexible in their attempts to meet the needs of the low income majority, more protest can be expected, despite the latter's past lack of political voice.

The supply of housing

Many of the constraints on housing production said to be typical of developing countries are not serious problems in Harare. Even though the supply of serviced and subdivided smaller plots for low and middle income families is inadequate, physical land availability is not a major constraint—though the absence of a systematic advance land purchase programme is a problem. The capacity of the construction sector to install infrastructure is considerable and the supply of many building materials is adequate, though inadequate foreign exchange to repair/replace vehicles and equipment, poorly administered price controls, and increased demand gave rise to shortages of some basic materials in the late 1980s. Delays in recognising the significance of these shortages on the part of the government and in instituting necessary policy and action resulted in growing accumulated shortages, with undesirable knock-on effects on public sector programmes, building materials manufacturers and construction firms. Although the problems have been alleviated for the construction sector as a whole by trade liberalisation, it is quite possible that the benefits will be disproportionately enjoyed by firms engaged in the construction of commercial buildings and luxury housing.

The public sector has continued to accept responsibility for the supply of housing for low income urban people, though the historical reasons for the introduction of this system are no longer valid. In other countries, for example Zaire, Uganda, Sudan or Nigeria, the public sector had less of a role in providing houses for low income residents, and private sector construction was relied upon to a greater extent (Stren 1989). Since independence in some countries, urban growth has been accompanied by housing shortages and increased overcrowding. Elsewhere, the continued view of spatial planning as a technical/regulatory activity and failure to reconsider land administration has meant that, although the private sector has continued to produce large quantities of housing, much of it has been built without reference to any guiding framework. In countries where the public sector has regarded the provision of low cost housing as its responsibility, supply has invariably fallen well below demand, because of the limited administrative, technical and financial capacity of public authorities. In Zimbabwe, however, the shortfall in low income housing supply cannot be blamed entirely on shortages of public sector capacity because considerable (if inadequate) funds have been directed to serviced plot programmes since 1980. These resources have been misapplied due to continued insistence on unrealistically high standards. The results have been, firstly, a reduced supply of plots and, secondly, home ownership benefiting, to a considerable extent, households who do not fall into the lowest income category. The middle class is also increasingly adversely affected by the lag of supply behind demand for medium cost housing.

Rent control, rigid and high planning standards, and other policies, notably attempts to control squatting and subletting, have actually constrained supply and resulted in considerable overcrowding. At least half of all low income households are likely to be renting a single room, and the prospect of them obtaining access to owner-occupied housing seems to be diminishing rather than increasing as the years go by. The nature of housing demand and need in Harare since independence has changed, and the inherited dual system of land and housing supply has only coped with difficulty. The private market which provides housing for middle and high income households is subject to recurrent speculative booms and crises because it is tied in, through financial capital, to the wider capitalist economy. The greatest volume of demand today comes from middle and low income residents, whose needs are only partially met by the private market and public sector respectively. Not only is action needed to relieve constraints on quantitative supply, but also adjustments to policy, administration and practice are needed to make them more realistic in the face of growing pressures.

Development and planning

Since 1980, the new political system, changing government priorities, and reorganisation at central and local government levels have changed the context in which the development planning system operates. The current urban development planning process is a hybrid. It is a combination of an older system based on zoning which benefited European property owners, in terms of values generated on land and standards enforced (Wekwete 1989a, 1989b), but which was criticised for its narrow scope, inflexibility and reliance on the negative instrument of development control for implementation. Since 1976, the master and local plan system, provides, in theory, an adequate planning framework for urban development, based on reasonably up to date legislation and enforceable controls and backed by a good resource base, including extensive public land holdings. In theory also, the master plan could provide a basis for strategic decision making with respect to urban development in the absence of local authority corporate policy statements.

In practice, the philosophy on which the legislation was based remained unchanged. It continues to aim at creating conditions suitable for capital investment in property and production and to protect property values and environmental conditions, especially in high income areas. There have been no major changes in property relations and in the fabric of laws related to land and property, of which the land use planning legislation is part (Wekwete 1989b, 1992). The present system is inadequate for dealing with strategic conurbation-wide issues, as is reflected in the lack of clarity as to the nature and functions of a strategic master plan which is evident in the recent plan prepared for the Harare Combination Master Plan area. An underlying weakness of a physical planning system like Zimbabwe's, based on the British model, is that it is not tied into resource allocation procedures and to a large extent can only respond to private sector initiative, rather than take a proactive role in achieving development goals.

The association of plans with engineering and public works, and thus with land use and physical infrastructure provision, and the preoccupations with maintenance of control, enforcing high standards and keeping physical order, reflect an outdated view of planning. This view is held by planners (Davies 1992), other central and local government officials and councillors alike. None of these appears to recognise firstly, the need to link land use planning with investment in and management of other services, or secondly, its potential as a vehicle for strategic decision making, innovation, monitoring and evaluation of project and policy performance, and a promotional approach to not only physical but also economic and social development (Devas and Rakodi 1993). In addition, the system is non-participatory and does not reflect the views of the urban majority in decision making, as seen in the continued priority given to maintaining a road network suitable for the minority of private car owners, for example. This is not to say that effective development control and land registration systems, rare in developing countries, should not be valued and maintained. Signs of strain on the systems are beginning to emerge, while the appropriateness of their complex requirements as large low income areas begin to be integrated into the system has not been reassessed. Procedures need to be streamlined and simplified, not so much for development in commercial and industrial areas, as for low income residential areas.

However, the planning system needs to be challenged, both in terms of its sufficiency as a means of promoting and guiding development in the course of plan implementation and in terms of whose interests it serves. The climate of certainty provided by the strict control over development benefits property capital but penalises the urban poor, who suffer from 'planning standards' supposedly imposed in the public interest and periodic demolition of illegal structures. These hinder the attempts, especially of the poorest, to meet their housing needs and to carry on informal economic activities.

Although the 1976 Act (and other legislation) gives local authorities powers to acquire land and implement planning policies, resource availability, safeguards for white owners under the Lancaster House Agreement, and reliance on the reactive rather than initiatory or developmental mechanism of development control have limited their scope to achieve positive planning goals or to challenge property interests (Wekwete 1992). As the pressures on urban administration in a context of economic austerity and population growth increase, making decisions between competing priorities will become more and more difficult. While the intention is to reduce inequality and segregation by income, an administrative culture which emphasises caution, entrenched and new property interests, a concern not to alienate and drive out white capital and skills, the absence of a political constituency pressing for radical change, and the enduring legacy of a built environment result in little happening. Changes to the planning system, to emphasise development promotion, relaxation of unrealistic and inappropriate standards and facilitation of informal sector activities have not occurred, and in their absence discriminatory segregation by race is being replaced by equally discriminatory segregation by class and income group.

The wage income available for purchase of goods and services produced by informal sector enterprises has historically been and continues to be substantial in Harare. Despite this, although the available estimates of the scale and nature of informal sector activities are rough and incomplete, these activities are clearly much less extensive in Harare than in other African cities. The original reasons for this lie in the policies of the settler government towards urban labour and patterns of urban development, which were analysed in Chapter 2. These policies, and the attitudes and assumptions that underlay them, have been continued since independence. Although some expansion of informal sector activities occurred in the 1980s, this was constrained by ambivalent official attitudes which, on the one hand, recognised that formal sector job creation was increasingly lagging behind growth in the labour force and the number of school leavers, but on the other hand desired to maintain control over it. The attempt, especially by local authorities, to formalise the informal by insisting on licences for all informal sector enterprises and confining their operation to approved sites, while doomed to failure, was backed up by spasmodic but effective use of the police. The inappropriate nature of most attempts to assist small scale enterprises to date stems in part from this desire to control them, but also from a lack of understanding of their operation and a dearth of research which could correct mistaken assumptions about the nature of informal sector entrepreneurs and enterprises.

To control the black population socially and politically, while harnessing its labour, the settler government employed a variety of tactics, including housing policies, as we have seen (Malaba 1980). Demolition of squatter areas was consistent with these wider aims. The policy of strict control over illegal housing, before and since independence, has gone hand in hand with attempts to control informal economic activities. Since 1980, waves of demolition have often coincided with round-ups of unlicensed informal sector traders and so-called vagrants and prostitutes, often with the aim of returning people to the rural areas.

The continuing priority attached to control (of physical development and urban residents) and the dislike of uncontrolled activities in urban areas have been attributed by some analysts to the class base either of ZANU's leadership (petty bourgeois) or its support (peasant) (Astrow 1983; Drakakis-Smith 1986). Drakakis-Smith (1986) attributes the Central Committee attitude to these activities to the unimportance of urban popular support to the ZANU base, both during the liberation struggle and since. However, this appears to be an oversimplified view ('Yates', 1980). Periodic opposition to the settler regime was, as we have seen in Chapter 1, expressed by urban wage labour and the urban African population in general, despite the successful emasculation of trade unions which left labour politically and organisationally too weak to play a leading role in the liberation struggle (Astrow 1983). The Mugabe government has shown little tolerance for protest by the urban wage labour force. However, it did increase minimum wages, despite the inequalities between urban and rural areas where its support base is supposed to primarily rest, and in the face of opposition from the business community. The populist support for ZANU is not only rural and runs considerable risk of erosion from punitive measures against groups of low income urban dwellers (Libby 1984). That such measures, in addition to the erosion of wage gains by inflation and the elimination of price subsidies (Riddell 1984; Davies and Sanders 1988) (see also Chapter 3), have given rise to remarkably little social unrest illustrates that public support for the Mugabe government has not been exhausted, notwithstanding the recent growth of political opposition as illustrated in the 1990 elections. Further explanations of the repressive control of urban activity, which do not rest entirely on the class base of ZANU, must be sought.

One potential source of explanation is in local culture. The cultural system at any point in time is a 'parallelogram of forces' in which the relationship between dominant or ruling cultures, subcultures and rebellious counter-cultures is continuously redefined as social power relations change (Kaarsholm 1990). Zimbabwe is typical in the sense that colonisation imposed cultural change and notions of European cultural superiority on pre-existing indigenous cultures (Mungazi 1992), and atypical in that settler cultural hegemony lasted until unusually recently.

> white Rhodesian society aimed at developing an 'almost surrealistic Europeanness', an enclave of modern enlightenment in the midst of African primitivity whose institutions, genres and manifestations could match the latest fashions at home. (Kaarsholm 1990: 47).

Nowhere was this more evident than in the planning and construction of urban areas.

As in other newly independent countries, attempts to create a new national culture on the basis of a resurrection of local traditions, themselves modified, manipulated and reinvented in the course of colonisation, have been contradictory and limited (Kaarsholm 1990). With respect to urban development, not only had the black Zimbabwean officials and politicians mostly been educated and trained in the European professional tradition (see also Davies 1992), but also the absence of an indigenous urban culture and built environment, whether transformed or not by colonialism, provided no alternative source of inspiration for the formulation of alternative urban development paths. It is only since 1987, Kaarsholm suggests, that independent theatre, literature and political protest have begun to challenge the perceived betrayal of the ideals of the independence struggle by corrupt and self-interested politicians, and a non-traditional spirit of anti-authoritarianism has begun to emerge. So far, the expression and impact of these new cultural forms is limited, and active political protest is restricted. In the urban sphere, there are signs of a change in attitudes which seems to be originating with local politicians, who previously backed council attempts at control but are increasingly recognising the lack of alternatives for those who lose their jobs or whose incomes are no longer sufficient to support their families. However, such a relaxation of attitudes towards both informal economic activities (income earning and reproductive such as urban agriculture), and illegal development (such as backyard shacks), if it continues, is not sufficient in itself to provide an alternative to current policies.

There is no short term prospect of extensive opposition to national and local urban development and housing policies, whether articulated through the political system or community organisations, or expressed through increasingly widespread evasion of bureaucratic regulatory systems, especially those related to land. The increasing inadequacy of wage incomes to support households may be accompanied by a change in attitudes to women's work, while marginal changes may be made to policies to increase their flexibility and appropriateness. This will not be enough to generate the hoped for large increase in employment in small scale activities. Although some expansion is likely to occur, the urban economy will continue to be dominated by the large scale formal sector and by wage employment. Unless other constraints on the operation of small enterprises and microenterprises are addressed, the shrinking size of the formal sector wage bill will merely result in the informal sector's income earning capacity being split between an ever-increasing number of new entrants. Nor will a softening of attitudes towards informal sector activities necessarily generate a radically different vision of cities, the built environment, urban life, or ways of managing the urban development process.

Assumptions about order, control and the role of the state have been carried over from the settler regime and the military order of the liberation struggle, and have been internalised by current leaders. A preoccupation with order and control, fuelled by the deteriorating situation in other African cities and, during the 1980s, by a desire to 'succeed' in terms of criteria which residents of South Africa might find reassuring, have found expression in a desire for tidiness in the built environment to which unusual emphasis is given compared to other African countries. Perhaps the lack of protest against controls on unlicensed activity is also partly due to people's inherited expectation that this is how governments behave. That strict control of the physical environment bears little relationship to social well-being and cohesion, or to popular political support, does not appear to have been appreciated.

The inherited urban form

The existing built environment embodies earlier ideological and planning principles and reinforces discriminatory standards and segregation by income group, as well as being a costly and wasteful form of urban development. The result of the twin policy emphases of maintaining standards and restraining illegal development (see above) has been an increasing lag of housing supply behind demand, especially for low and middle income households, reflected in growing housing waiting lists, increased backyard shack construction and increased overcrowding. At the other end of the income spectrum, a desire to maintain controls and standards in low density suburbs, in part to avoid alienating the white residents, has served the interests of an emerging bourgeoisie of professionals, bureaucrats and businessmen. This new property-owning elite is unlikely to welcome desegregationist measures which might affect their living standards and property values in future.

Harare's widely varying and extravagant densities, when allied to the extensive land left undeveloped, both within and between residential areas, are a major problem of the colonial legacy. The low densities of urban development, even in so-called 'high density' areas, increase infrastructure and transport costs, and the existence of undeveloped land within the built-up area is wasteful (Figure 7.1). Some areas of undeveloped land are poorly drained vleis and other soils which require expensive foundations. However, others are physically suitable for development. As part of the long term restructuring of the segregated city, and in order to make the use of land and infrastructure more efficient, densification has periodically been discussed. This could occur by redevelopment at higher densities (say the replacement of a single house on a stand of 4000 or 8000 square metres by row houses or a block of walk-up flats), by infilling vacant stands at higher densities, by subdivision of existing stands (allowing existing owners to sell off part of their stands for development), and by rezoning areas currently zoned for open space.

A study by Swedeplan (1989) for the Ministry of Local Government and Rural and Urban Development, in a study area in Hatfield, concluded that it was physically possible to subdivide many existing stands, certainly into 1000 square metre stands, and in some cases into 500 square metre stands, thus increasing the density from 1.5 to 3.4 or 5.0 stands per hectare. To increase the density further, to 8.3 dwellings per hectare, a more radical restructuring would be necessary, to develop row housing in the internal core of a street block, leaving individual houses on reduced plots round the periphery. It was noted that densification would have implications for infrastructure and the capacity of social facilities, but these implications were not explored. It was thought that septic tank sanitation would be feasible on plots of 1000 square metres and might even be possible on plots of 500 square metres, though this was not investigated. While there are physical issues to be dealt with, and changes to zoning would be necessary, there appear to be no insoluble problems.

Figure 7.1   Harare is a sprawling, low density city: a view of Kuwadzana sites and services scheme

More significant are the issues of how densification might be achieved, which were not investigated by the Swedeplan study. One possible obstacle to densification could be the views of existing residents. These were, therefore, solicited in the course of interviews in Mount Pleasant, Hatfield and Mabelreign (Rakodi with Withers 1993). In Mabelreign, the plots themselves are generally relatively small, but large areas were left at the rear of plots as 'greenways'. Respondents in this area overwhelmingly reacted adversely to the greenways in their current form—few if any considered them visually attractive or suitable for leisure activities, none walked in them, all thought them unsafe at night and none thought the council maintained them adequately. As the greenways were too narrow for subdivision into separate stands, owners were universally in favour of the council permitting them to buy the land adjacent to their plots. Most would build on such an enlarged plot, for their children or for rent.

Respondents in Mount Pleasant and Hatfield were asked first for their views on the suggestion that owners subdivide their plots to build extra 'cottages' for sale or rent. This was portrayed as a means of reducing the per household cost of service provision. The response was over- whelmingly negative in Mount Pleasant, though a couple of respondents liked the idea of being able to build a second house for use by relatives. In Hatfield, however, the reaction was more positive (three-quarters supported the idea, mainly to help ease the housing shortage and to earn extra income). Most wanted to be able to build between one and three houses for rent. When asked whether higher density development of town houses or flats for high income households should be permitted on vacant stands, a more positive response was received in Mount Pleasant, where nearly a third of respondents supported the idea (it was considered better than having idle land), as long as their own properties were not affected. Half the owner heads of household in Hatfield also supported the idea, in part because vacant land was seen as hindering their attempts to make their own properties secure against intruders. Relatively few (28% in Mount Pleasant, 21% in Hatfield) were in favour of using undeveloped land for medium and low cost houses. Among those who did support this, the most common reason was to ease the housing shortage. Almost universally, respondents who opposed densification of one sort or another were concerned that it would adversely affect the character, standard and amenity of the area (that is, their property values and lifestyles). Concern was also expressed that higher density development would increase noise, create overcrowding, increase crime, strain the facilities and reduce privacy. Some concern was expressed that building housing for lower income groups would 'introduce socio-economic disparities', which they can ignore while housing is segregated by income group. Such attitudes are predictable, and may change if densification is incremental and not too radical.

It has been suggested that the council may be able to repossess some undeveloped stands when rates arrears exceed the value of the land. The 1992 Land Acquisition Act maintains compulsory purchase powers, with their associated requirement for the payment of 'fair' and 'reasonable' compensation, but to use these powers extensively would not be affordable. Only if land can be declared 'derelict' or unused can it be compulsorily acquired without the payment of compensation. The provisions of the Act, which were enacted despite noisy opposition from commercial farmers, are primarily directed at achieving the rural land reform objectives of the government via its resettlement programme, and it is not clear whether they will be extended to urban areas.

Another possibility that is being discussed is to increase rates on undeveloped land to a value reflecting the use for which the land is zoned. Although the rate for land has, from early in the city's development, been higher than that for improvements, no distinction is made between developed land and land ripe for development but lying idle. A tax rate has to be set at a level which would erode anticipated profits sufficiently to induce either development or sale of a large enough supply of land to bring down the price to that affordable by those who wish to use it. The use of a financial disincentive to the hoarding of undeveloped land assumes that current owners are price responsive. While it is highly likely that corporate owners are, this cannot be assumed of private owners, who may be holding on to land for their children, as insurance against future uncertainty and need, or for nostalgic or emotional reasons. Little is known about the proportion of undeveloped land which is owned by emigrants; the motives of private owners and their likely responsiveness to price signals; or the significance of other constraints on development, such as escalating costs of new construction, lack of capital in the construction sector or limited availability of housing finance. Unless some of these information gaps are filled, the results of the proposed increase in property taxes on undeveloped land will be unpredictable.

Conclusion

Harare is an African city, and yet it is not. It could not be in Europe, and yet in many ways European influences, distorted through a settler prism, have formed the city. It is a recent, planned, orderly, pleasant city characterised by rigid residential segregation and low density sprawl—a garden city. The privileged lifestyle of the rich has survived independence unscathed, and the city administration ensures that the quality of their environment and services is maintained. By contrast, despite the availability of much regular wage employment, and adoption of high standards of construction and infrastructure in high density housing areas, the urban life experience of most low income residents has been impoverished. Nowhere is this more evident than in Chitungwiza, a planning disaster promulgated for ideological reasons, which has left a legacy of intractable administrative, financial and transport problems.

The spatial pattern of development in Harare is not unlike the apartheid cities of South Africa, but in the latter the excesses of apartheid policy, and the long deterioration in administration of African residential areas in the face of urban unrest, rent strikes and massive rural–urban migration since the 1970s, have resulted in poor quality infrastructure, extensive illegal development of squatter areas and backyard shacks, and a politically mobilised, vocal and volatile population speaking through the civics (community-based organisations initiated during the 1980s as an alternative to the distrusted, discredited and often inoperative local government system in black residential areas/townships) and now the political parties. In Harare, unlike cities in South Africa and elsewhere in Africa, strict control has been maintained over illegal development, while infrastructure and services have been maintained. Although conditions have deteriorated for many poor urban residents, the fact of majority rule, some progress in providing new housing areas, the continued availability of wage employment and post-independence reforms in wages, education and health care, together with the tolerance, charm and patience of Zimbabweans themselves, have defused urban protest. For the moment, the city works. However, as the pressures arising from population growth, inflexible and traditional administration and planning, and economic hardship and liberalisation build up, it is becoming a little like a pressure cooker. If Harare is to continue to provide economic opportunities and a pleasant and healthy environment for its residents in future, more responsive urban administrations, implementing more realistic and innovative policies, are needed quickly.

Bibliography

Amin, S. (1971) *Neo-colonialism in West Africa* (transl. 1973). Penguin, Harmondsworth.

Ashton, E. H. (1969) Economics of African housing. *Rhodesian Journal of Economics*, 3 (4): 29–33.

Astrow, A. (1983) *Zimbabwe: A Revolution that Lost its Way?* Zed Press, London.

Atkins, G. (1983) Town planning and economic design. *Zimbabwe Environment and Design*, 5 (Jan.): 5–9.

Auret, D. (1990) *A Decade of Development: Zimbabwe 1980–1990*. Mambo Press, Gweru.

Batezat, E., Mwalo, M. and Truscott, K. (1988) Women and independence: The heritage and the struggle. In C. Stoneman (ed.) *Zimbabwe's Prospects: Issues of Race, Class, State and Capital in Southern Africa*, pp. 153–174. Macmillan, London.

Bell, M. (1986) *Contemporary Africa*. Longman, London.

Beresford, W. M. P. (1990a) The role of building societies in mobilising finance for low income housing. Paper presented to the Zimbabwe Institute of Rural and Urban Planners' Annual School.

Beresford, W. M. P. (1990b) Private finance of low cost shelter and infrastructure: Building Societies in Zimbabwe. Paper presented to the RHUDO/ESA Regional Office Policy Workshop.

Beresford, W. M. P. (1990c) A review of Zimbabwe low income housing policy and the roles of the public and private sectors. Paper presented to Namibia National Housing Conference.

Bond, P. (1991) Geopolitics, international finance and national capital accumulation: Zimbabwe in the 1980s and 1990s. *Tijdschrift voor Economische en Sociale Geografie*, 82 (5): 325–37.

Bond, P. (1992) Finance and uneven urban development in 1950s Salisbury: contradictions in the Central Business District. *Geographical Journal of Zimbabwe*, 23: 1–19.

Bond, P. (1993a) Economic origins of black townships in Zimbabwe: Contradictions of industrial and financial capital in the 1950s and 1960s. *Economic Geography*, 69 (1): 72–89.

Bond, P. (1993b) The rise and fall of the Rhodesian economy. Witwatersrand African Studies Institute, Johannesburg (mimeo).

Bond, P. (1993c) Housing as an Investment: A Report on Zimbabwe's Housing Crisis and on Public–Private Reform of the Housing Finance System through

Pension / Provident Fund Investments. Unpublished draft report to the Zimbabwe Congress of Trade Unions.

Bourdillon, M. F. C. (1977) Labour migrants from Korekore Country. *Zambezia*, 5 (1): 1–29.

Brand, V. (1986) One dollar workplaces: A study of informal sector activities in Magaba, Harare. *Journal of Social Development in Africa*, 1 (2): 53–74.

Bratton, M. (1981) Development in Zimbabwe: Strategy and tactics. *Journal of Modern African Studies*, 19 (3): 447–75.

Bratton, M. and Burgess, S. (1987) Afro-Marxism in a market economy: Public policy in Zimbabwe. In E. J. Keller and D. Rothchild (eds) *Afro-Marxist Regimes: Ideology and Public Policy*, pp. 199–222. Lynne Rienner, Boulder, CO.

Brokonsult AB (1985) Study on Urban Passenger Transport in Harare, Bulawayo, Gweru and Mutare. Vol. II: *City Reports*. Brokonsult for Swedish International Development Agency and Government of Zimbabwe, Harare.

Bromley, R. and Gerry, C. (eds) (1979) *Casual Work and Poverty in Third World Cities*. Wiley, Chichester.

Building Societies' Role in Zimbabwe (1987) *Housing Finance International*, (Nov.): 20–6.

Butcher, C. (1986) *Low Income Housing in Zimbabwe: A Case Study of the Epworth Squatter Upgrading Programme, Harare*. Occasional Paper No. 6, Department of Rural and Urban Planning, University of Zimbabwe, Harare.

Butcher, C. (1989) *Land Delivery for Low Cost Housing in Zimbabwe. Phase 1: Report of Findings*. Plan Inc. Zimbabwe (Pvt) Ltd., Report for the Ministry of Public Construction and Housing and United States Agency for International Development, Harare.

Butcher, C. (1990) The potential and possible role of housing cooperatives in meeting the shelter needs of low income urban households. Paper presented to the Zimbabwe Institute of Rural and Urban Planners' Annual School.

Butcher, C. (1993) Urban low-income housing: A case study of the Epworth squatter settlement upgrading programme. In L. Zinyama, D. Tevera and S. Cumming (eds) *Harare: The Growth and Problems of the City*, pp. 61–75. University of Zimbabwe Publications, Harare.

Chadwick, G. (1987) *Models of Urban and Regional Systems in Developing Countries*. Pergamon, Oxford.

Chazan, N., Mortimer, R., Ravenhill, J. and Rothchild, D. (1988) *Politics and Society in Contemporary Africa*. Macmillan, Basingstoke.

Child, G. and Heath, R. (1989) Outdoor recreation patterns and preferences among the residents of Harare, Zimbabwe. Supplement to *Zambezia*, University of Zimbabwe Publications, Harare.

Choto, R. (1991) Factory filth severely polluting Lake Chivero. *Horizon* (Sept): 14–15, 17.

Christopher, A. J. (1973) Land ownership in the rural–urban fringe of Salisbury, Rhodesia. *South African Geographer* IV (2): 139–56.

Christopher, A. J. (1977) Early settlement and the cadastral framework. In G. Kay and M. A. H. Smout (eds) *Salisbury: A Geographical Survey of the Capital of Rhodesia*, pp. 14–25. Hodder & Stoughton, London.

Clarke, D. G. (1977) *The Distribution of Income and Wealth in Rhodesia*. Occasional Papers, Socioeconomic Series, No. 7. Mambo Press, Gweru.

Cokorinos, L. (1984) The political economy of state and party formation in Zimbabwe. In M. Schatzberg (ed.) *The Political Economy of Zimbabwe*, pp. 8–54. Praeger, New York.

Colombard-Prout, M., Marciano, M. and Mansell, M. (1986) Construction materials industries: Technical and economic study of the various industrial branches producing materials and components for roof structures in Zimbabwe. Mimeo, Department of Civil Engineering, University of Zimbabwe, Harare.

Colquhoun, B., O'Donnell and Partners (1985) *Overview of Construction and Materials Production Sectors for Inclusion in the National Housing Corporation Study.* Report to the Ministry of Public Construction and National Housing, Harare.

Colquhoun, S. (1993) Present problems facing the Harare City Council. In L. Zinyama, D. Tevera and S. Cumming (eds) *Harare: The Growth and Problems of the City,* pp. 33–41. University of Zimbabwe Publications, Harare.

Coquery-Vidrovitch, C. (1991) The process of urbanization in Africa (From the origins to the beginning of independence). *African Studies Review,* 34 (1): 1–98.

CSO (Central Statistical Office) (1987a) *Zimbabwe National Income and Expenditure Report.*

CSO (Central Statistical Office) (1987b) *Quarterly Digest of Statistics.* March.

CSO (Central Statistical Office) (1988) *The Economy of Households in Zimbabwe 1985.*

CSO (Central Statistical Office) (1989) *Main Demographic Features of the Population of Mashonaland E. Province.*

CSO (Central Statistical Office) (1990) *Quarterly Digest of Statistics.* December.

CSO (Central Statistical Office) (1991) *Quarterly Digest of Statistics.* August, December.

CSO (Central Statistical Office) (1993) *Quarterly Digest of Statistics.* December.

Cubitt, V. S. (1979) *Supplement to Urban Poverty Datum Line in Rhodesia: A Study of the Minimum Consumption Needs of Families (1974).* University of Rhodesia Faculty of Social Studies, Salisbury.

Cubitt, V. S. and Riddell, R. C. (1974) *The Urban Poverty Datum Line in Rhodesia: A Study of the Minimum Consumption Needs of Families.* Faculty of Social Studies, University of Rhodesia, Salisbury.

Cumming, S. (1990) Post-colonial urban residential change in Zimbabwe: A case study. In R. B. Potter and A. T. Salau (eds) *Cities and Development in the Third World,* pp. 32–50. Mansell, London and New York.

Cumming, S. (1993) Post-colonial residential change in Harare: A case study. In L. Zinyama, D. Tevera and S. Cumming (eds) *Harare: The Growth and Problems of the City,* pp. 153–76. University of Zimbabwe Publications, Harare.

Davies, D. H. (1986) Harare, Zimbabwe: Origins, development and post-colonial change. *African Urban Quarterly,* 1 (2): 131–8.

Davies, D. H. (1987) Population growth, distribution and density changes, and urbanization in Zimbabwe: A preliminary assessment following the 1982 census. *African Urban Quarterly,* 2 (13): 13–23.

Davies, D. H. (1992) Urban developments. In S. Baynham (ed.) *Zimbabwe in Transition,* pp. 149–75. Almqvist and Wiksell, Stockholm.

Davies, R. (1988) The transition to socialism in Zimbabwe: Some areas for debate. In C. Stoneman (ed.) *Zimbabwe's Prospects: Issues of Race, Class, State and Capital in Southern Africa,* pp. 18–31. Macmillan, London.

Davies, R. and Sanders, D. (1988) Adjustment policies and the welfare of children: Zimbabwe, 1980–1985. In G. A. Cornia, R. Jolly and F. Stewart (eds) *Adjustment with a Human Face.* Vol. II: *Country Case Studies,* pp. 272–300. Clarendon Press, Oxford.

Devas, N. and Rakodi, C. (eds) (1993) *Managing Fast Growing Cities: New Approaches to Urban Planning and Management in the Developing World*. Longman, Harlow.

Dewar, N. (1987) Salisbury to Harare: Citizen participation in public decision making under changing ideological circumstances in Zimbabwe. *African Urban Quarterly*, 2 (1): 38-48.

Dizanadzo, M. C. (1987) Ward Development Committee Structures as Framework for Development Planning Participation: Case Study of Ward 25, Glen Norah B of the Harare City Council. M.Sc. dissertation, Department of Rural and Urban Planning, University of Zimbabwe, Harare.

Drakakis-Smith, D. (1985) The changing economic role of women in the urbanization process: A preliminary report from Zimbabwe. *International Migration Review*, XVIII (4): 1278-92.

Drakakis-Smith, D. (1986) Urbanisation in the socialist third world: The case of Zimbabwe. In D. Drakakis-Smith (ed.) *Urbanisation in the Developing World*, pp. 141-57. Croom Helm, London.

Drakakis-Smith, D. (1987a) Zimbabwe: The slow struggle towards socialism. *Geography*, 72 (4): 348-51.

Drakakis-Smith, D. (1987b) Urban and regional development in Zimbabwe. In D. Forbes and N. Thrift (eds) *The Socialist Third World: Urban Development and Territorial Planning*, pp. 194-213. Basil Blackwell, Oxford.

Drakakis-Smith, D. (1992) Strategies for meeting basic food needs in Harare. In J. Baker and P. O. Pedersen (eds) *The Rural-Urban Interface in Africa: Expansion and Adaptation*, pp. 258-283. Scandinavian Institute of African Studies, Uppsala.

Drakakis-Smith, D. and Kivell, P. (1990) Urban food distribution and household consumption: A study of Harare. In R. Paddison and J. A. Dawson (eds) *Retailing Environments in Developing Countries*, pp. 156-80. Routledge, London.

Epworth Local Government Board (1989) *Urban Upgrading Programme: Socio-economic Study*. Urban Development Corporation, Harare.

Farvacque, C. and McAuslan, P. (1991) *Reforming Urban Land Policies and Institutions in Developing Countries*. Urban Management Program Policy Paper 5. World Bank, United Nations Development Programme and UN Center for Human Settlements, Washington, New York and Nairobi.

Gann, L. H. (1986) Malawi, Zambia and Zimbabwe. In P. Duignan and R. H. Jackson (eds) *Politics and Government in African States 1960–1985*, pp. 162-201. Croom Helm, London.

Giersing Rose, A. S. (1991) *Construction Industry Development Study—Draft final report*. Report to the World Bank, Ministry of Finance, Economic Planning and Development and Ministry of Public Construction and National Housing, Harare.

Gore, C. with Wegge, J. and Munasireyi, D. K. (1985) Small scale informal construction sector at Kuwadzana low-income housing project. Mimeo, Report to the Ministry of Public Construction and National Housing, Harare.

Green, R. H. and Kadhani, X. (1986) Zimbabwe: Transition to economic crises, 1981-83: Retrospect and prospect. *World Development*, 14 (8): 1059-83.

Grown, C. A. and Sebstad, J. (1989) Introduction: Toward a wider perspective on women's employment. *World Development*, 17 (7): 937-52.

Gugler, J. and Flanagan, W. G. (1978) *Urbanization and Social Change in West Africa*. Cambridge University Press, Cambridge.

Hansen, K. T. (1989) *Distant Companions: Servants and Employers in Zambia 1900–1985*. Cornell University Press, Ithaca NY.

Harare City Council, Department of Works (1980/1–1988/9) Annual *Report of the Director of Works*.

Harare City Council, Department of Housing and Community Services (1985–90) Annual *Report of the Director of Housing and Community Services*.

Hardwick, P. A. (1973) Salisbury's urban transportation problems in the light of current overseas trends. *Geographical Association of Rhodesia Proceedings*, 6 (Dec.): 20–31.

Hardwick, P. A. (1977) The transportation system. In G. Kay and M. A. H. Smout (eds) *Salisbury: A Geographical Survey of the Capital of Rhodesia*, pp. 94–112. Hodder & Stoughton, London.

Harvey, S. D. (1987) Black residential mobility in a post-independent Zimbabwean city. In G. J. Williams and A. P. Wood (eds) *Geographical Perspectives on Development in Southern Africa*. Papers from the Regional Conference of the Commonwealth Geographical Bureau, Lusaka, 1982, pp. 179–87. James Cook University and the Commonwealth Geographical Bureau, North Queensland.

Hawkins, A. M., McBurney, P. J., Shadur, M. A. and Clatonoff, W. (1988) *Formal Sector Employment Demand Conditions in Zimbabwe*. University of Zimbabwe, Harare.

HCMPPA (Harare Combination Master Plan Preparation Authority) (1984a) *Industrial Development Study Report*. HCMPPA, Harare.

HCMPPA (Harare Combination Master Plan Preparation Authority) (1984b) *Commercial and Shopping Study Report*. HCMPPA, Harare.

HCMPPA (Harare Combination Master Plan Preparation Authority) (1987) *Draft Report of Study*. HCMPPA, Harare

HCMPPA (Harare Combination Master Plan Preparation Authority) (1988a) *Traffic and Transportation Study Report*. HCMPPA, Harare.

HCMPPA (Harare Combination Master Plan Preparation Authority) (1988b) *Employment Study Report*. HCMPPA, Harare.

HCMPPA (Harare Combination Master Plan Preparation Authority) (1988c) *Housing Study Report*. HCMPPA, Harare.

HCMPPA (Harare Combination Master Plan Preparation Authority) (1988d) *Population Study Report*. HCMPPA, Harare.

HCMPPA (Harare Combination Master Plan Preparation Authority) (1989) *Report of Study*. HCMPPA, Harare.

HCMPPA (Harare Combination Master Plan Preparation Authority) (1991) *Draft Written Statement*. HCMPPA, Harare.

Heath, R. A. (1986) The socio-economic characteristics of selected Harare suburbs three years after independence. *Proceedings of the Geographical Association of Zimbabwe*, 17: 34–67.

Heath, R. A. (1990) Service centres and service regions in Rhodesia. Supplement to *Zambezia*, University of Zimbabwe Publications, Harare.

Herbst, J. (1989) Political impediments to economic rationality: Explaining Zimbabwe's failure to reform its public sector. *Journal of Modern African Studies*, 27 (1): 67-84.

Herbst, J. (1990) *State Politics in Zimbabwe*. University of Zimbabwe Publications, Harare.

Hoek-Smit, M. (1982) *Housing Preferences and Potential Housing Demand of Low-income Urban Households in Zimbabwe*. National Savings and Loan League for United States Agency for International Development, Washington DC.

Holin, M. J. (1985) *Evaluation of the Kuwadzana (Parkridge–Fontainbleau) Low-Income Shelter Project, Phase 1, Report on a Survey of the Beneficiaries of the Kuwadzana Housing Project*. USAID, Nairobi.

Hosford, P. J. and Whittle, A. G. (1979) Background and functions of the Department of Physical Planning. *Zimbabwe Rhodesia Science News*, 13 (11): 252–5.

Jackson, P. (1986) *Historic Buildings of Harare*. Quest Publishing, Harare.

Jackson, P. (1993) Local initiatives in the conservation of historic buildings. In L. M. Zinyama, D. S. Tevera and S. D. Cumming (eds) *Harare: the Growth and Problems of the City*, pp. 139–52. University of Zimbabwe Publications, Harare.

Jamal, V. and Weeks, J. (1993) *Africa Misunderstood or Whatever Happened to the Rural–Urban Gap?* Macmillan, London

Jesperson, E. (1992) External shocks, adjustment policies and economic and social performance. In G. A. Cornia, R. Van der Hoeven and T. Mkandawire (eds) *Africa's Recovery in the 1990s: From Stagnation and Adjustment to Human Development*, pp. 9–90. St Martin's Press, New York.

Jordan, J. D. (1984) *Local Government in Zimbabwe*. Occasional Papers, Socioeconomic Series, No. 17. Mambo Press, Gweru.

Kaarsholm, P. (1990) The development of culture and the contradictions of modernisation in the Third World: The case of Zimbabwe. *European Journal of Development Research*, 2 (1): 36–58.

Kanji, N. and Jazdowska, N. (1993) Structural adjustment and women in Zimbabwe. *Review of African Political Economy*, 56: 11–26.

Kazembe, J. (1986) The women issue. In I. Mandaza (ed.) *Zimbabwe: The Political Economy of Transition 1980–1986*, pp. 377–404. CODESRIA, Dakar.

Kazembe, J. and Mol, M. (1987) The changing legal status of women in Zimbabwe since independence. *Canadian Woman Studies*, 7 (1/2): 53–9.

Kileff, C. (1975) Black suburbanites: An African elite in Salisbury, Rhodesia. In C. Kileff and W. D. Pendleton (eds) *Urban Man in Southern Africa*, pp. 81–97. Mambo Press, Gwelo.

King, A. D. (1990) *Urbanism, Colonialism, and the World-Economy: Cultural and Spatial Foundations of the World Urban System*. London, Routledge.

Leiman, A. (1984/5) Formal/informal sector articulation in the Zimbabwean economy. *Journal of Contemporary African Studies*, 4 (1/2): 119–37.

Lemon, A. (1988) The Zimbabwe general election of 1985. *The Journal of Commonwealth and Comparative Politics*, XXVI (1): 3–21.

Libby, R. T. (1984) Developmental strategies and political divisions within the Zimbabwean state. In M. Schatzberg (ed.) *The Political Economy of Zimbabwe*, pp. 144–63. Praeger, New York.

Lipton, M. (1977) *Why Poor People Stay Poor: Urban Bias in World Development*. London, Temple Smith.

Lister, L. A. (1975) A note on aspects of geomorphology in the Salisbury area. *Geographical Association of Rhodesia Proceedings*, 8: 35–7.

Lloyds Bank (1985) *Zimbabwe*. Lloyds Bank Group Economic Report, London.

Loewenson, R. and Sanders, D. (1988) The political economy of health and nutrition. In C. Stoneman (ed.) *Zimbabwe's Prospects*, pp. 133–52. Macmillan, London.

MacGarry, B. (1993) *Growth? Without Equity?* Silveira House Social Series, No. 4. Mambo Press, Gweru.

Mafico, C. J. C. (1991) *Urban Low Income Housing in Zimbabwe*. Avebury, Aldershot.

Makamure, D. M. (1970) Cattle and social status. In C. Kileff and P. Kileff (eds) *Shona Customs: Essays by African Writers*, pp. 14–16. Mambo Press, Gweru.

Malaba, L. (1980) Supply, control and organisation of African labour in Rhodesia. *Review of African Political Economy*, 18: 7–28.

Mandaza, I. (1986a) The state and politics in the post-white settler colonial situation. In I. Mandaza (ed.) *Zimbabwe: The Political Economy of Transition 1980–1986*, pp. 21–74. CODESRIA, Dakar.

Mandaza, I. (1986b) Introduction: The political economy of Zimbabwe. In I. Mandaza (ed.) *Zimbabwe: The Political Economy of Transition 1980–1986*, pp. 1–20. CODESRIA, Dakar.

Manyere, A. (1989) Development control in Harare: Delay in the process and determination of planning applications. Unpublished B.Sc. dissertation. Department of Rural and Urban Planning, University of Zimbabwe, Harare.

Martin, R., Coleman, D. S., Lintz, R. S., Hall, T. and Austin, R. (1985) *National Housing Corporation: Feasibility Study for the Republic of Zimbabwe*. USAID and UNCHS, Nairobi.

Maunder, D., Mbara, T. and Khezwana, M. (1993) Assessing the impact of government control on Harare's bus services. *Transport*, 14 (3): 3–4.

May, J. (1973) *Drinking in a Rhodesian African Township*. Occasional Paper 8, Department of Sociology, University of Rhodesia, Salisbury.

May, J. (1979) *African Women in Urban Employment*. Mambo Press, Gweru.

May, J. (1983) *Zimbabwean Women in Customary and Colonial Law*. Mambo Press, Gweru and Holmes McDougall, Edinburgh.

Mazur, R. E. (1986/7) Reversal of migration in the labor reserves of Zimbabwe? Prospects for change. *Studies in Comparative International Development*, 21 (4): 55–87.

Mbiba, B. (1993) Urban agriculture, the poor and planners: Harare case study. In A. O. Elgohary (ed.) *Proceedings of the 10th Interschools Conference on Development*, pp. 129–35. University College London.

Mbiba, B. (1994) Institutional responses to uncontrolled urban cultivation in Harare: Prohibitive or accommodative? *Environment and Urbanisation*, 6 (1): 188–202.

Mehretu, (1983) Cities of SubSaharan Africa. In S. D. Brunn and J. F. Williams (eds) *Cities of the World*, pp. 243–79. Harper & Row, New York.

Mills, G. M. (1979) Planning of low-cost housing. *Zimbabwe Rhodesia Science News*, 13 (11): 265–9.

Moller, V. (1974) Some aspects of mobility patterns of urban Africans in Salisbury. *Geographical Association of Rhodesia Proceedings*, 7: 22–32.

Moyo, N. P. (1988) The state, planning and labour: Towards transforming the colonial labour process in Zimbabwe. *The Journal of Development Studies*, 24 (4): 203–17.

Moyo, S. (1986) The land question. In I. Mandaza (ed.) *Zimbabwe: The Political Economy of Transition 1980–1986*, pp. 165–202. CODESRIA, Dakar.

MPCNH (Ministry of Public Construction and National Housing) (1986) Public and private partnership in housing. *Zimbabwe Science News*, 20 (3/4): 31–9.

MPCNH (Ministry of Public Construction and National Housing) (1991) *Monitoring the Shelter Performance in Zimbabwe using the Shelter Indicator Methodology*. MPCNH, Harare.

Mungazi, D. (1992) *Colonial Policy and Conflict in Zimbabwe: A Study of Cultures in Collision*. Crane Russak Publishers, New York.

Murongazvombo, M. N. (1989) Social neutrality vs development control in twenty-first century urban development: A case study of Epworth as an ad hoc residential settlement in Harare/Zimbabwe. B.Sc. dissertation, University of Zimbabwe, Department of Rural and Urban Planning, Harare.

Musandu-Nyamayaro, O. (1992) Municipal water development and management practice in Zimbabwe: Some critical comments with special reference to the impact of drought on urban development. *Review of Rural and Urban Planning in Southern and Eastern Africa*, 1: 21–48.

Musandu-Nyamayaro, O. (1993) Housing design standards for urban low-income people in Zimbabwe. *Third World Planning Review*, 15 (4): 329–54.

Musekiwa, A. (1993) Low-income housing development in Harare: A historical perspective. In L. Zinyama, D. Tevera and S. Cumming (eds) *Harare: The Growth and Problems of the City*, pp. 51–60. Harare, University of Zimbabwe Publications.

Mutizwa-Mangiza, N. D. (1985a) *An Analysis of Low-income Housing Strategies in Harare*. Discussion Paper 111, Project Planning Centre for Developing Countries, University of Bradford.

Mutizwa-Mangiza, N. D. (1985b) Post-independence urban low-income shelter policies in Zimbabwe: A preliminary appraisal of affordability. In S. D. Romaya and G. H. Franklin (eds) *Shelter, Services and the Urban Poor*. University of Wales Institute of Science and Technology, Cardiff.

Mutizwa-Mangiza, N. D. (1986) Urban centres in Zimbabwe: Inter-censal changes, 1962–1982. *Geography*, 71 (2): 311, 148–51.

Mutizwa-Mangiza, N. D. (1991a) The organisation and management of urban local authorities in Zimbabwe: A case study of Bulawayo. *Third World Planning Review*, 13 (4): 357–80.

Mutizwa-Mangiza, N. D. (1991b) Land title registration process: The case of Zimbabwe. Mimeo, Department of Rural and Urban Planning, University of Zimbabwe, Harare.

Mutizwa-Mangiza, N. D. (1991c) Financing urban shelter development in Zimbabwe: A review of existing institutions, problems and prospects. *Habitat International*, 15 (1/2): 51–68.

Mutizwa-Mangiza, N. D. (1991d) Planning suburban shopping centres in Harare, Zimbabwe: A study of structure, use, patterns and needs, with special reference to retailing in High Density Residential Areas. Supplement to *Zambezia*, University of Zimbabwe Publications, Harare.

Mutizwa-Mangiza, N. D. (1993) Urban informal transport policy: The case of emergency taxis in Harare. In L. M. Zinyama, D. S. Tevera and S. D. Cumming (eds) *Harare: The Growth and Problems of the City*, pp. 97–108. University of Zimbabwe Publications, Harare.

Mutizwa-Mangiza, N. D. and Marciano, M. (1987) Building brigades and urban low-cost shelter provision in Zimbabwe: A preliminary evaluation. Paper presented at the International Conference on Urban Shelter in Developing Countries, International Centre for Technical Research, London, September (mimeo).

NCSI (National Council of Savings Institutions) (1985) *Housing Finance in Zimbabwe*. Report prepared for the United States Agency for International Development, Washington DC.

Ncube, M. (1991) *Development Dynamics: Theories and Lessons from Zimbabwe*. Avebury, Aldershot.

Ndlela, D. B. (1986) Problems of industrialisation: Structural and policy issues. In I. Mandaza (ed.) *Zimbabwe: The Political Economy of Transition 1980–1986*, pp. 141–63. CODESRIA, Dakar.

Oberai, A. S. (1993) Urbanization, development and economic efficiency. In J. D. Kasarda and A. M. Parnell (eds) *Third World Cities: Problems, Policies and Prospects*, pp. 58–73. Sage, Newbury Park, California.

O'Connor, A. (1983) *The African City*. Hutchinson, London.

Pasteur, D. (1992) *Good Local Government in Zimbabwe: A Case Study of Bulawayo and Mutare City Councils 1980–1991*. Institutional Framework of Local Government Case Study No. 6. Institute of Local Government Studies, Development Administration Group, Birmingham.

Patel, D. (1984) Housing the urban poor in the socialist transformation of Zimbabwe. In M. Schatzberg (ed.) *The Political Economy of Zimbabwe*, pp. 182–96. Praeger, New York.

Patel, D. (1985) *Evaluation of Kuwadzana (Parkridge–Fountainbleau) Low Income Shelter Project Phase 1, Evaluation of Secondary Sources of Data*. Report for USAID, Harare.

Patel, D. (1988) Government policy and squatter settlements in Harare, Zimbabwe. In R. A. Obudho and C. C. Mhlanga (eds) *Slum and Squatter Settlements in Sub-Saharan Africa*, pp. 205–17. Praeger, New York.

Patel, D. and Adams, R. J. (1981) *Chirambahuyo: A Case Study in Low-income Housing*. Mambo Press, Gweru.

Potts, D. and Mutambirwa, C. (1990) Rural–urban linkages in contemporary Harare: Why migrants need their land. *Journal of Southern African Studies*, 16 (4): 677–97.

Potts, D. with Mutambirwa, C. (1991) High-density housing in Zimbabwe: Commodification and overcrowding. *Third World Planning Review*, 13 (1): 1–25.

Pritchard, C. R. (1989) Rented housing in Zimbabwe: A case study of the development of flats in Harare 1980–8. B.Sc. dissertation, Department of Rural and Urban Planning, University of Zimbabwe, Harare.

Quantin, P. (1992) The 1990 general elections in Zimbabwe: Steps towards a one-party state? In S. Baynham (ed.) *Zimbabwe in Transition*, pp. 24–44. Almqvist and Wiksell, Stockholm.

Raftopoulos, B. (1986) Human resources development and the problem of labour utilisation. In I. Mandaza (ed.) *Zimbabwe: the Political Economy of Transition 1980–1986*, pp. 275–317. CODESRIA, Dakar.

Rakodi, C. (1986) State and class in Africa: A case for extending analyses of the form and functions of the national state to the urban local state. *Society and Space*, 4: 419–446.

Rakodi, C. (1990) Housing production and housing policy in Harare, Zimbabwe. *Journal of Urban Affairs*, 12 (2): 135–56.

Rakodi, C. (1991a) Women's work or household strategies? *Environment and Urbanisation*, 3 (2): 39–45.

Rakodi, C. (1991b) Developing institutional capacity to meet the housing needs of the urban poor: Experience in Kenya, Tanzania and Zambia. *Cities*, 8 (3): 228–43.

Rakodi, C. (1992) Housing markets in Third World cities: Research and policy into the 1990s. *World Development*, 20 (1): 39–55.

Rakodi, C. (1993) *Trends in the Residential Property Market in Harare and Gweru.* Occasional Paper 24, Department of Rural and Urban Planning, University of Zimbabwe, Harare.

Rakodi, C. (1994) *Household Strategies and the Urban Poor: Coping with Structural Adjustment in Gweru, Zimbabwe.* Papers in Planning Research 149, Department of City and Regional Planning, University of Wales College of Cardiff, Cardiff.

Rakodi, C. and Mutizwa-Mangiza, N. D. (1990) Housing policy, production and consumption in Harare, Zimbabwe: A review, Parts I and II. *Zambezia*, XVII (1): 1–30 and (2): 111–31.

Rakodi, C. with Withers, P. (1993) *Land, Housing and Urban Development in Zimbabwe: Markets and Policy in Harare and Gweru.* Final Report to Overseas Development Administration Economic and Social Research Committee, Occasional Paper in Planning Research, Department of City and Regional Planning, University of Wales, Cardiff.

Rakodi, C. with Withers, P. (forthcoming) Home ownership and commodification of housing in Zimbabwe. *International Journal of Urban and Regional Research.*

RAL Merchant Bank (various dates) *Executive Guide to the Economy* (From September 1988: RAL Merchant Bank, *Quarterly Guide to the Economy*; from June 1990: First Merchant Bank of Zimbabwe Ltd, *Quarterly Guide to the Economy*).

RBZ (Reserve Bank of Zimbabwe) (1991) *Quarterly Economic and Statistical Review*, 12: 1.

Rhodesia, Government of (1979) *Urban Development in the Main Centres.* Ministry of Finance, Harare.

Riddell, R. C. (1978) *The Land Problem in Rhodesia.* Socioeconomic Series, No. 11. Mambo Press, Gweru.

Riddell, R. C. (1984) Zimbabwe: The economy four years after independence. *African Affairs*, 83: No. 333, 463–76.

Riddell, R. C. (1992) Manufacturing sector development in Zimbabwe and the Côte d'Ivoire. In F. Stewart, S. Lall and S. Wangwe (eds) *Alternative Development Strategies in SubSaharan Africa*, pp. 215–37. Macmillan, Basingstoke.

Rondinelli, D. A. (1988) Giant and secondary city growth in Africa. In M. Dogan and J. D. Kasarda (eds) *The Metropolis Era.* Vol. 1: *A World of Giant Cities*, pp. 291–321. Sage, Newbury Park, CA.

Sachikonye, L. M. (1986) State, capital and trade unions. In I. Mandaza (ed.) *Zimbabwe: The Political Economy of Transition 1980–1986*, pp. 243–74. CODESRIA, Dakar.

Sachikonye, L. M. (1989) The debate on democracy in contemporary Zimbabwe. *Review of African Political Economy*, 45 (6): 117–25.

Sachikonye, L. M. (1990) The 1990 elections: A post mortem. *Review of African Political Economy*, 48: 92–98.

Salau, A. T. (1990) Urbanization and spatial strategies in West Africa. In R. B. Potter and A. T. Salau (eds) *Cities and Development in the Third World*, pp. 157–171. Mansell, London.

Salisbury, City Council of (1973) *Outline Plan II, Part II—Written Statement.* Salisbury City Council, Salisbury.

Schlyter, A. (1985) Housing strategies: The case of Zimbabwe. *Trialog,* 6 (Summer): 7–17.

Schlyter, A. (1989) *Women Householders and Housing Strategies: The Case of Harare, Zimbabwe.* The National Swedish Institute for Building Research, Gavle.

Schlyter, A. (1990) Zimbabwe. In K. Mathey (ed.) *Housing Policies in Socialist Third World Countries,* pp. 197–226. Profil Verlag, Munich; Mansell, London and New York.

Seidman, G. W. (1984) Women in Zimbabwe: Postindependence struggles. *Feminist Studies,* 10 (3): 419–40.

Seki Project Team (1976) *Seki New Town Master Plan.* Department of Physical Planning, Ministry of Local Government and Housing, Harare.

Seralgeldin, I. (1989) *Poverty, Adjustment and Growth in Africa.* World Bank, Washington DC.

Shaw, T. M. (1989) Corporatism in Zimbabwe: Revolution restrained. In J. E. Nyang'oro and T. M. Shaw (eds) *Corporatism in Africa: Comparative Analysis and Practice,* pp. 149–65. Westview, Boulder CO.

Sibanda, A. E. (1988) IMF–World Bank impact on Zimbabwe. In B. Onimode (ed.) *The IMF, the World Bank and the African Debt: The Economic Impact,* pp. 149–59. Zed Press, London.

Sijaona, S. T. (1987) Women's Income Generating Activities in Epworth, Harare. Diploma Project, Department of Rural and Urban Planning, University of Zimbabwe, Harare.

Simon, D. (1986) Regional inequality, migration and development: The case of Zimbabwe. *Tijdschrift voor Economische en Sociale Geografie,* 77 (1): 7–17.

Simon, D. (1992) *Cities, Capital and Development: African Cities in the World Economy.* Belhaven, London.

Sit, F.-S. (1993) Transnational capital flows, foreign investments, and urban growth in developing countries. In J. D. Kasarda and A. M. Parnell (eds) *Third World Cities: Problems, Policies and Prospects,* pp. 180–98. Sage, Newbury Park, CA.

Situma, I. (1987) Problems of public transportation in Zimbabwe. *African Urban Quarterly,* 2 (1): 49–54.

Skalnes, T. (1993) The state, interest groups and Structural Adjustment in Zimbabwe. *Journal of Development Studies,* 29 (3): 401–28.

Skinner, E. P. (1986) Urbanization in Francophone Africa. *African Urban Quarterly,* 1 (3–4): 191–5.

Smout, M. A. H. (1977a) The townscape. In G. Kay and M. A. H. Smout (eds) *Salisbury: A Geographical Survey of the Capital of Rhodesia,* pp. 26–40. Hodder & Stoughton, London.

Smout, M. A. H. (1977b) The city centre. In G. Kay and M. A. H. Smout (eds) *Salisbury: A Geographical Survey of the Capital of Rhodesia,* pp. 57–71. Hodder & Stoughton, London.

Smout, M. A. H. (1977c) The suburban shopping centres. In G. Kay and M. A. H. Smout (eds) *Salisbury: A Geographical Survey of the Capital of Rhodesia,* pp. 72–87. Hodder & Stoughton, London.

Smout, M. A. H. (1977d) Urbanization and development problems in Rhodesia. *Journal of Tropical Geography,* 45: 43–51.

Sparrow, C. A. (1979) Urban planning. *Zimbabwe Rhodesia Science News,* 13 (11): 256–60.

Standing, G. (1984) *Population Mobility and Productive Relations: Demographic Links and Policy Evolution.* World Bank Staff Working Paper 695. World Bank, Washington DC.

Stoneman, C. (1988) The economy: Recognising the reality. In C. Stoneman (ed.) *Zimbabwe's Prospects: Issues of Race, Class, State and Capital in Southern Africa,* pp. 43–62. Macmillan, London.

Stoneman, C. and Cliffe, L. (1989) *Zimbabwe: Politics, Economics and Society.* Pinter Publishers, London.

Stopforth, P. (1972) *Two Aspects of Social Change in Highfield African Township, Salisbury.* Occasional Paper 7, Department of Sociology, University of Rhodesia, Salisbury.

Stopforth, P. (1977) Some local impediments to social change among urban Africans. *Zambezia,* 5 (1): 31–40.

Stren, R. E. (1989) Urban local government in Africa. In R. E. Stren and R. R. White (eds) *African Cities in Crisis: Managing Rapid Urban Growth,* pp. 20–36. Westview, Boulder CO.

Stren R. E. and White, R. R. (eds) 1989 *African Cities in Crisis: Managing Rapid Urban Growth.* Westview, Boulder CO.

Sutcliffe, R. B. (1971) Stagnation and inequality in Rhodesia 1946–1968. *Bulletin of the Oxford University Institute of Economics and Statistics,* 33 (1): 38. Quoted in Clarke 1977.

Swedeplan (1988) *The Harare Combination Master Plan: A Second Opinion.* Swedeplan, Harare.

Swedeplan (1989) *Harare Infilling Study.* Swedeplan, for the Department of Physical Planning, Ministry of Local Government, Rural and Urban Development.

Taylor, J. C. B. (1985) Zimbabwe: One local authority's response to the challenge of decent shelter. In T. Blair (ed.) *Strengthening Urban Management,* pp. 24–8. Plenum, New York.

Teedon, P. (1990) An analysis of aided-self-help housing schemes: A study of a former colonial city, Harare, Zimbabwe. Unpublished Ph.D. thesis. University of Keele.

Teedon, P. and Drakakis-Smith, D. (1986) Urbanisation and socialism in Zimbabwe: The case of low-cost urban housing. *Geoforum,* 17 (2): 309–24.

Tekere, A. B. C. (1993) Redevelopment of the Harare Kopje area. In L. M. Zinyama, D. S. Tevera and S. D. Cumming (eds) *Harare: The Growth and Problems of the City,* pp. 131–8. University of Zimbabwe Publications, Harare.

Tevera, D. S. (1991) Solid waste disposal in Harare and its effects on the environment: Some preliminary observations. *Zimbabwe Science News,* 25 (1/3): 9–13.

Tevera, D. S. (1993) Waste recycling as a livelihood in the informal sector: The case of Harare's Teviotdale dump scavengers. In L. M. Zinyama, D. S. Tevera and S. D. Cumming (eds) *Harare: The Growth and Problems of the City,* pp. 83–96. University of Zimbabwe Publications, Harare.

Thrift, N. (1987) The fixers: The urban geography of international commercial capital. In J. Henderson and M. Castells (eds) *Global Restructuring and Territorial Development,* pp. 203–33. Sage, London.

Todaro, M. P. (1994) *Economic Development,* 5th edition. Longman, Harlow.

Tomlinson, R. W. and Wurzel, P. (1977) Aspects of site and situation. In G. Kay and M. A. H. Smout (eds) *Salisbury: A Geographical Survey of the Capital of Rhodesia,* pp. 1–13. Hodder & Stoughton, London.

Tordoff, W. (1984) *Government and Politics in Africa*. Macmillan, London.

Trinder, J. (1977) The industrial areas. In G. Kay and M. A. H. Smout (eds) *Salisbury: A Geographical Survey of the Capital of Rhodesia*, pp. 88–93. Hodder & Stoughton, London.

UN (1991) *World Urbanization Prospects 1990*. UN Department for International Economic and Social Affairs, New York.

Underwood, G. C. (1986) Zimbabwe. In N. Patricios (ed.) *International Handbook of Land Use Planning*, pp. 185–218. Greenwood, Hartford CT.

Underwood, G. C. (1987) Zimbabwe's low cost housing areas: A planner's perspective. *African Urban Quarterly*, 2 (1): 24–36.

UNDP (1991) *Human Development Report*. Oxford University Press, New York.

Urban Transport Unit (nd) *Technical Papers: Transport Issues*. Department of Physical Planning, Ministry of Local Government and Rural and Urban Development, Harare.

USAID (United States Agency for International Development) (1992) *Zimbabwe Private Sector Housing Program*. Harare, USAID.

Ushewokunze, H. (1982) Zimbabwe: Problems and prospects of socialist development. *Race and Class*, 23 (4): 275–85.

van der Linden, J. (1986) *The Sites and Services Approach Reviewed*. Gower, Aldershot.

Weiner, D. (1988) Land and agricultural development. In C. Stoneman (ed.) *Zimbabwe's Prospects: Issues of Race, Class, State and Capital in Southern Africa*, pp. 63–89. Macmillan, London.

Weiner, D., Moyo, S., Munslow, B. and O'Keefe, P. (1984) Land use and agricultural productivity in Zimbabwe. *Journal of Modern African Studies*, 22 (4): 529–57.

Wekwete, K. H. (1989a) Physical planning in Zimbabwe: A review of the legislative, administrative and operational framework. *Third World Planning Review*, 11 (1): 49–69.

Wekwete, K. H. (1989b) *Planning Laws for Urban and Regional Planning in Zimbabwe: A Review*. Occasional Paper 20, Department of Rural and Urban Planning, University of Zimbabwe, Harare.

Wekwete, K. H. (1989c) Urban local government finance: The case of Harare City in Zimbabwe. Mimeo, Department of Rural and Urban Planning, University of Zimbabwe, Harare.

Wekwete, K. H. (1992) New directions for urban development in rapidly urbanising countries: The case of Zimbabwe. *Habitat International*, 16 (2): 53–63.

Whitsun Foundation (1980) *Data Bank No. 3: The Urban Sector*. Whitsun Foundation, Harare.

Winters, C. (1983) The classification of traditional African cities. *Journal of Urban History*, 1 (1): 3–31.

Withers, P. M. and Rakodi, C. (1993) *Self-help Housing in Harare and Gweru*. Occasional Paper 25, Department of Rural and Urban Planning, University of Zimbabwe, Harare.

Wood, B. (1988) Trade-union organisation and the working class. In C. Stoneman (ed.) *Zimbabwe's Prospects*, pp. 285–308. Macmillan, London.

Woodward, D. (1992) *Debt, Adjustment and Poverty in Developing Countries*. Pinter, London (in association with Save the Children), 2 vols.

World Bank (1984) *Zimbabwe Urban Development Project Staff Appraisal.* East African Projects Department, Water Supply and Urban Development Division, World Bank, Washington DC.

World Bank (1985) *Zimbabwe Urban Sector Review.* East African Projects Department, Water Supply and Urban Development Division, Nairobi.

World Bank (1989) *Zimbabwe Urban Sector and Regional Development Project.* Staff Appraisal Report, Southern Africa Department, Infrastructure Operations Division, Washington DC.

World Bank (1993) *Housing: Enabling Markets to Work.* World Bank, Washington DC.

World Bank (1994) *World Development Report 1994.* Oxford University Press, Oxford.

'Yates', P. (1980) The prospects for socialist transition in Zimbabwe. *Review of African Political Economy,* 18: 68–88.

Zachariah, K. C. and Condé, J. (1981) *Migration in West Africa: Demographic Aspects.* Oxford University Press, Oxford.

ZANU (PF) (1985) *Zimbabwe at 5 Years of Independence: Achievements, Problems and Prospects.* ZANU (PF), Harare.

Zimbabwe, Government of (nda) *Census of Production 1988/9.* Central Statistical Office, Harare.

Zimbabwe, Government of (ndb, probably early 1980s) *Urban Housing Policy Implementation Manual.* Ministry of Public Construction and National Housing, Harare.

Zimbabwe, Government of (1982) *Transitional National Development Plan 1982/3—1984/5,* Vol. 1. Ministry of Finance, Harare.

Zimbabwe, Government of (1985a) *Main Demographic Features of the Population of Zimbabwe: An Advance Report Based on a Ten Per Cent Sample.* Central Statistical Office, Harare.

Zimbabwe, Government of (1985b) *Long Term Plan 1985–2000.* Ministry of Public Construction and National Housing, Harare.

Zimbabwe, Government of (1986a) *Report of the Commission of Enquiry into Taxation.* Government Printer, Harare.

Zimbabwe, Government of (1986b) *Report on Housing and Urban Development in Zimbabwe: Public and Private Sector Partnership.* Report by the Ministry of Public Construction and National Housing to the Tenth Conference on Housing and Urban Development in Sub-Saharan Africa, Harare.

Zimbabwe, Government of (1987a) *National Action and National Shelter Strategies up to the Year 2000.* Submission to the tenth session of the UN Commission for Human Settlements, Nairobi.

Zimbabwe, Government of (1987b) *Government Should Take Interest in Housing Co-ops.* Department of Information, Ministry of Cooperative Development, Harare.

Zimbabwe, Government of (1989) *Statistical Yearbook 1989.* Central Statistical Office, Harare.

Zimbabwe, Government of (1991a) *Zimbabwe: A Framework for Economic Reform (1991–95).* Harare.

Zimbabwe, Government of (1991b) *Report on Development of Human Settlements in Zimbabwe.* Ministry of Public Construction and National Housing. Paper presented at the 13th Session of the Commission on Human Settlements, 29 April to 8 May, Harare.

Zimbabwe, Government of (1991c) *Monitoring the Shelter Performance in Zimbabwe using the Shelter Indicator Method.* Ministry of Public Construction and National Housing, Harare.

Zimbabwe, Government of (1992) *Census 1992: Preliminary Report.* Central Statistical Office, Harare.

Zinyama, L. M. (1987) Assessing spatial variations in social conditions in the African rural areas of Zimbabwe. *Tijdschrift voor Econ. en Soc. Geografie,* 78, 1: 30–43.

Zinyama, L. M. (1993) The evolution of the spatial structure of Greater Harare: 1890–1990. In L. M. Zinyama, D. S. Tevera and S. D. Cumming (eds) *Harare: The Growth and Problems of the City,* pp. 7–32. University of Zimbabwe Publications, Harare.

Index

Index compiled by Geoffrey Jones